Across the Territories

Born in Glasgow and raised on the west coast of Scotland, Kenneth White studied French, German and philosophy at the Universities of Glasgow, Munich and Paris. He was first published in London in the mid-sixties (*The Cold Wind of Dawn, Letters from Gourgounel, The Most Difficult Area* – all at Jonathan Cape), but broke with the British scene in 1967, settling in the Pyrenees, where he lived in concentrated silence for a while before beginning to publish again, this time in Paris. A whole series of books – narrative, poetry, essays – won not only wide-spread recognition in France, but also some of its most prestigious literary prizes: the Prix Médicis Etranger for his book *La Route bleue*, the Prix Alfred de Vigny for his poetry, the French Academy's Grand Prix du Rayonnement Français and the Prix Roger Caillois for his work as a whole. These books have been translated into several languages. Since his return, via Scotland, to the English-language context in 1989, White's work has been published by Mainstream (Edinburgh): *The Bird Path, Handbook for the Diamond Country, Travels in the Drifting Dawn, The Blue Road, Pilgrim of the Void*, and by Polygon (Edinburgh): *On Scottish Ground, House of Tides*. When Birlinn Ltd (also of Edinburgh) took over Polygon, its first act was to publish White's collected poems, *Open World*, as a gateway to White's complete work. From 1983 to 1996, Kenneth White held the Chair of XXth Century Poetics at Paris-Sorbonne. In 1989, he founded the International Institute of Geopoetics, which now has centres in various countries, including Scotland, and he directs its transdisciplinary review, *Cahiers de Géopoétique*. Kenneth White lives at present with his wife Marie-Claude, translator and photographer, on the north coast of Brittany.

Other books by Kenneth White

The Cold Wind of Dawn, poems, London, Jonathan Cape, 1966.

Letters from Gourgounel, narrative, London, Jonathan Cape, 1966.

The Most Difficult Area, poems, London, Jonathan Cape, 1968.

The Bird Path, collected longer poems, Edinburgh and London, Mainstream Publishing, 1989; also in Penguin paperback edition.

Travels in the Drifting Dawn, narrative, Edinburgh and London, Mainstream Publishing, 1989; also in Penguin paperback edition.

Handbook for the Diamond Country, collected shorter poems, Edinburgh and London, Mainstream Publishing, 1990.

The Blue Road, narrative, Edinburgh and London, Mainstream Publishing, 1990.

Pilgrim of the Void, narrative, Edinburgh and London, Mainstream Publishing, 1992.

Van Gogh and Kenneth White, an encounter, Paris, Flohic Éditions, 1994

Coast to Coast, interviews, Glasgow, Open World Editions and Mythic Horse Press, 1996.

On Scottish Ground, essays, Edinburgh, Polygon Press, 1998.

House of Tides, narrative, Edinburgh, Polygon Press, 2000.

Open World, Collected Poems 1960–2000, Edinburgh, Birlinn-Polygon, 2003.

The Wanderer and his Charts, essays, Edinburgh, Birlinn-Polygon, 2004.

KENNETH WHITE

Across the Territories
Territories

Travels from Orkney to Rangiroa

First published in Great Britain in 2004 by Polygon Books

Polygon an imprint of Birlinn Ltd
West Newington House
10 Newington Road
Edinburgh EH9 1QS

British Library Cataloguing in Publication Data

A catalogue record is available on request from the British Library

ISBN 1 904598 14 5

Typeset in Scotch Roman by Koinonia, Manchester
Printed in Great Britain by Creative Print and Design, Ebbw Vale,
Wales

Contents

The Isles of the Orks   1

The Dancing Cranes   8

Aurora Borealis   20

Winds of the Skagerrak   36

Travels in a Sea of Vodka   52

The Cry of the Loon on the Kennebec   63

Around Corsica   82

The Big Andalusian Trip   118

Rainy Margins and Misty Horizons   144

The Lights of the Atlas   163

The Road to Rangiroa   197

'Thus do they live as rovers...'
(Cleveland, *The Rebel Scot*)

'In his travels, he always takes
things right to the limit.'
(Ernst Jünger, *Visit to Godenholm*)

'From the middle zones of existence
to the sharp edge of life.'
(Leon Chestov, *Life's Limits*)

The Isles of the Orks

The flight to the Orkneys started late. As the pilot explained when we'd been about ten minutes in the air, 'Edinburgh airport just can't handle the traffic any more.' The plane, a kind of square bus with blunt wings, containing about a dozen passengers, was throbbing and droning through a fog that was now rainily grey, now incandescent white. From time to time it cleared, and you had a bird's eye glimpse of the land down below, all ice-scored and complicatedly watercoursed.

At Inverness, five passengers left us, one of them teasingly wishing the young air hostess 'a nice night in Kirkwall'. Up in the air again, the pilot apologised once more for the delay, insisting it was 'due to congestion at the capital', and announced that the weather over Kirkwall was lousy, with a tough easterly wind. However, 'hopefully, we should get in'. Maybe more than one passenger thought fleetingly of the life jacket under the seat, equipped, as we'd been told, 'with a light and a whistle to attract attention'. Though, looking out into the murky turmoil, who wouldn't be thinking too that, in a storm like that, a wee light and a pink plastic whistle would have about half the chance of a snowball in hell.

However, get in we did, seeing first a huddle of islands wrapped in sheepskin cloud, then a white-flecked blue leaden sea, finally two yellow cargo-boats getting tossed about like corks.

★

Ninety-odd islands and skerries off the north-eastern tip of Scotland, the Orkneys are a scattered continuation of the Scottish mainland. Over millions of years, sediments were eroded from the old Caledonian rocks and dragged out into the gaping maw of the North Sea. Later, the ice came grinding down over them – ice from the Moray Firth, deflected to the north-east by the great, glowering glacier from Scandinavia. It is low land, except for some rugged, rounded hills on Hoy: nothing so dramatic or spectacular as the wildly upheavaled Scottish Highlands. But there is a sensation over the archipelago of something very ancient, archaic even. And wind and waves have written the foreground into fantastic shapes, creating towering cliffs here, deep inlets there, lone stacks elsewhere, and liable at any time to leave anywhere a new storm-beach of sand and broken shell.

★

Around Grimsetter, the airport area, stretched a wan and gloomy expanse of moorland. I made off in a taxi for the little port of Stromness away there over the big island to the west.

'That's Finstown', said the taxi-driver as we passed through it, 'that's where I live', and relapsed into a fathomless silence.

I was reminded of the story about the Orcadian who disappeared from home one day and turned up again, via Nova Scotia and Labrador, twenty years later: 'Where have you been?', said his brother. 'Out for a walk.'

At the Stromness hotel, the wind had got in before me, and was howling along the hallway as though it owned the joint. I took the asthmatic lift, made a long time ago in Glasgow, that wheezed its way up to the top floor and deposited me in front of the room that was going to be my headquarters for the next few days.

I laid out my things, set out books (among them, the *Orkneyinga Saga*) on the table by the window, pinned a map of the archipelago on the wall, and felt immediately quite at home – as in a captain's cabin, or maybe rather a monk's cell.

★

Next morning, early on, I was standing at the window of my observation post looking out over the sea. A fierce north wind was still blustering its way across the sky and the rain was coming down in torrents. Through the blur, I could just make out, down there in the spumy harbour, the silhouettes of the *St Ola* and the *St Sunniva* (both registered in Aberdeen) that do the ferry service between the islands and the Scottish mainland.

At the beginning of the century, here in Stromness, the best sheltered anchorage north of the Cromarty Firth, it might have been the SS *Esquimaux* that was moored down there, or the *Scotia*, bound for Cape Farewell in Greenland, and beyond Greenland into Davis Strait and Baffin Bay, on the hunt for whales:

*O 'twas in the year of '94, of June the 2nd day
that our gallant ship her anchor weighed
and from Stromness bore away...*

The work conditions on those expeditions were horrendous. For those who managed to make it back, so many suffering from the intense cold, scurvy and mind-boggling isolation, there was a first-aid hospital right there on the shore front.

At breakfast, down in the big room, at the long table, I had for neighbours a group of divers from Birmingham. Amid an unmistakably British guff of fried sausage, bacon and black pudding, they were talking about wrecks, of which there are quite a few in these parts – Rackwick, a place-name on Hoy, must mean 'the bay of wreckage'. Hearing the divers describe Scapa Flow, I thought it must be like the nightmare of history deluged by the elemental ocean.

Later that morning, still windy and rainy, I went down the long steep main street, lined with great plainstones (on every single one, a wavering chart of geological time-tides), to the packed little Stromness museum, where I spent a couple of hours with harpoons, Eskimo whalebone sculptures, a fossil fish, a Greenland falcon, a big lump of blue-glinting labradorite, and a biography of John Rae, born here in these islands.

What interests me about John Rae, Arctic explorer and Hudson's Bay company doctor (a good proportion of the Hudson's Bay men were Orcadians, known along the canoe routes of northern Canada as 'Les Orknays'), is that he practised a kind of field-tactics very different from the orthodox strategy of the established authorities. He learned directly from the Inuit how to move about in the frozen wilderness. To the company of colleagues and officials he preferred, by far, that of Eskimos, Cree Indians and Canadian half-breeds, crossing the Arctic not in pukka European garb, but wrapped in hides and furs, and not lugging with him huge loads of processed food, but living off the land. It was because of this that Rae was heartily disliked by those said 'authorities' and never became so nationally well known a figure as the Franklins and Shackletons who regularly made a heroic and resounding mess of things.

When I came back up the Plainstanes the rain had slackened and the cats were out. There are a lot of cats in Stromness. They were a necessary element of boats' crews – brought on board, not just as pleasant company, but also as having a job to do. They must have come back from the Arctic with frozen paws and crazier even than the men.

★

The rain had started to pour down again, but the sun had come out when I emerged from the hotel and my meditations that afternoon, and its sheen through the after-rain made for a strangely beautiful light.

I decided to make for the place called Skara Brae.

Skara Brae is a small village of eight dwellings that was built, just above the tideline on the shore of Skaill Bay, about five thousand years ago by people who had wandered up from Spain and France, looking for a quiet place to stay somewhere on the rim of the world. Trees being rare on the islands, every-thing in the village was of stone, from roof to furniture. Which is one of the reasons why it has been preserved in such a perfect state. The other reason is that, about 2500 BC, at a time when, after about four centuries of habitation, the place was clogged up by its own middens (that happens to civilizations), a big storm blew up and buried it in the sand. It was to remain embedded in the sand forty-three centuries, till, in 1850, another big storm uncovered it.

I continued my stone age pilgrimage the next day with a visit to Maeshowe, a massive chambered tomb of Orkney flagstones that must have been built about 3000 BC. Norsemen who had been on a crusading trip to Byzantium and Jerusalem visited it in the mid-twelfth century, leaving inscriptions. One of these says that the runes were carved with an Icelandic axe by 'the foremost writer in the Western seas'.

Coming back to my hotel I noticed a plaque set in a wall giving the distances from Stromness to Brodgar, Skara Brae, Kirkwall. In the Viking times, it would have been the distance to Reykjavik, Novgorod, Istanbul.

★

That night, in my cabin-cell, to the accompaniment of the ever-falling rain, I read the *Orkneyinga Saga*, from start to finish:

> After the death of Earl Sigurd, three of his sons, Sumarlidi, Brusi and Einar, took over the earldom and divided it between

them, for Thorfinn was only five years old when his father was killed, and he living from then on with his grandfather, King Malcolm of Scotland. The King of Scots gave Thorfinn Caithness and Sutherland...

The 'history of the Earls of Orkney', written in Icelandic about 1200, is a story of territorial rights, family bickerings, bloody fights and sadistic butcherings. It makes for pretty heavy reading, especially when you hit the genealogies: Hrolf Bandy-Legs was the son of Rognvald the One-Eyed who was the son of Bjarg the Big Drinker who was the son of Einar the Skull-Basher... This stodgy genealogical dough is relieved, fortunately, here and there by some stark phrases about 'crows croaking over cold carrion' and 'a grey wolf with a red gub padding over the wounded' and by the unconscious humour of the laconic, monosyllabic style: 'Kol was killed, so that's him out of the story.' Now and then too we get wind of a larger, mythic dimension. It's there at the beginning, in the evocation of Logi (flame), Kari (storm), Frosti (frost), Snaer (snow), Aegir (sea), and it's in this shamanic dimension that at one point in the story we're told of one who was 'keen on the old practices and spent many a night in the open air with the spirits'. At times, also, we actually hear, beyond the human context, of the islands themselves, that come across as a myth older than myths: 'At the far end of the island of Rousay is a big headland with a pile of broken rock at its foot, where otters can be seen...'

While piling up the facts about plundering expeditions to the Hebrides, Ireland and Strathclyde, the *Orkneyinga Saga* is also the story of a saint: Saint Magnus. This Magnus died in 1117, brutally murdered by his cousin, Haakon Paulson, who later went to wash off his bloody sins in the River Jordan. No sooner had Magnus been laid away than miracles started to happen: a light shone over the grave, and a holy odour was wafted on the air. People came on pilgrimage: the blind saw, the mad recovered their wits. By invoking the name of Magnus, a gambler even won the jackpot, and what better guarantee can you get than that? One of his advisers told chief Rognvald it might be a good stunt to build a lofty cathedral in Magnus's name, and crafty politics forbye, since it would manifest in a massive way the filiation the said Rognvald had with his uncle and put his rival once and for all in the shade. Neat, eh? Meanwhile Magnus was getting saintlier all the time. When a sceptical bishop (too many miracles can kill the market) had his body dug up, one of his knuckle bones, believe it or not, had turned into a gold nugget. And then somebody had a dream, in which Magnus, buried on Birsay, declared in an otherworldy voice: 'I want to go to Kirkwall.'

The next morning, I went to Kirkwall myself.

★

The young guy driving the taxi I took from Stromness had a book lying beside him on the seat, a book on the Kabbala. He'd just had his fortune told by a famous kabbalist in Kirkwall: 'Oh, he is a clever man, a very clever man, he knew all about me.' Ross Duncan usually went south in the Summer, to work in the sunny paradise of the Channel Islands. This year he'd had it all lined up, or thought he had: a great job as cocktail waiter in a slick hotel on Jersey, but it hadn't worked out. However, the kabbalist in Kirkwall had told him that after 'a bizarre reverse of fortune', his life would take 'a considerable turn for the better'. That had fair bucked him up. 'Oh, it was well worth the twelve pounds, I tell you.'

The first idea that crosses your mind when you get to Kirkwall is: why the hell did I come to Kirkwall? Of course you can think of all kinds of good historical reasons. Kirkwall was a big trade centre, on the sea-road from Bergen to Dublin. It was here Haakon of Norway died after his defeat at the battle of Largs, 1263, the first date in history I ever learned, living as I did just next to the monument on the Scottish west coast commemorating that event. In the fourteenth century, rebel Scots involved in the movement created by Robert the Bruce took refuge here. Architecturally, there are fourteenth, seventeenth and eighteenth-century houses, one built with contorted volcanic stones that were ballast on Johnny Gow the Orkney pirate's ship, the hero of one of those interminable, garrulous novels by Walter Scott.

But Kirkwall was bleak, very grim and bleak, that late afternoon, and the Latin mottoes graven on the walls here and there didn't help to relieve the atmosphere: *Soli dei gloria* (glory to God alone), *Si Deus nobiscum* (if God be with us). By God, it was lugubrious. Nevertheless, I went up and down, to and fro, and round and round the town: Broad Street, Tankerness Lane, Harbour Street, Bridge Street, King Street, Water-gate, the Strynd. I must have walked about ten kilometres that day in Kirkwall. It was like a perambulating pluviose penance.

When darkness fell, I took refuge at an inn. I thought I would enjoy, as compensation for all the God-ridden gloom, a hearty meal, with a good beer to accompany it, and a superlative island whisky to follow it up. Why I ordered the home-made lasagne God only knows. But there it was: a mushy, glubby, slobbery, slabbery mess. I forked at it despondently for a couple of minutes, then, resigning all hopes of restauration, went back out into the rain.

★

I was just about ready to give up the ghost entirely in Kirkwall when, down by the harbour, I came upon this howff, and it was there I made the acquaintance of Eric Sinclair.

Eric was holding forth, would you believe it, on literature: 'There's been damn little here since the sagas', he was saying. 'Only primary school versions of the saga material and reams of community stuff.'

I pricked up my ears. It's rare to hear anyone talking like that anywhere any more (resignation in the name of realism is the motto), and I hadn't expected to find it here.

'And when all this grubbing about in the archetypes, all this steeping in the stereotypes, is thrown out as garbage, all you'll have in its place will be autistic pathology.'

I liked this Eric Sinclair.

'I don't know why I bother talking like this at all', he said later, when we'd got into a one-to-one conversation. 'I suppose I just feel I have to get it off my chest. But it's high time there was something with a bit more amplitude going on.'

We talked about that idea the next few days, but spent most of the time just moving around the islands in Eric's boat, *The Whitemaa:* Westray, Eday, Egilsay, Rousay, Stronsay, Shapinsay, Sanday...

Every one of them was saying something, in a language of dark consonantal rock, tidal noise and wandering light.

Every one of them was like the illuminated and elaborate first letter on the page of some manuscript of the open sea, an open world.

The Dancing Cranes

A letter had come out of the blue, from Falköping, in south-west Sweden: 'Come and see five thousand cranes on a Scandinavian lake.'

I was interested. It was January. I said I'd come up that very Spring. I'd make a composite little Swedish trip out of it. In addition to seeing the migrant birds, I'd stay in Stockholm for a while, then move farther north. That was the idea. Here's how it was.

★

Birger Jarl's city was just emerging from the ice. The whole of northern Europe was still wintry. I'd come up on an SAS flight via Lille, Amsterdam, Copenhagen. Away to the right there, the foggy, frosty fuzz of the Kiel and Lübeck coast. The sea ice-grey, with here and there streaks of darkblue and green.

Arlanda airport, Stockholm, is a silent airport, and the silence was striking – none of those heavenly voiced announcements. What I did hear though was a series of little *bip-bip-bips*. It was the beginning of the mobile telephone craze, and the Swedes seemed to have gone for it in a big way (Posters everywhere: 'Get a real deal. The leader in mobile telephony. Ericcson'). Glancing around, I could see a dozen guys, in different postures, looking as if a bee had stung them on the ear.

The taxi-man who drove me to the Old Town, the Gamla Stan, was of Greek origin, but had lived in Sweden from the age of eleven, all in all twenty years. It was fine, he said, the social system was good, but conditions were far from rosy, there was a lot of unemployment, a lot of poverty – you didn't always see it, of course, people hid away in their apartments, but they might be living on bread and water. And there were more and more neo-Nazi skinheads in the streets: 'They think they're carrying on the Viking tradition – jackbooted, with blue and yellow blood in their veins.' As to Swedish women, he went on, they were OK for fun, but not on a steady basis. 'Once it's steady, they expect you to work fourteen hours a day – and then they don't even make the meals.' He'd have guys in his car, head office execs, with their mobile phones: 'Hello, darling

8

– what's for dinner?' Big pause. 'OK, I'll make something up myself.'

The hotel I'd booked a room in lay close to the Big Church, the Storkyrkan, just off the Västerlänggatan – not far away in fact from the spot where René Descartes nearly froze to death when he was teaching radical modern philosophy to the blue-stocking Queen Christina. It was a long narrow room at the top of the building, with furniture of seasoned browngold birch.

The inner Old Town of Stockholm consists of Petticoat Lanes full of musty little haberdashery stores alternating with snack-bars selling bulky sausages with an abundance of mustard alongside plastic cups of Coca-Cola. I wandered down those little streets as far as the underground station, the Tunnelbana, then came back up the Västerlänggatan to the outer façade of the same Old Town constituted by the Big Church, the Swedish Academy and the Royal Palace, the Kungliga Slottet.

The palace square is not only spacious, it's strangely empty, with a distinctly unfinished feeling about it. You can suddenly get that empty feeling all over Stockholm. There was another square I saw that evening, up by the Opera House, with statues of rider-less horses at either end – like a theatrical decor, and no play.

That said, Stockholm is a beautiful city. This is what I was saying to myself as I crossed the Strömbron to the Strömgatan and the Strömkajen. It's a sea city: Venice of the North, as they say – but with strong salt sea streaming in rather than the torpid water of malarial canals.

★

In coming to Stockholm, I had two characters on my mind – well, maybe three: Swedenborg, Rudbeck and Strindberg.

I'd read Swedenborg years before in Glasgow. As a fetish, I had a copy of his *Heaven and Hell*, in Japanese, borrowed from the University library, in my student's room. Later on, in Paris, I'd got interested in him again, thanks to Strindberg. In his book *Inferno*, Strindberg tells how one day in 1896 he left his room at the Hotel Orfila, in the Rue d'Assas, crossed the Luxembourg Gardens, and at a bookstall in the arcades of the Odeon theatre, picked up a novel by Balzac called *Seraphita*. This is the story of how a certain Wilfrid, of uncertain origins (but his name ought to mean 'seeker of peace') is blocked by the snow in a Norwegian village, where he makes the acquaintance of the girl Seraphita, whose father was Swedish, in fact a nephew of Swedenborg. Wilfrid, a sceptical scientist, falls in love with her – in other words, is initiated into the full range and the intimate depths of Swedenborgian philosophy. *Seraphita* is a strange phenomenon in Balzac's development. Here was a writer out, apparently, to depict French society and, through it, the 'human condition', who suddenly deviated from the social-realist track to plunge into a metaphysical wilderness. For Strindberg, it was a revelation. He'd read Swedenborg, cursorily, in Sweden, where this eighteenth-century figure had been relegated more or less to the category of a nutcase. He now plunged into the fifty volumes of Swedenborg's work, convinced that he had touched on an unmapped continent of the mind.

Who then was this Swedenborg?

Up to the age of about sixty, Emmanuel Swedenborg was a straight scientist and mathematician living a well-filled social life. As a young man, he had studied biology, physics, geology, mathematics, music and poetry (his first book was a collection of poems written in Latin). He had done work in paleontology, the formation of planets, magnetism, crystallography and the brain. He had written books on anatomy, minerals, tides, algebra, copper-smelting and salt-making. With all this behind him, he planned a great astronomical observatory in Sweden, but the authorities, as so often, were sluggish. Which is why Emmanuel started travelling, staying whenever possible with craftsmen (watchmakers, cabinet makers, mathematical instrument makers), from whom he could learn the secrets of a trade, publishing his books, in Latin, wherever (England, Holland, France) an opportunity offered. Then, in April 1744, a tremendous break occurred. He had a vision, he heard a roaring noise, like a high wind, saw a great light. He began a *Dream Book*, dividing it initially into three sections: dreams of my youth; dreams of Venice and the beautiful palaces; dreams of Sweden and 'the white clouds of heaven'. He piled up manuscripts: *Clavis Hieroglyphica, Diarium Spirituale, Arcana Caelestia, De Coelo et de Inferno, Apocalypsis Revelata*. Instead of talking in terms of mechanics, he embarked, via all this 'unworldly writing', on an exploration of 'the greater brain', an investigation of 'life's master plan'. He declared that intuition, inspiration, insight (associated always, in Swedenborg's texts, with experiences of light) could reveal a synthesis of which rationality was incapable, and elaborated a theory of 'correspondences' for reading the universe. He began, there in the streets and cafés of Stockholm, to say things like: 'One day as I was strolling around hell', or 'As I was saying the other day to St Paul...'

What had happened?

Was this the case of a hard-working, overwrought brain gone astray, undergoing precocious senile decay? Possible, but unlikely. Was this a mind desiring to expand science and reason into unedited areas, and who for this had only religious language at his disposal? Maybe. Was this someone eager to communicate the 'light' he had experienced and who felt the only way to communicate it was through celestial cinema? Maybe again. But I don't see a mind like Swedenborg's bent primarily on communication. Otherwise, why would he have written in Latin and published his books so haphazardly? No, communication isn't Swedenborg's main motivation, it's the excitement of discovery, it's the pleasure of pathfinding, the delight of synthetical composition. Maybe he wanted to explore in depth that part of his brain labelled 'religion' (his father was bishop of Skara and he had been brought up on the Bible). Maybe, by a kind of kabbalism, he wanted to find in the holy text the same kind of correspondences that he'd found in the world of matter. Maybe he wanted to transcend not only the inconsequential chitchat of normal social discourse but also intellectual controversy, and penetrate into a great still centre. Maybe he felt he had to go esoterically underground (as for any fundamental work one may have to adopt strategies outside the normal circuits). To come back to the accusation of madness, it's no more mad maybe for Swedenborg to say: 'I was talking the other day in the suburbs of heaven with St Paul' than for me to say here, as I might: 'The other day in Stockholm I was talking with Strindberg and Swedenborg.'

Wandering around Stockholm, I went into one antiquarian bookshop after another, looking for a particular text of Swedenborg's that I wanted to have with me – and finally found it. This was his *Opera Philosophica et Mineralia* ('Mineral and Philosophical Works'), in which one can read this: 'In the former part of our treatise, we arrived at that element of the world that may be called the magnetic, the first in which elementary nature presents herself as visible to the eye. Here it is that she begins to emerge out of her hiding place, and from darkness to issue forth into light...'

That notion of 'magnetic field' was one of the ideas occupying my mind in those days.

The other was the world of birds.

That's where Rudbeck comes in.

It was at an old bookshop in Paris, only a few yards away from where Strindberg picked up Balzac's *Seraphita*, that, in 1989, I came across Olof Rudbeck's *Book of Birds*, in a facsimile edition of the original manuscript that had lain dormant in a library (that of the little town of Lufsta in Sweden) for close on three hundred years. This was the first compendious and consequential bird-book ever undertaken.

Enormous projects, sometimes never completed, ran in the family.

It had begun with the grandfather, Johannes, who started off in mathematics, went from mathematics to Hebrew, and from Hebrew to nature study – as though he was looking for a greater and greater language.

His son, Olof, Olof the Younger's father, born in 1630, specialized in medicine, but got more and more interested in botany outside medicine, and projected the biggest album of botany the world had ever seen, calling it the *Campus Elysii*, 'The Field of the Blessed'.

Olof the Younger, born 1660, also specialized in medicine, with a particular interest in botany – he worked for years with his father on the *Campus Elysii*. But gradually he distanced himself from medicine, while still occupying his chair at Uppsala. At one point, he left on a mission to the north, from which he brought back his *Iter Lapponicum*. Later, he'd just wander off – sometimes for years on end, doing 'research' on something he called his *Lexicon Harmonicum*: the search for some kind of fundamental harmony. Once, after such an absence, he came back to lecture from his university chair and talked to the mesmerized students – about birds: whitehead eagles, ospreys, goshawks, gyrfalcons, kestrels and snowy owls.

The Rudbecks were precursors to the better known Linné (as a student, he was preceptor in the family), who did more systematic work, but they were, it appears, intellectually wilder and more speculative.

At the Royal Library of Stockholm, I was able to see one of Rudbeck's manuscripts, a massive thing bound in white parchment. And then I took the train to Uppsala where, at the University, I saw the original manuscript of the *Book of Birds* as well as that of the *Lexicon Harmonicum*.

I then left for western Gothland.

★

It was five in the evening, and a heavy rain falling. Passing Flemingsberg, I got glimpses of furzy land with patches of snow, and here and there skoggy forest. I was on the express train, the X2000, from Stockholm to Falköping.

In conversation with my neighbour, I realized that he was using the word 'landscape' in a way unfamiliar to me. He'd said he lived in the landscape south of Falköping. It turned out that in Swedish the word *landskap* indicates not only the lie of the land but a regional unit.

When we got to Falköping station, Leif Äkerman, the man who'd suggested I come and see the cranes, was waiting for me.

As we drove to his house, I told him about what I'd learned on the train. He confirmed the fact, saying that backcountry Swedish would have a whole lot of other things to interest me. He then quoted a line from a poem: *'Jag trivs bäst i öppna landskap'* ('I live best in the open landscape'), saying that the Swedes were very attached to their territory. It was there even in their national anthem, things usually full of blood, sweat, tears, breast-beating and pomposity:

> *Du gamla du fria*
> *Du fjällhöga nord*
> *Du fysta*
> *Du glädjerika*
> ...
> *ja jag vill leva*
> *jag vill dö*
> *i norden*

('You old one, you free one, you mountainhigh northland, you trustful one, you gladsome one... yes, I want to live, I want to die, in the North').

Leif's wife, Ulla, had prepared an abundant meal, the central part of which was, she said, a homely dish which all Swedes knew: potatoes with onions and anchovies, known familiarly as *Janssons Frestelse*, 'Mr Johnson's Temptation'.

We went to bed early, intending to get up early the next morning to go to see the cranes.

Leif told me the normal word for early was *tidgit*, but that the archaic, poetic word was *arla: arlamorgentid* is the early morning time – 'a sort of animal early', he said.

We were up at dawn, drove up to Lake Hornborga and by just a little after sunrise were at Tjurum, at the southern tip of the lake, on a field edged with sumpy, tussocky, reedy marshland, here and there birch copses.

And there they were, the cranes – thousands of them: wings grey, white, blacktipped; neck white, black, with a red patch on the head; body feathers grey and fawn.

Some were still flying with outstretched neck and wings widespread, limbs held rigid, the feathers close-set at the bone ridge and splaying out at the back. Some were stepping daintily through the misty fen, doubled in the smoothly reflecting water. Some were standing tall with curved breast, beak raised open to the sky and calling. Others were dancing, in a style that made even the taoist tactics of Chinese mountain monks look clumsy. They leapt and gestured and adopted magnificent stances – like living ideograms.

Hornborga is the principal resting-place for migratory birds in Sweden. The cranes come from North Africa, Portugal and Spain. They leave their winter quarters in February, and fly up over France and Germany, taking time to rest and feed up on the way. The last resting-place before Falköping is the island of Rügen on the German Baltic coast. From Rügen to Falköping is about 400 kilometres, and the birds do the journey in about seven hours.

If Hornborga is so unanimously appreciated by the cranes, it's because its waters are shallow and nutritious, but also because there, in addition to a diet of worms, frogs, berries, they can enjoy potatoes. Cranes apparently have a craving for potatoes – especially frosted potatoes. There used to be a distillery on the lake side that left a lot of potato mash piled up. Word at one time must have got around among the Crane

Folk. The distillery has long since closed down, but local people see that plenty of potatoes are still available. After feeding and resting at Hornborga, the birds move on to the Swedish Norrland, Finland, Russia.

Within the next few days, we went several times to watch the cranes, morning and evening. But Leif was keen for me also to make acquaintance with the whole region, the whole 'landscape'.

★

Leif liked to feel that he was living in what at one time had been the edge of the human world. And he had reasons to think and feel so. The last great ice sheet stopped only a little north of here. Maybe the two great table-mountains that dominate the area, the Mosseberg and the Ålleberg, are what remains of the great loads of earth pushed by the glacier, elsewhere, on the plain, weathered down to granite and gneiss, but there preserved in the mass by a crust of hard rock. You could imagine people wandering up here and living with the ice on their horizon. You can count about twenty neolithic tombs right in the middle of Falköping: they loom up at street corners, or in behind buildings. One neolithic queenie died just after eating raspberries. Her bones are laid out in the Falköping museum and she is known locally, in a charming kind of way, as The Raspberry Girl.

So much for fore-history.

As to history, it's there most obviously in the rune stones that dot the landscape. People here must have been raising stones, and cutting and colouring runes, for centuries, but perhaps more often during the Viking times. One stone in particular attracted me by its forms. As to its meaning, it read like this: 'Buve had this stone raised for Olof, his son, a good man, who was cut down in Estonia.'

Then there were the political wars and frontier fighting, between Swedes and Germans, between Svenskar and Danskar. In 1389, at the Battle of Falköping, the people of Sweden were fighting against a German domination represented by Albert of Mecklemburg. That was the time when Stockholm was held by a band calling themselves The Big Hat Boys (the Hättebrödrar) and when the Baltic was overrun by pirates calling themselves the Vitalie Brödrar, ('the Victualler Fellows') because they were supposed to be bringing in food to succour the capital. As to Swede and Dane, they were at it hammer and tongs for ages, both before and after the triple treaty of Union (Norway, Sweden, Denmark) negotiated by Margaret of Denmark. In 1455, the Swedish hero, Tord Bonde, changed the name of a Danish fortress from Danaborg ('the stronghold of the Danes') to Danasorg ('the sorrow of the Danes'), which sums up the story. Those were tough times. The Bishop of Uppsala, a disreputable Dane, ended up tied in a sack and drowned, in Iceland.

Meanwhile, pilgrims were moving across the land – the Pilgrim's Trail to St Olav's grave in Trondheim passed by here.

We went through towns and villages such as Odensberg ('Odin's hill'), Friggeråker ('Freya's field'), Håkantorp ('Haakon's village'), Gudhem ('God's home'), Ugglum ('Owl town'), Gökhem ('Cuckoo town'), Dala, Borgunda, Skara, the old centre of learning, where, as aforesaid, Swedenborg's father was pastor. In some stood beautiful little whitewashed churches with painted walls ('Mäster Amund painted this') and woodwork done by the same hands that made the Viking ships.

We went up to Lake Vättern, talking in a fish-shop about *röd-fish* (charr) and *öring* (trout), walking among beeches and birches, listening to the slash-slosh of the lakeside waters, sitting, at Hjo, in a *hamn-krog* (a harbour eatery), and the rain falling.

But mainly it was the land itself, the great dun yellow sweep of it, crossed by grey crows, gulls, magpies and thrushes. Cultivated fields too, of rich dark loam, that yet always left an uncultivated 'island' at the centre, the *äkerö*.

I could have stayed longer there in west Gothland, but I was keen to go further north.

Which is why, after a week, I was back in Stockholm, waiting at Stockholm's Central Station for the train to Falun.

★

We pulled out by Märsta, and pretty soon we were humming across the landscape: birchy, piney country, with a lot of erratic boulders, here and there darkred farmhouses.

Avesta Krylbo.

Some snow patches still on the hills.

Borlänge.

A sky shot with incredible blues.

I checked in at the Miners' Hotel, Falun, had a meal, and went for a walk through the town.

When Carl Linné was up in these parts in 1734 (this was two years after his Lapland journey), he called Falun copper mountain mine the most grandiose image of hell he'd ever seen or was ever likely to see. He crept among the stones of the mines and at night sat near the smelting furnaces:

> A pungent smell issues continuously from the depths of the mine, poisoning the air and corroding the soil so that no grass can grow. Underground are countless passageways where the sun never reaches, fouled with fumes, heat and damp. In these underground labyrinths toil a thousand minehands, surrounded by smoke, fumes and darkness on all sides. The walls are sooty, the floor is slippery and the passageways narrow. The risk of cave-ins is great. The workers go about half-naked with a woollen cloth over their mouths to keep them from inhaling smoke and damp. The sweat runs from their bodies like water from a bag.

Linné made Falun the point of departure for a study-trip through the quarries and mines of Sweden: *Iter ad fodinas*. On his return to Falun, he drew up a treatise concerning the classification of minerals: *Pluto Svevicus* (1735) – 'A Description of the Kingdom of Rocks'. His criterion for classification was based on external marks, mainly crystalline structure, and was outdated even before it was included in the complete edition of his *Systema Naturae* (1768), but it is still worth reading, because it was Linné who wrote it, and any movement of a mind with that amplitude and acuity is interesting.

The next morning, after spending half the night reading that text, I went to visit the mine myself.

You stand there at the surface, looking at the many-coloured chasm of the Great Pit, 400 metres wide, 150 metres deep, the result of the tremendous cave-in of 1687. Then you take the cage to go underground and move along the galleries. The rock is still sweating black blood. It's not hard to imagine the bodies at work, the forges for the sharpening of tools shedding a fuliginous glow, and horses neighing dementedly. In the early Middle Ages, it was hard to find people willing to work down there. In order to recruit a work force, the king had to offer pardon to criminals, so that the place turned into a kind of underground penitentiary. Later, when the mine had become the hub of Sweden's industry and economy, people lined up for jobs, because the wages were good. You might suffer from perpetual dizziness, muscle spasms, haemorrhaging of the lungs, but there were those good wages.

Coming up from the mine, I went to examine the maps and mineral collections of the mine's museum.

What interested me particularly about the old copper mountain maps – Olof Swart's of 1629, Hans Ranie's of 1683 – was that they made out a different sheet for each level, with the cavities and shafts cut out, so that you have not only a surface level with indications of depth, but a multi-dimensional mass.

As to the stones of the mineral collection, it was their sheer beauty first of all: that pink feldspar; that other bit of feldspar, pale-coloured, with gleaming black gadolinite crystals; that mica schist with quartz intrusions; that chalcopyrite in quartz... But there was also the context and the process. Granite in the first place, then limestone changing into dolomite, leptite into quartz and mica schist, and thereafter chalcopyrite, sulphur pyrite, zinc, pitchblende and galenite.

You don't think the same once you're into that kind of thing.

★

I'd long been used to pinning up maps in hotel rooms. There in Falun, it was a map of the magnetic field present around the earth and that extends into space – caused by electrical currents in the fluid core of the planet, influenced also by the solar wind; constant for long periods, but liable also to sudden changes in strength and direction; varying according to differences in the density of the bedrock.

At least one poetic movement in the twentieth century had taken the magnetic field analogy: Surrealism. But it was only as an analogy, the 'magnetic field' for the Surrealists being the unconscious.

But might it not be more than analogy?

Might it be possible at least to extend the analogy, thinking not only of the unconscious, but of the brain, the nervous system, the whole body in its relationship to the universe?

Make of existence a field of poetic density?

I left Falun for Lake Siljan.

On the way, I saw again one of the grey, red-topped cranes I'd seen at Hornborga. It made me feel I was on the right migratory track. Though I was a bit puzzled to come across only one, after all the thousands I'd seen at Hornborga. Was this a loner on his (or her) well-loved secret path?

Late afternoon, and the lake waters absolutely limpid, with bluewhite cloud exactly and impeccably reflected. Then, as evening came, a slight breeze set to fluttering the thin shreds and tatters of fine paperbark on the birchtrees. Later still, it was sunset, with the strangest redness I've ever seen and the strongest blue on the horizon. Then an owl began to hoot, amplifying the space.

During the next couple of days, I moved round the lake. I went to see the kirk at Rättvik, with its huddle of cabins and stables on the shore. I visited the house of the painter Zorn at Mora, interested mainly in some very quick 'Atlantic sketches' (a mass of white, a few lines of darkblue) he painted when returning from America in 1894. I went to Leks, seeing the little excursion steamers moored in an arm of the lake, walking round the wooden fire-tower and the graveyard where Olof Sandberg lies next to Gustav Olsson.

Then, near Tällberg, I came upon this cabin on a little promontory: weathered grey wood, with darkred facings at door and windows. Inside, two rooms and a little kitchen. It was to let, like many others I'd seen round the lake.

I rented it.

There may be many people around Siljan in Summer, but there were very few that April.

My main company for the next week consisted of a black and grey crow, two magpies, a squirrel, a blackbird, and, at night, an owl.

Not forgetting the lake itself, with its amazing colours, the little promontory with its birches, and the shore with its mossy rocks.

How good it can feel to get out of all the agitation, all the opining and the discoursing, and just be at peace for a while with the planet.

Aurora Borealis

It was a soppingly rainy grey-green morning in the town of Gothenberg, on the west side of Sweden. Gulls were wailing and squawking on the station square. In my hip pocket, I had a ticket entitling me to *Plass* 29 (*Vindu*) on the 6:35 for Oslo, which was a redcoloured ICE (Inter City Express) marked 'till Oslo S'.

'*God Morgen* – Good morning and welcome on board.'

There were very few passengers.

We pulled out past the Post Terminal, the building of an export business (*Expert på Export*) and a tower bearing the message Quaker State Motor Oil.

Then we were into the landscape: a dank misty stretch of river, grey-green, grey-yellow, followed by tussocky moorland.

★

On the first page of my Norway notebook, I had this, from Balzac's *Seraphita*:

> Looking at a map of the Norwegian coast, what imagination could fail to marvel at that fantastic tracery of granite over which the waters of the North Sea moan incessantly? Who has never dreamt of the magnificent spectacle afforded by those rocky shores, that multitude of creeks, bays and fjords no one of which ressembles another, all of them places of pathless depth?

Places of pathless depth...

Öxnered.

After that, it was more open country, with the sky clearing. Here and there, patches of snow, and a silvery glow on the birches.

Huge magpie nests.

Tawny yellow fields, a grey ice-covered lake.

Then *skogland*, forest country.

Thereafter, reedy marshland.

Ting, tong, at the level crossings.

In Gothenberg last night, a Swede told me he'd travelled all the way up north by train. Before taking to his bunk at night-time, he was looking out at a certain landscape. When he woke up hundreds of kilometres later, he was looking out at the very same landscape.

But I wouldn't say that here. There are subtle variations of brown, black, grey and white in the misty monotony.

Halden – a huddled little harbour.

We pass through a tunnel and blue bulbs light up in the bluegrey of the carriage.

Skjeberg.

A huge factory belching smoke.

Sarpsborg.

More people have come on board. Speaking with more rising intonations than I've become used to in Sweden.

Fredrikstad.

Moss – a big number of Chinese containers massed in the harbour front.

Vestby.

Oslo.

★

Either weekends are the time for religion in Norway, or some Billy Graham kind of character had just passed that way. What's sure is that, on that Saturday afternoon in Oslo, religion was everywhere. You couldn't move for it. Everywhere voices were bawling: 'Choose the Lord today!' Rock-bands were chanting: 'He reigns, he reigns, he reigns, he reigns – forever.' Children's choirs were sing-singing: 'He's got the whole world in his hands.'

Christ almighty, what a cacophony!

I went into the Grand Café for some peace. This was where Henrik Ibsen used to hang out. They serve a 'Henrik Ibsen literary menu' here. It ends up with caramel pudding. I abstained.

There are a lot of statues in Oslo. At one point, I thought they were all of Winston Churchill. Then I saw a figure that obviously wasn't Winston Churchill – it was Theodore Roosevelt. In front of the Oslo Kommune Information Centre stood a line of sturdy statues in honour of Industrial Labour. On the square nearby, another row – hymns to motherhood.

Maybe the spruce and dapper little chap I saw as evening was coming down in the Karl Johann Street, wearing a black coat, a bowler, and spats, with his beard dyed a bright blue, was just trying, desperately, to get away from all that humano-historical weight.

Back in the hotel, a rough-looking lout waiting in the hall let out an expressionist howl as his three companions came out of the lift. These four constituted a folk group called The Yorkshire Yokels, here in Oslo for a Culture Festival of European Peoples.

I was beginning to think more and more that Oslo was a place to leave, fast.

In no time at all, this mixture of War Memory, Social Realism, Religiosity, not forgetting Folky Yokeldom, would have had me in the throes of a mammoth depression.

Norway had to be more than all that stuff.

I checked out of the hotel the next morning at the same time as an air-crew, of which one member said:

'Back up into the snow.'

That sounded like a good idea.

★

I'm standing at the SAS bus-stop in front of the Sentralstasjon, beside a green box full of salt. The red face on the glass tower of the clock tower marks 6:58. It's raining. I'm making for Fornery airport. There's a flight for Tromsø, away up there in the Arctic Circle, at eight o'clock.

On the plane, the announcements are made in Norwegian, English and Russian: 'Flying conditions are good, but there is a thick cloud cover... The temperature at ground level in Tromsø is 3°... *Spassibo.*'

I have a map of Norway in front of me.

We'll be flying up via Lillehammer, Trondheim and Narvik, but it's to the ragged coast of fjords and islands that my eye is attracted:

Boknafjord
Hardanfjord
Osterfjord
Nordfjord
Romsdalfjord
Velfjord
Randfjord

Saltfjord
Solbergfjord

...

and, among the islands, in particular, the Vesterälen and the Lofoten.

It's just above Randfjord that the Polar Circle begins.

My eye follows the line up beyond Tromsø to the North Cape, where the south–north line becomes a west–east line that goes by Laksefjord and Tanafjord and Varangerfjord over into Russia: Murmansk, the Kola peninsula, the White Sea, Arkhangelesk.

So far as its Norwegian boundaries are concerned, this area is called Hålogaland, Nordlandene og Finnmarken, Nordlandet, or Nord-Norge. It has, in Norway, something of an aura. I realized that down in Oslo, when, after a little conversation, the girl behind the reception counter at the hotel said, 'Ah, you are going to our Northland?' From about the middle of the nineteenth century, but with increasing insistence as from the end of that century, the Northland has been considered both as Norway's backcountry (place of origins, land of sources) and as its frontier: 'Go North young man and grow up with the country.' There's even a North-Norwegian regional anthem: '*Å eg veit meg eit land...*'

From a transnational point of view, Norway's Nord-Norge joins up with Sweden's Norrland, Finland's Lapland and Russia's White Sea Region to form Euro-Arctica.

Europeans have been going up to the North Cape and beyond, both north and east, for at least ten thousand years. A rock painting at the head of the Altafjord shows a long boat and men fishing from it. For centuries, folk were sending down fish from there to feed Catholic Europe on Fridays. Vikings, during their great out-going activity, passed by that way on their route to the White Sea, in ships like that beautiful Gokstad ship, a *karvi*, I saw in the Ship Hall at Oslo: built of oak, 24 metres long, 16 pairs of oars. By the sixteenth century, Europe was looking for a North-East Passage to China. In 1553, Captain Richard Chancellor left London on the *Edward Bonaventure* bearing a letter addressed by the king of England to 'all the kings of the North-East part of the world as far as China'. At Vardø, east of the North Cape, he met a band of Scotsmen who'd been around there for a while and told him it was too late in the year (November) to continue. Chancellor pushed on regardless. He made it, just – but he was wrecked off the Scottish coast three years later. He should have paid more attention to those Aberdonians.

In 1664, at the age of forty, Francesco Negri, a Franciscan priest of Ravenna, student not only of Latin, theology and philosophy, but also of astronomy, geology, geography, botany and zoology, set out on the long journey in the North he had been dreaming of for years, ever since, as a young man, he had read that *Historia de Gentibus Septentrionalibus*, written by Olav Magnus, the last Catholic archbishop of Sweden, who had left his homeland for Rome at the time of the Reform. Negri brought back voluminous notes on which he worked right up to the end of his life. His book, *Viaggio Settentrionale*, was published, posthumously, at Padua, in 1700. So it went on, till, towards the end of the nineteenth century, the North Cape became a point of attraction for the kind of English or American traveller who would strike a pose on the plateau and recite a poem by Longfellow.

I don't think I'll go up to the Cape. They probably don't recite Longfellow any more, but I'm pretty sure that every day in the week a hundred gentlemen from Tokyo get themselves photographed in Viking helmets.

No, I won't go up to the Cape, I'll stay in Tromsø.

★

Coming through Tromsø airport, I pass the Arctic Gate Pub, where the beer is pulled out of the gub of a polar bear. Outside, waiting for a taxi, I see a big black van pull up and wonder if it isn't a kind of bus-taxi, till I see emblazoned on its side the words Arctic Conversions. That's heartening. It means some people still haven't been converted.

'Where do you want to go?'

'The centre of town.'

Once there, I walk along the Storgata, Main Street, then along the Skippergata, into the old fisher town. It's there I come across a mustard yellow wooden building bearing the name Nordhuset (North House) and advertising itself as a hotel. I ask if there's a room available. There is. Once in it, I see I've got nine square yards of space, a bed, a cupboard, a table and chair. And on one wall there's a photo of the Lofoten Islands.

I go back out into town.

An icy rain is falling. There aren't many people about. The impression is of some frontier settlement. I go into a newspaper shop and buy the *Svalbard Posten*. The owner's dog is a husky, snowy white, with amazing blue eyes, a female. 'What's her name?', I ask. 'Bella', I'm told. I'd have preferred something huskier...

My steps lead me then to the Nordnorsk Kunstmuseum. Again, the heavy maternity–paternity thing, this time due to Vigeland. Next to that, a photography exhibition showing a series of fat bulging bodies, mostly women, one of them bound from head to foot in tape. But some paintings indicate another space: a view of Svolvaer by one Gunnar Berg; a landscape of the Finnmark, yellow sun on the tundra, by Gustav Mordt.

I go back out into the streets.

Strand Street.

A battered Russian cargo-boat, registered Murmansk, is beating its way south.

I walk up to the Arctic Cathedral, over the long bridge, then come back down again into the town centre.

That icy rain is still falling.

I pass a green metal statue of Amundsen, with a crow perched on his shoulder, like some Odin of the ice.

In the evening I go into a restaurant: Peppermöllen ('the pepper mill'). That's where I meet Amundsen again. The walls are lined with photos of him, and of other Arctic explorers: Henry Rudi, Waldemar Kralmer, Hetman Nøys, Arthur Oxaas, Heimar Hansen, Guttorm Jakobsen, Hjolmar Johansen, Paul Bjøvig, Olaf Starstad. There's a special notice on one wall about Amundsen and, since I'm having trouble with the Norwegian, I call over the waitress and ask her to translate: 'When Roald Amundsen was in Tromsø on his travels north he always was a guest here of the pharmacist Zappfen and was often in this room.'

Those travels north. Mostly about 'conquering the Pole', about peril and survival, with anthropologists in the wake of the explorers revelling in accounts of the seal hunt, delighting to describe their faces smeared with blood. Very little about what the Inuit mind can get at in its furthest reaches. For example, the state of mind called in Eskimo *quiiuinaqtuk*, which an old Inuit I met once in Montreal (he'd come down for treatment at the hospital) described to me as follows: 'It's like a window you can look through into a bigger world, you can see the world whole beyond the shadows, some say it's dreaming, but it's not dreaming and, I can tell you, it's a lot deeper than happiness.'

I take my time over the Peppermill dinner, and leave about eleven o'clock, making my way back up to the Nordhuset.

There will be no Aurora Borealis these nights. But I can *imagine* it up there, leaping sixty miles or so above the earth, an immense phenomenon – the solar wind taking about three days to travel the millions of miles between the sun and the earth, its electrons entering the earth's magnetic field, running along its lines into the earth's atmosphere and bursting into light, a great sheet of flickering, dancing light. I had it, secretively, in my head, where I translated it, but not too much, into humanese.

★

Next morning, at breakfast, I make the acquaintance of Yuri Akanazov.

In English spiced by Norwegian and some Russian he tells me that he is from Arkangelesk, and that he has been coming to Tromsø for some time now, since 1992. His great-grandfather used to frequent Tromsø a lot. When Spring came, making navigation once again possible in the White Sea, he'd sail his ketch loaded with flour and timber and come to trade direct with the Norwegian fishermen for dried cod, *stockfisch*. It was an old practice, he says, going back long into the past – a way for the fishermen of the North to get round the monopolies of Bergen and Copenhagen. That was the famous Pomor Trade (Pomor – 'people of the sea'). But Russia had put an end to this private enterprise after the revolution of 1917 and the setting-up of the Soviets. It was only after the collapse of the Communist bloc that it had started up again, in a small way, oh, a very small way. He and several others like him had started coming by boat or by bus, bringing with them what they could: military uniforms and medals, binoculars, samovars, old icons. They'd sell what they had in three or four days, change their loks (Norwegian kroners) into USD (US dollars) in Tromsø and then convert their dollars into rubles, making profit in the process, at Murmansk. In four days they could earn the equivalent of a month's salary in Russia. But then some fellows had begun to bring in drugs, and some women had started to come in awhoring, so the Norwegian government were out to put an end to it all. But Yuri keeps coming, doing a little trade in a quiet way, especially in the innocuous domain of arts and crafts.

I spend the day at the Tromsø Museum, looking at the drawings on Saami shaman drums, listening to recordings of the wolf song, the reindeer calf song, the long-tailed duck song, which contain phonetic imitations of these animals. *There* was a culture. There's something essential in that relationship to the earth. No need, of course, to accept all the mental cinema present there too. But the contact, the permanent, grounded relationship, that's what matters.

In the evening, I share a meal with Yuri at an underground pizza place. He tells me about Nova Zembla, where he did his military service, at the Nuclear Polygon: 'I hated it, and it will kill me with cancer... I hated not only the Army routine, but the way people lived there. The greatest sport was to shoot at polar bears from helicopters. And I will tell you one thing. There is still a bomb up there, a huge bomb, that will explode some day, it may destroy the whole world.'

Yuri leaves the next day for Arkangelesk.

I keep stravaiging about Tromsø.

★

Midnight, and I'm at the harbour café in Tromsø, waiting for the boat to the Lofoten. Insomniac gulls are yelling in the darkness, and a black ship is throbbing up the black waters.

A great blast, and it's the *Vesterålen* coming into harbour.

I wait in the queue to see the purser, get my key, and retire to my cabin.

A very pleasant little place, immaculately white, with a little nineteenth-century painting by P. S. Krøyer on the wall: *Summer evening in Skagen.*

Next morning, I'm up early, eager to get the feel of the fjords and islands from the sea.

During the night, we've come down the Grøtsund, through the Rustraum, along the Gibosund into the Solbergfjord. Now we've left Stangsnes on the island of Senja and are making towards Harstad in the Vesterålen (the Western Isles). The boat noses its way slowly among islands now tawny and fuzzy brown, now grey-white. Higher summits are smothered in cloud. At times, a salmony flush. Gulls gliding. Black duck scudding across the darkgreen waters.

Speculum boreale.

There's been a lot of 'boreal' speculation over the past century. It's Nietzsche speaking of a 'hyperborean' distance from society and humanity. It's Valéry (a Southerner) saying that 'Nobody ever goes to the North of being.' This has nothing to do with expeditions. It has everything to do with getting in touch with the non-human. That's what gives an edge to human existence, space to the mind, light to the eyes.

At Harstad, there's an hour's stop, so I go ashore for a walk through town, passing a hotel called The Viking Nordic, a restaurant called The Viking Grillen, a statue of Generalmajor Carl C. Fleischer (1883–1942), another statue to Musikh-løytnant Alfred Evensen (1883–1942), a bingo hall and an advertisement for Willie Nelson's Country & Western appearance at the Harstad Kulturhus.

We then continue along the Risøy Sound to Risøyhamn, through a landscape–seascape of anthracite and salt. The weather report is 'Slight north-easterly wind (*nordostig swak vind*), sky slightly overcast.' Which is true to fact. It's late April, and for a while I'm alone on the observation deck. Then, after breakfast, I'm joined by an American couple from Minnesota. I get bits of conversation: 'At least we've been to the North Cape. We've done it', says the woman. 'Yeah, and we've got a certificate to prove it too.' Jane is a very neat sixty, white-haired, dressed in a blue-black-white Norwegian knitted sweater and jeans. Bob is burly, wears a tartan shirt. Silence for a longish while, then Bob says he thinks he'll go down to the bar, 'blow a 100 an' have a coke – high livin'.' Jane says she'll just sit there. When Bob comes back, Jane has raised her head from her crossword puzzle and is staring into space. Bob comes up behind her, puts his hands on her shoulders and says softly, 'Yeah, that's life.'

After unloading sacks of plant earth at Risøyhamn (this isn't just a passenger boat, it also provides the outlying districts with supplies), we're moving right down the middle of the Western Isles towards Sortland and Stokmarknes.

Then it's the Raftsund.

Rocks grey-black, violet purple, with waterfalls cascading down them into the fjord. Low cloud hanging on the heights. A cold wind blowing at times through the gaps. Moss thick on the stone.

The gulls are close: red-eyed, golden-beaked. Up against the rock face, a sea-eagle.

I get off the boat at Svolvaer, on the east side of the Lofoten.

★

When I've set foot on the pier at Svolvaer, the first thing I see are two graffiti on a wall: 'Fuck da police', followed a few inches later by 'Fuck you.' The English language sure is becoming a great means of universal communication.

On all sides, piles of mucky snow, and over it a cold rain falling.

I pass by the Methodist Church (Metodiskkirke), then a Centre for Psychic Health (Senter på Psykisk Helse), then a poster advertising the project of some folk singer: 'Get the kids together.'

The hotel I'm vaguely looking for turns out to be that cinema-looking building up there at the top of the street. I check in. The proprietrix is a surly slob. As to the premises, they have a pervasive guffy stench. And the predominant colours are meaty red and dirty yellow. The lamps in the hall are like big mamma-breasts with protuberant nipples.

I stand at my window, looking out into the dusk gathering over Svolvaer.

Down below, heaps of grey snow, outcroppings of darkgrey rock and piles of refuse. A gull flies back and forth. The lift of the hotel gives a whine and a thud, as of bombs dropping: *wheeeee boom, wheeeee boom.*

I decide to look elsewhere for an evening meal. On the way, I go into a newspaper shop to buy a map of the Lofoten. I have to work my way through tangled bunches of technicolour trolls and rows upon rows of plump sex magazines. I get the map, not so detailed as I'd hoped, and while I'm at it, buy the *Lofotposten*. On the front page, a photograph of all the recent mothers with their progeniture in their arms. I then continue my search for a place to eat. Find one that looks not too bad. As a meal, what I get is glairy soup that feels as if it's been ladled out of a spittoon, and a dish of boiled catfish with double-boiled potatoes – no, on second thoughts, boiled potatoes with doubled-boiled catfish.

And so to bed. *Wheeeee boom, wheeeee boom.*

★

The curtains grow redder, and it's sunrise, with gulls clamouring loudly over the harbour.

When I open the curtains, I see the sky is unbelievably blue.

My eyes take in a rack of drying fish, two huge gulls with great hooked yellow beaks sitting among their starry shit-splashings, and in the lee of a big moss-covered rock, eleven darkblue crocuses, the advance guard of Spring.

'Good morning, Norge – hello, Lofoten.'

There's a tremendous sensation of freshness and unbesullied reality.

You don't have to move about a lot in the Lofoten to see not only that the landscape is strangely beautiful but that it's a complex unity, made up largely of two types of rock: old Caledonian masses, rugged, worn; and younger ranges of sharp Alpine crests. It's perhaps especially beautiful at this time of the year, when Winter is still close enough for great stretches of whiteness to subsist, while early Spring has melted enough of the snow for stark, black lines to appear.

I've come out on the East Way, moving up the shore of the Austnesfjord towards Fiskebøl. This is 'outerside Lofoten'.

The light's varying fast, from glowering through glaring to glowing. The fjord's waters, a deep blue, are whipped by the wind into white and violet.

Beyond Fiskebøl, at the head of the Morfjord, still waters and brilliant light. The shore is first sand, then tussocky grass, then a marshy, mossy ground with stunted birches.

All along the fjords, whether the Austnesfjord, the Mosfjord, or now the Grunnførfjord, icy streams trickling down into their waters from the rocky hills.

Coming down from Laukvika, those hills are bulky jetblack masses and behind these, sharp ghostly-white crags. While I'm looking at one such jetblack mass, a big cloud comes swooping down over it, covering it almost to ground level.

★

The next day I go down the West Way, across the islands of Gimsø, Vestvå, Flakstad and Moskenes, this last name probably stemming from a Saami word *moski*, meaning 'a far and with difficulty accessible place'. At one time, when the Lapps were still around these parts before they were driven farther north, it may have been the name for all the Lofoten.

I'm standing on the pier at Å, at the end of the road, down at the tip of Moskenes, watching how the gulls have used the pier as a cliff, building nests in the tyres that line its sides as dunters for the fishing boats, when a man of about forty comes up to me and engages me in conversation. His name is Ole Nilsen, from an old fishing family he says, and he wants to tell me about cod-fishing in the Lofoten:

'These are the biggest cod fisheries in the whole wide world. Do you know about the cod?'

In fact, I know quite a lot about cod. One of my red-haired ancestors spent years of his life on the Banks of Newfoundland, as a fishing minister. He even left a manuscript: 'The Book of Cod and God'.

'A bit, not that much.'

'Like for me to tell you?'

'Sure.'

So, he goes on, the Arctic cod, the *skrei*, as they call it in Norwegian, after seven or eight years gambolling about in the Barents Sea, come down to the Lofoten to spawn. They begin their journey in, say, November, and arrive in the West Fjord, 800 kilometres later, in January. That's when the fishing season starts, and it lasts into April.

And why do the fish come to the Lofoten?

Because of the good water temperature and the just right degree of saltiness. Then there's plenty of food: crawfish and copepod larvae. And it's good water too, because the number of cross-currents and the melting of tides make for a maelstroming.

Back in the old times, the Lofoten would be packed every

31

January with men lugging Lofoten chests full of warm clothing and food from all over the Nordland. They'd be lodged in those red cabins there, the fishermen's shanties, 'what we call *rorbuer*', maybe ten to twelve men in one hut, sleeping two or three to a bunk. A hard life. They'd be out every day, in boats owned by 'the kings of the fjord'. Many still come, but in their own boats; times have changed... Everybody joins in. As a boy, like other kids, he got the job of pulling out the cods' tongues: 'It's good for you: you get to know blood, production and money.' After the fishing and gutting, the fish have to be put out on racks, tied in pairs by the tail. That's a risky business. It's true that conditions on the Lofoten are the most favourable in the world: cold enough to keep off flies and maggots, warm enough to avoid freezing. But still and all, it's good to have someone about who knows his business, and who can keep an eye or rather a nose on the drying fish, to 'see if it's sour or if it smells of money'. It hangs out in the wind till June. At the moment, Ole reckons there must be about 20 million kilos of *stockfish* on the Lofoten racks. That is a lot, but nothing compared with the old days. In 1895, they caught 38 million cod, can you imagine?! After the drying, it goes into bales of 50 kilos and is shipped off mainly to Italy and Nigeria...

I thanked Ole for the information. He said he was practising. He was thinking of opening a museum on the stockfish curing, and on the making of cod liver oil which every child used to imbibe by the tablespoonful (I can remember that myself). Did I think it was a good idea, would it work? 'Who knows?' I said. Would I like to come in the shed and see what he had already gathered together? I said, no, thanks, I'd maybe visit his museum some other day when it would be all ready.

He then asked me if I'd like to hire a fisherman's shanty for a while. He had been buying them up in the neighbourhood, with the idea of converting them into cabins for travellers. He even had one out there on the island of Røst, out beyond the maelstrom, away at the end of the end, where only birds live. I must admit I was attracted to this proposal, but I'd begun to have a great liking for Svolvaer, so I turned it down.

I really was beginning to like Svolvaer (probably Saami *Svolo-Vearra*, 'the island village').

I liked walking the streets of the little gull-yelling burg. In the mornings, I'd be down at the harbour to see what cargo was being brought in: these last few days, big 1,000-kilo bags of salt from Finland. I'd found a place where I could get a good dish of stockfish and bacon and mashed beans. I'd found a café laid out like an old-fashioned dining-room with armchairs and sofas, where I could sit, with no muzak playing, and watch the Spring sun streaming in through the windows in which the craggy snow-covered Lofoten mountains were profiled.

I spent a week like that, then decided to get on the move again.

★

When I got on the Coastal Cruiser again that afternoon at Svolvaer, I wasn't too happy. Especially as it wasn't the same type of boat, but a newer one, more vulgar in its effects. There were more people on board too.

By dusk, we were at Stamsund, between the dark rocks and the rosy rocks.

After Stamsund, the Lofotens fanned out into a crescent. At the centre, the Stamsund hills turned from tawny brown to dark and, at the extreme ends of the crescent, the hills faded away into a ghostlier and ghostlier bluegrey.

A gull followed the boat for a while, as though enjoying its last manoeuvres for the day, letting itself be wind-carried down the stretch, then beating up again. But after a while it winged its way resolutely back to the islands.

A lighthouse began to blink back there on the Lofoten. Ahead, another blinked on the mainland coast.

The next morning, at 9:20, we came out of the Polar Circle. I said farewell to the Lofoten with regret.

Not that things weren't still beautiful. We were hardly out of the Polar Circle, at 66° 33', when I saw a polar fujiyama – blue, with a white summit: absolute serenity, beyond everything thinkable.

We came down through the islands of the North Sea (Norskehavet), the wind whistling, along a series of bluegrey meditations. Then along a hardgrey, snowwhite coastline. Seeing here and there fleet lines of migratory birds.

We passed by Rørvik, Trondheim, Kristiansund, then along the Atlantic Road.

Moving down to Bergen.

At eight on the following morning, it was a grey sea, and the cloud cover thick. But when the grey bank broke, a flood of brilliant paleblue light was shed over the snow-streaked hills on the horizon. Later on, shafts of sunlight through the grey mist lit up grey, lichen-covered rock.

I said there were more people on board. There definitely were, and more and more.

Of the men, some looked like lumberjacks, but broke out now and then into infantile tee-hee laughter. Others were business-looking characters with mobile phones attached to their belts.

A bevy of older Norwegian women were chewing sweets, knitting ski-gloves for the family, while a bunch of younger ones were engaged in a discussion group.

★

Bergen.

The hotel room I found looked over a park (small, green-curled leaves on the tree by the window) and then on to the harbour. On the wall there was a copy of a sixteenth-century map by Waghenaer: *Vers Bergues en Norvège.*

That first afternoon, I laid out my things, notably several pieces of rock I'd picked up on the Lofoten.

Wanting to identify these bits of rock, check on their context, I went out on the hunt for a bookshop. The first one I came across sold only religious books: *Andaktbøker* – I passed on my way. The next had boxes full of mystical kitsch, stories about trolls, and albums about the Vikings that they were selling in 3-kilo packets at a special rate. Then I came to this modern-looking, spick-and-span establishment:

'I'm looking for books on geology – stones and minerals.'

'We don't have that. We're not interested in that kind of thing in Norway. Maybe in the children's section – school-books.'

I could hardly believe my ears. So knowledge was only for children? What do you do after childhood? Just grow up to be a sociable ignoramus? I looked around nonetheless. Saw all kinds of sections: Psychology, Religion, Sociology – but nothing like what I was looking for.

Leaving the bookshops, I went wandering about the town.

Imagine a thin inroad into a great mass of mountain – that's Bergen harbour. It's a long, thin harbour, Bergen. And there are boats in every corner: big boats, little boats, in-between boats, going from a sleek and immaculately graceful white-painted three-master to a dirty wee orange-bedaubed cargo hauler from Aberdeen.

Around the harbour, the old wharves, where the houses hold each other up, shoulder to shoulder, Madam Felle's wine-house beside Brun's bakehouse. Among them, the old Hanseatic warehouses, like merchant monasteries, where the 'Bergen travellers' lived in little wooden cells till they'd worn them-selves out, enough tallying up incoming fish, sending out flour, to merit a Hansa medal for good and loyal service.

I must have walked more than twenty times between Haakon's Fort and Scruffy Murphy's Pub. I sat in the Lido Café, looking down at the booth selling *Bakte Poteter* and the shoeshine stall, *Skopuss*, and farther on, the skin-merchant selling wolf and reindeer pelts.

I was beginning to get to know Bergen.

And finally I found a man who could talk about the stones of Norway. He had a shop full of quartz and mica and feldspath and andradite and *leirstein* and *eklogitt*.

To my pieces of rock from the Lofoten I added a bit of jasper from the island of Bemlo, south of Bergen – paleblue, old rose, like a North Sea April twilight.

Looking out over Bergen from my quiet room, I felt content, rockbottomly content.

Winds of the Skagerrak

I'm standing at a top-floor window in an old part of Copenhagen with a mug of coffee in my hand, listening to the twittering of birds and the roaring of buses, looking out over the city's youth hostel (kids lying out on the grass, drinking coke, playing guitar), and the Town Museum (among other items, I have been told, it houses Søren Kierkegaard's writing desk). To the right lie the City Archives, and to the left, first, a Bio & Café, i.e. a café and cinema (cinema: *biograf* in Danish), then a murky little bric-a-brac shop in which, beside a doll and an old sewing-machine, you see a pair of Eskimo boots and yellow photographs of Greenlanders. You cannot forget that, if Copenhagen is Kierkegaard's city, it is also Knud Rasmussen's.

If you go along the Absalonsgade to the left, you come to the Istedgade, a little cultural cul-de-sac full of tattoo shops and all kinds of sex-shops: the Copenhagen Gay Centre, the Sex-Bio Centre, the Homo Bio Centre, the Intim Bio Centre, the Sexy Keyhole, the Spunk Bar. Not forgetting the Hot 'n' Rock Café with announcements of the music-groups that are to be performing within its walls during the next few months:
Swineherd
Jigsaw Puzzle
Lovemilk
Mother of Mary
Strawberry Slaughterhouse
Screaming Eric and the Erections.

★

On 15 February 1843, at Reitzel's Bookshop here in Copenhagen, appeared *Either-or, a life fragment* by Viktor Eremita, alias Søren Kierkegaard, then twenty-nine years old.

This use of pseudonyms was to become a habit with Kierkegaard. When he brought out his second book, *Fear and Trembling*, later that same year, he signed it 'Johannes de Silentio'. Two years later, in 1845, it was as 'Hilarius Bookbinder' that he published his *Stages on a Life-journey*. When he brings out his *Unscientific Postcript*, that 'mimetic, pathetic, dialectical and existential' contribution to philosophy, in 1846, he signs it 'Johannes Climacus'. The *Training for Christianity* is presented as being by 'Anti-Climacus', edited by Søren Kierkegaard. And it's Anti-Climacus, again edited by Søren Kierkegaard, who publishes *The Sickness unto Death* in 1849.

The 'hermit', the 'silent one', the 'hilarious bookbinder' – these pseudonyms illustrate not only Kierkegaard's humour, but his fundamental life-stance, that of an absolute individual whose attitude to society can only be sardonic and satirical.

In 1846, a journal in Copenhagen decided to write an article in favour of 'our rising local author', Mr Kierkegaard. Kierkegaard retorted, in a cold fury, that he wanted none of *their* praise, he was writing for *individuals*, for individuals alone, not for any local society. The result of course was that the paper didn't go silent on his behalf, but turned vociferously and viciously against him.

It was not easy to be incognito or a silent hermit in the little city of Copenhagen. But Brother Taciturnus, another of Kierkegaard's pseudonyms, did the best he could.

The thing as he saw it, from his radically existential point of view, was to overcome boredom, the 'sickness unto death'. In one of his essays, Kierkegaard, the cosmo-comedian, writes this:

God was bored, so he created Adam. Adam was bored, and so Eve got created. Adam had been bored alone, now Adam and Eve were bored together. Pretty soon, Adam and Eve, Cain and Abel and the rest were all bored *en famille*. The population of the world went on boringly increasing, and the nations were very soon more and more bored *en masse*. It was then they got the idea of building a tower high enough to reach the heavens, which is the most boring idea conceivable...

How to get out of this boredom? There are moments of joyance: Kierkegaard recorded one in his *Journal*, under the date 19 May 1838: 'A heavenly chorus that suddenly breaks in on the ordinary sing-song, something that cools and refreshes like a breeze.' But that was rare, and not to be depended upon. You needed an *attitude*: based on aesthetics or ethics, maybe a mixture of both.

I'm thinking of Kierkegaard's attitude, and his solitary passion here in Copenhagen, as I make my visit this May morning to the Town Museum.

There, then, is his writing desk, there are his books ('If an ape looks in, an apostle won't look out'), hardly read during his lifetime but, after his death, translated round the world, and there are the drawings, paintings and caricatures of the man wandering, pathetically and peripatetically, with a distinct limp and a slightly curved spine, through the streets of Copenhagen, the city loved and hated.

It's to get an idea of Kierkegaard's Copenhagen that I take a close and lingering look at those little paintings by Skovgaard done around 1835 that you can also see in the Town Museum: *Den gamle Langebro* – two men crossing a square on a moonlit night; or *Parti fra Langebro med Christianskirken* – two men leaning on a railing under the full moon. Or, again, those by Køske, of the Sortedam, where Kierkegaard's brother-in-law, Ferdinand Lund, lived, and which was one of the philosopher's favourite walks. These little paintings, along with the drawings by H. G. F. Holm (*Landstedet Blidah, Strandsvejen i Skovshoved*) remind me of nothing more than some Japanese prints I know – those of the 'last master of the floating world', Kobayashi Kiyochika, for example, whose views of Edo, particularly those of the Mukojima dyke, with the lights of Imado reflected in the waters of the Sumida and the cherry trees in flower, have always been the expression for me of something deeper than nostalgia.

★

Since this flat on the Absalonsgade contains a good library, and since I'm wakened up early by the light and the birds, I spend the mornings reading. In the afternoons, I wander round the city. As to the evenings, well, that depends.

Tonight, at what in Danish is called *de lyse natters tid* (the light night time), I went for a stroll along the lakes: the Skt. Jørgens Sø, the Peblinge Sø and the Sortedams Sø, those expanses of water that now fill what used to be the city's ramparts.

I went down the Absalonsgade to the Gammel Kongevej, with the Tycho Brahe observatory there on the right, and set out, past a bunch of young Copenhagers laden with bottles of beer in preparation for a sloshy nocturne, along the Suineryggen which turned into the Peblinge Dossering, then the Sortedam Dossering.

Villa after villa – these must be among the quietest dwelling-places in Copenhagen. A strong fragrance of lilac, hawthorn in bloom, all kinds of duck among the reeds at the lake's edge.

On my way back, after about an hour's walk, under the stars, I came across, at one point, among the reeds, a grey heron, standing there, still and vigilant, like a sentinel of eternity.

The gas lamps were lit when I got back into the Absalonsgade.

★

It was because of Saxo Grammaticus that I decided to go to Helsingør.

I'd been reading that old book, the *Gesta Danorum*, early down the morning. I knew it was from it that Shakespeare had got the story of Hamlet, so it was the Hamlet part I looked up.

In the original, Hamlet isn't Hamlet, he's Amled, a legendary figure, living in Jutland. A foreign army (Swedes? Germans?) has invaded Denmark, and its champion, a giant of a fellow, has challenged any one of the Danes who dares to single combat. After cannily debating some time with his chiefs as to what kind of reward he could expect if he won (which was unlikely), if he was honorably wounded, or, posthumously, if he got himself killed, a certain Hrdvendel takes up the challenge. He fights furiously, and wins. As a reward, he is given the fair and gentle Gerut (the one Will Shakespeare turns into Gertrude), and Amled (Hamlet) is born of their union. All might have been well, but Finge, Hrdvendel's brother, Hamlet's uncle, is jealous. He kills Hrdvendel (who opens Shakespeare's play as an 'extravagant and errant spirit') and marries Gerut. To gain time, and to conceal his strategy of revenge, Amled pretends to go stark raving mad: 'He stayed close to his mother's fire, sleeping in the mud, covered with ashes, talking nonsense.' People can hardly believe he's a human being any more: 'He was like an animal.' Finge thinks a girl in his bed might cure him – or maybe he wants to find out if Amled is really crazy. He arranges a meeting between his nephew and Opelia (Shakespeare's Ophelia) in a convenient and cosy wood. Amled might have been tempted. But his boyhood friend tells him it's a trap. So Amled rides away, having mounted his horse with his back to its head... In the end, he manages to kill his uncle, and lives a long life thereafter. He is supposed to be buried at a place called Ammlhede, near Raenders, in Jutland.

The reason why Shakespeare sets him at Helsingør (Elsinore) is that, at the end of the sixteenth century, Helsingør was chock-full of Englishmen and Scotsmen: merchants, skippers and ambassadors, who sometimes brought actors and musicians with them. William Kemp clowned about there and clumped his Morris dance. Dowland's *Second Book of Songs* was dated 'Helsingøre, June 1st, 1600'. News of the town, and of its great castle, Kronborg, which commanded the entrance to the Sund Straits and hence the Baltic, must have got through to Shakespeare in stuffy London and fired his imagination.

I was making along the Vesterbrogade towards the station. All the little Ophelias in Copenhagen at the moment seem to be wearing tights with short skirts over them. Sometimes the tights sport holes – but maybe in that case, the girls are *roligan* girls. *Roligan* is the Danish equivalent of hooligan. But whereas a hooligan bashes and smashes, a *roligan* just gets drunk, vomits and sleeps. And the girls let holes grow in their tights. It is, they tell me, a question of identity.

At Copenhagen Central, I got myself a return ticket to Elsinore, had five minutes to admire the roof of the station (ribbed like a ship with wood), and boarded one of the cherryred trains of the DSB.

So, we're on the 10:25, passing through Østerport, Hellerup, Skosborg, Smidstrup, Rungsted, Kokkedal, Sletten, Humlebaek, Espergaerde and Sulkesten.

Villas with well-kept gardens. Wooden piers. Here and there a roof of thatch. The sea brown, then green, then blue.

You're not long in Helsingør before you come up against the Hotel Hamlet and the Restaurant Ophelia, where you can order Shakespeare American Spareribs.

Wine and spirit shops are plentiful too in Helsingør, and they do a great trade. The streets are full of Swedes with a bulky clinking plastic bag in each fist. One I see without a plastic bag: lying stretched out beside a hollybush in the grounds of St Olai's kirk, dead to the world, with a look of total bliss on his face.

I like St Olai's. I like its whitewashed, or rather white-painted brick, and the wind howling round it. I finger the fat

little Danish psalm-book (*Den Danske Salme Bog*), and read the
verses of the 'psalm-poet' (*Salmedigteren*) Hans Christensen
Sthen, who was born at Roskilde in 1540, and died at Malmø,
in 1610:

> Raek us o Jesus din Frelserhaand
> I dag ug i alle stunde
> Udløs os alle af mørkers baand
> At ret vi dig tjene kunde...

After the church, I go over to the sea-museum at the windy
and vigilant Kronborg castle, built by Erik of Pomerania as a
place for collecting the dues from ships passing up and down
the Sound. This collection of dues, a lucrative enterprise,
which made for the prosperity of Helsingør and all the bustle
that went on there (skippers, shipchandlers, hustlers of all
kinds, bars and hostelries...), went on from 1420 till 1857. The
sea-museum, with its collections of books and maps, was
started up in 1915. I spend a couple of delectable hours with
old charts and with data concerning Denmark's trade with
China and the West Indies.

Back in town, I walk along the Skyttenstraede, admiring the
old houses, at times looking in through a window, which a
Danish woman, in passing, tells me, quite rightly, is an
improper thing to do, before going over to the St Marial Kirke,
where the caretaker tells me they have had no vicar in six
months, the last one having left to take up the post of port
chaplain in Singapore.

Passing by St Olai's again, I see that my Swede has left his
hollybush and is now pissing dreamily into a yew tree. He is a
tall, thin fellow, with a crop of shaggy yellow hair, and with a
small black knapsack on his back, wearing pink track pants
tucked into green socks, and with very thick blue sports shoes
on his feet. I watch him take a little brown knitted cap from his
pocket and place it carefully, very carefully, on his occiput.
Then, feeling he's ready, he puts one leg way out to the right,
tests it, then puts the other leg way out to the left, tests it, and,
like some pantomime daddy longlegs, lurches off in the
direction of the harbour, to board the last boat for Malmø.

In my mind, I situated Copenhagen's pleasure-gardens, Tivoli, somewhere between the Disneylands of America and Old Tokyo's pleasure-quarter, the Yoshiwara, but definitely closer to the infantile fantasia of the one than to the floating-world sophistication of the other. Which is to say that, when some Copenhageners invited me to the gardens, I was not over-enthusiastic. But I went.

The rendezvous was at Tivoli's main entrance, on the Hans Christian Andersen Boulevard, at seven o'clock.

Crowds passing through the turnstiles and, once inside, a great milling around, dust and smoke, cries of *wheeee* and *whoooo* from Ferris wheel and flying carpet and roller-coaster – but behind all the noise, the flowers on the chestnut trees, the quiet globes of tulips, and the black swans on the lake.

First stop, the open air theatre, where the act I witness might be called the Apple Elephant and the Carrot Elephant. Man strolls across the stage, and drops an apple and a carrot behind him. One of the great brown wrinkled pachyderms picks up the apple in its trunk, stuffs it into its mouth, then picks up the carrot and trunks it to the other, who accepts it and stuffs it into its mouth. The man now takes another apple and another carrot out of his pocket. He offers the carrot to Elephant no. 1. Elephant no. 1 shakes its head in negation. The man then offers the carrot to Elephant no. 2, who already has its mouth open. He then offers the apple to Elephant no. 1, who nods assent, accepts the apple in its trunk and stuffs it into its mouth.

Applause. The man looks happy, and bows. The elephants look sad, and bow. But maybe the man is sad, and the elephants are quite happy. Maybe.

We pass the Chinese pagoda, the Japanese restaurant, the Las Vegas saloon, and move along alleys on the walls of which are inscribed rhymes by a certain Halfden Rasmussen, such as this one:

> *Rottefaenger Rasmus*
> *fanged fire Glasmus*
> *tog dem med til sit Palads*
> *ovre i Damascus*

> (Ratcatcher Rasmus
> caught five glass mouses

and took them to his palace
way over in Damascus)

then go to a beer-garden.

Night's coming down now. There are lights, pink and yellow, hanging in the chestnut trees. And on the pond, big electric mosquitoes blink in and out, giving the impression that they are flitting here and there.

At 11:45, it's firework time. *Splutter, swoosh, bang* – and brilliant blossoms, gushes of light, explode and scatter in the sky.

One of the popular bands then plays the last waltz.

And everybody flocks to the gates.

Midnight, Tivoli, Copenhagen.

Kierkegaard hated Tivoli. Hans Christian Andersen loved it.

★

In the year of the word, 1834, Andersen wrote a letter to the authorities at the Royal Library in Copenhagen, asking for a job there that would free him 'from the burden of writing for a living'.

That letter, along with Andersen's rough drafts and manuscripts, are now part of the archives of the Royal Library.

It was Frederik the Third who started it up, in the second half of the seventeenth century. To begin with, he just piled up the books he had bought and had had bought (in Paris, Amsterdam, Venice) in the old castle of Copenhagen. But pretty soon he had the idea of a library like the one Cardinal Mazarin had set up in Paris.

Books began to pour in. And manuscripts. Count Otto Thott bequeathed two hundred thousand volumes. Other private collectors did the same: Henrik Hielmstrierne, for example, who collected everything Danish. Carsten Niebuhr brought in manuscripts from India and Persia.

How do you classify hundreds of thousands of volumes coming from all over the world and covering various fields of knowledge and creation? The original catalogue made a four-fold division: theology, law, medicine, philosophy.

In the nineteenth century, with the rise of the nation states and cultural nationalism, a special Danish section was set up and a catalogue produced.

At first, the books are the choice of an individual, then, gradually, *everything* is collected, or as near as possible. Where do you make the intellectual divisions, where do you make the value distinctions? You try, then you give up. Comes a time when the library isn't measured in books at all, it's measured in kilometres. The Royal Library in Copenhagen now has holdings of over a hundred kilometres, and there's a kilometre or two (or three) added every year.

It's with something like relief that I go to the Map Room and consult the 'Maps of the North' made by Sigurdur Stefansson, Hans Poulson Resen and Gudbrandur Thorlaksson, in 1590, 1605 and 1606 respectively. There's Poulson's map, with Norway, Scotland, Ireland to the east, then, out in the Atlantic, Iceland, and, to the west, Estotiland, Markland and Terra Corterealis. I follow with particular interest that line of driftwood stretching across the Atlantic, borne by the current from the Isles of America to Iceland.

The mind craves, beyond all the accumulations, lost connections, hidden currents, unsuspected passages.

★

Between the Kronprinsessegade and the Øster Voldgade lie the Rosenborg Gardens, a pleasant place, especially in Summer. Young Copenhagen girls lie out there with their breasts bare to the grass or to the air, and I have seen more than one unembarrassed mamma sitting beside her pram dressed only in her knickers, with plastic curlers in her hair.

I'm sitting for the moment in the little garden of a restaurant called the Kongens Have (the King's Garden), which has taken over the ancient premises of Nielsens Konditorei. The original building is still there, with its little private rooms hung with paintings of Copenhagen's streets and quays, and it fills up around four every day for tea. But with this hot Summer weather, it's more pleasant to be out here in the garden, at this table with its yellow cloth, its bunch of flowers, its white parasol, and its cool breeze, enjoying a pot of coffee after a meal of 'summer salad' and cold red-fruit soup.

Around the railings of the Rosenborg there are little

buildings that must at one time have been guard posts for the King's Palace, but which now house all kinds of shops and businesses.

In one I found an amber-worker.

I'd seen amber before, but never had I seen such variety as here. On display in the window there was not only the transparent caramel sort, but pieces that were yellowwhite, or palegreen, or blue, either left in rough lumps, or worked into bracelets and necklaces. I went in for a closer look and the look turned into a long and rambling talk.

Mr Sørensen told me that, according to legend, amber came into being in some special dream time when the rays of the setting sun lit up the brown waters of a stormy sea. But in fact it goes back about fifty million years, to a period when the climate here in the north was warm and wet, and when Scandinavia was covered with tropical forest. Certain trees in that forest exuded abundant resin. The resin was borne by streams down to the sea, where it slowly petrified. What we call amber, *rav* in Danish, is found all round the coasts of Denmark, you can even find it under Copenhagen, but the main deposits lie on the west coast of Jutland. Mr Sørensen goes out there, he tells me, every now and then. Particularly just after a stormy spell. He'll gather in some himself, and he'll buy a kilo or two from people who live out there permanently and have their eyes skinned every day of the year. He shows me his store of raw amber, and photos of extraordinary pieces that have come through his hands: a piece with a mouse's tail caught in it, another with a grasshopper, another again with a spider and its eggs.

★

It was Saturday morning, and I was making for the National Museum.

If I was making for the National Museum, it was because the Danish *National Museet* has the finest collection of Eskimo culture, both material and intellectual, in the world. That's partly because of what Knud Rasmussen gathered and learned in the course of the Fifth Thule Expedition.

It was in Glasgow, years ago, that I first read Rasmussen's *From Greenland to the Pacific,* an account of 'two years intimacy with unknown Eskimo tribes'. Born in Greenland, raised as an Eskimo, Rasmussen studied in Copenhagen before moving back up among the Hyperboreans. That Fifth Thule Expedition in particular took in the central part of the polar archipelago of North America, covering ground in Ellesmereland, North Devon, North Somerset, Baffinland, the Melville Peninsula and the Barren Grounds. I'd read that book of his with emotion and fervour, particularly interested in his conversations with shamans and in the fragments he quoted of Eskimo poetry:

> *I awake with the morning cry of the grey gull*
> *I rise with the morning cry of the grey gull*
> *I don't look towards the darkness*
> *I look into the light...*

In his meetings and conversations with individuals of the Netsilik and Iglulik people, Rasmussen had heard in particular tales from the mouth of Ivalvartjuk: tales about the great night-time of the earth, when darkness covered everything so that fox was able to steal meat from the hiding-places of human hunters; about crow who wanted light and he went to the sun to get it; about the old woman who turned into mist; about the man whose soul had lived inside the bodies of all animals; about the man who spent all of his time in the land of gulls and crows.

For Ivalvartjuk, that was a mess of old wives' tales. He'd been told to dismiss it all as such, and eliminate it from his consciousness. But back of it, as Rasmussen knew, was shamanism, and he asked the old man to talk about it.

So it was that Ivalvartjuk told the stranger how, in a time of dire stress and distress in the tribe, a man had said that, in order to find help, he'd go down to the Mother of the Sea Animals. He was the first shaman. A shaman has knowledge of secret things, he talks a different language, he can help people to live, and to die. You can become a shaman either by going out into the great solitude, or sometimes the spirit of the outside will come to fetch you. Older shamans can help you on your way. You set up a post, with gull's wings at the top, near the old shaman's house. That means: 'I want to be a winged spirit and a seer.' The older man can help you to become full of light. But to become a great shaman, you have to begin early, even before you are born. That's how it was with Ava. There was a long preparation, he didn't know what was going on, he just felt strange and a stranger. Then one day, out on his own, away out on the ice, he felt melancholy and fear, a long, long time, and then, suddenly, there was a deep change, he experienced great joy, he saw and heard in a new way. He had spirits to help him. His new name, Ava, came from a female spirit who lived at the edge of the sea, the 'little spirit of the beach'. Then there was a shark, which had come up to him one day as he was paddling in his kayak: the shark had come alongside his boat, turned over on its side, and whispered his name.

When he became a Christian, Ivalvartjuk told Rasmussen, he sent all his guardian spirits away to his sister in Baffinland.

I knew the book, but actually to see, there in the museum, beside the harpoons and the arrows and the kayaks and the shaman masks and the drums, the amulets and the drawings that had only been cursorily illustrated in the book's pages, not only renewed my emotion, but increased it. There was the necklet with the swan's beak, the owl's claws, the gull's head and the bear's teeth brought back from Netsilik by Rasmussen.

Primal poetics!

★

I'd decided to go over to Jutland.

It was a nine o'clock flight, in a Tord Viking at twenty thousand feet, to Ålborg. You leave Zealand over a long narrow spit of land called the Sjaellands Odde. Then it's the Kattegat, a bright blue expanse. Up there to the north, the island of Anholt. Towards the south-west, the island of Samsø. You arrive in Jutland over the port of Grenaa. Thereafter it's the Randers Fjord and the Mariager Fjord.

Neat farmlands, with blazing yellow fields of colza. Great eolians turning. Wind and light. Red ships of the Royal Arctic Line. A sensation of distance and of freshness.

Sunday morning in Ålborg.

I get myself a room in a street off the Vesterbro, and go to visit the town. First, the great white mass of the Budolfi Cathedral. I'm admiring the general look of the church, and the scallop shells with which the pews are decorated, when the beadle, dressed in a spruce bow-tie, comes up and asks me very amiably to leave by that exit down to the right because the service is about to begin. Sure enough the priest with the conspicuous ruff at his neck is already making an appearance, the beadle has gathered together into one box odd cash deposited here and there, soon the bells will begin to ring and the congregation will come pouring in. I make my exit and go to the Historical Museum, which starts with a fine display of the early hunter–gatherer community and moves up to the library of one Harald Jensen, distiller in the town of a famous Akvavit, but who was more interested in painting and in books. After that, I have the choice between the Museum of Modern Art, the Monastery of the Holy Ghost or the Viking burial ground, said to be the biggest in Scandinavia, at Lindholm Høje.

I make for Lindholm Høje.

It's a place of stones. At first it seems an informal mass. Then you see shapes: triangular shapes, boat shapes. You think of the life the people lived here: raising swine and children, ploughing the land, making long voyages.

'From Hermun in Norway', says an Icelandic manuscript, the *Hauksbok*, 'sail due West to Hvarf in Greenland, following the North about Hjaltland (the Shetlands), so that it can just be seen in clear weather, but sail South of the Faroes, so that only the top half of the braes can be seen on the horizon, and thereafter South of Iceland, so that you have the birds and the whales with you.'

Those people could handle their boat, and the leader of the trip, the *farmann*, knew the way, and had all kinds of place-images at his disposal: either written down, or drawn, or learnt by heart thanks to short rhymes. Long before he descried the White Shift and the Blue Shift of Greenland, he had his eyes open for 'Helmet Rock', or 'Flat Rock', or that jagged skerry he or somebody like him called 'Watch Out'.

But bad weather could drive them away off course, and leave them astray at sea. That was maybe how Bjarni Herjolfsson discovered America: Helluland, Markland, Vinland.

What claimed to be the first map of Vinland turned up in the United States (at New Haven, Connecticut) in October 1957, attached to an account of John de Plano Carpin's missionary expedition to the Mongols in the years 1245 to 1247. An antiquarian bookseller had said he'd got it from a private collection in Europe. Could be. Experts got together and said the map might have been made in the Upper Rhineland around 1440. Other experts got together and said it was all a fake. Whether fake or fact, I'm enthralled – because of a certain mental configuration. I'm interested just in the fact that this map, with its *Desideratae Insulae,* its *Beata insula fortuna,* its *Magnae insulae Beati Brandani Braziliae dictae* and its *Vinlandia insula* should have been connected to De Bridia's account of that Mongolian journey (from Lyons to Karakorum) made by the Italian Carpini, Benedict the Pole and Ceslaus of Bohemia. There you have the extension of the European consciousness west and east. And I'm intrigued to learn that at one point the Western map and the Eastern travel account were stitched into Vincent de Beauvais' *Speculum Historiale.* I'm thinking of an enlargement of speculation thanks to the extension of geographical and intellectual awareness.

I go back down to my room in Ålborg to read the Vinland Saga, that of events in the year 1000 or thereabouts:

> They sailed for two days before a northerly wind and sighted land ahead. This was a heavily wooded country abounding with animals. There was an island to the south-west, where they found bears, and so they named it Bjarn Isle. They named the wooded mainland itself Markland. After two days they sighted land again and held in towards it. It was a promontory they were approaching. They tacked along the coast, with the land to starboard. It was open and harbourless, with long beaches. They went ashore in boats and found a ship's keel on the headland, and so they called the place Kjalarness. They called this whole stretch of coast 'the marvellous shore'.

★

It's a wild country north of Ålborg, and the farther north you go, the wilder it gets. Farmland yields to moorland, beech woods to clumps of birch and fir, and along the coast runs a line of shaggy dunes. But with this austere beauty goes a more fragile and fragrant one: the roads are lined with rosy *armeria maritima* and here and there a rose-bush (*rosa rugosa*) is tousled in the wind.

Lyngdrup, Hjallerup, Hellum, Kirkholt, Mylund, Thorshøj, Søholt, Landum, Stensbalk, Sindal, Tversted, Klitlund, Hulsig...

It was late afternoon when I got into Skagen.

Skagen used to be a little fishing village which, in the late nineteenth century, attracted to it painters who came to paint the northern light and portray the fisher-folk. Something like Pont-Aven in Brittany. But it all remained strictly local – no extravagant Gauguin emerged from it.

I left the Main Street, passed the offices of the Saga Shipping Company, and the Sømandhjem (the Seamen's Home), the Skagen Skipperskole and the Trawlterminal, and went to drink a coffee at Det blaa Cafeteria (the Blue Café), looking out over the quays at the harbour, where I noted the *Santos* from Whalsay, the *Radiant Star* from Macduff and the *Mette Jensen* from Grenaa. They are very strange, those Danish North Sea boats, snub-nosed and well-covered at the bow, made for buffeting heavy seas.

The sky was a pale lead blue, with gulls gliding in over it in slow motion.

While there was still light, I went up to Grenen, the very northern tip of Jutland, where the waters of the Kattegat meet the waters of the Skagerrak.

Dunes, drab sands, the remains of a Nazi bunker.

Seventeen ships on the horizon.

★

Just under Skagen, lost in the dunes, with only its tower remaining, stands the *tilsandede kirke,* the 'sanded-up church'.

Hans Christian Andersen has a story about it.

It's a long story, because it starts in Spain before getting up here to Jutland, and it's full of episodes such as wars, drownings and losses of identity. I don't read the story for all that rigmarole, but for the feeling even Andersen obviously had for this Jutland landscape:

> Over there in Jutland it's easy to fancy yourself far back in distant times, further back than the reign of Christian the Seventh. Still in Jutland, as in those days, the brown heath stretches for miles with its Viking graves, its mirages, its bumpy intersecting roads that are often deep in sand. In the West, where large brooks fall into the fiords, meadow and moorland

spread out bounded by high sand-dunes that, like an Alpine
range with jagged peaks, rise up against the sea...

That 'Alpine range' is a bit of an exaggeration, and the sand-
dunes are in fact more interesting and attractive than that
comparison suggests. They are unique. If I had to liken them to
anything, it would be to the backs of Shetland ponies. But I'd
rather do without comparison at all. Just imagine mound after
mound covered with a thick matted coating of lyme and
marram grass, which the wind blows now grey, now green,
now silver, now black.

I was reading Andersen's story last night in the room of a
hotel I found just down from Skagen at a place called
Kandestederne: a plain little room, with a balcony looking out
over the dunes and the sea.

I went for a walk among the dunes.

At one time, there were huts among these dunes, built of
wreckage, covered with peat and heather, and tarred. The rude
huts have gone, but houses have been raised in their stead, and
they are still painted black.

I went down to the beach.

Foam, spindrift. the wailing of gulls and terns.

'The ocean itself', says Andersen in his *Story of the Sand-
dunes*, 'is a great textbook – every day it offers a fresh page.'

But to get at *that*, as Andersen himself well knew, you have
to do more than tell stories.

You have to go out.

You have to open space, and deepen place.

Fill your eyes with the changing light.

Travels in a Sea of Vodka

It was November – *Listopad* in Polish: 'the month of the falling leaves'.

They were falling all right, bright red, coppery-brown, yellow, and among them foraged crows: the big one they call *kruk*, the slightly smaller ones they call *vrona* or *gavron*, and the small ones with the thin white feathers round the neck, *kavka*.

★

The night I arrived in Poland, it was raining and as the plane taxied to a stop at Okecie airport, the letters WARSAW were shivering, crimson, through the darkness.

Yurek was waiting for me. I'd corresponded off and on with him over the years, but I did not know what he looked like. Now there he was: tall, thin, wearing a leather jacket and a skip cap of the kind that, at one time in London, denoted dangerous characters from Eastern Europe.

On the way to the Europa Hotel, we passed by the House of Culture, massive and stolid, looking like a New York sky-scraper of the 1930s. 'Stalin's gift to Poland', said Yurek. A few moments' silence, then: 'You should know that we are moving over the bones of Polish soldiers.'

That evening in the Europa, over a vodka from Cracow, Yurek told me about his own relationship to the army under the Communist régime.

When he turned up at the barracks with his call-up papers, he set the papers carefully on the ground, then straightened up, saluted, and shut his eyes tight. 'That made them think already I was maybe a nutcase. Especially as I had long hair reaching down to my backside and my face was covered in pimples.'

When, later, during instruction, he was asked to draw a battle field, he drew a cemetery:

'Why a cemetery?'

'Because we'll all be dead, man.'

Eventually he got examined by a psychiatrist, and they started to give him injections. Those jags reduced him to a state of passive inertia. One day, though, half-dead and barely conscious as he was, he knew he'd won when he heard the lieutenant-doctor say to the apprentice army doctors around him:

'A very difficult case... A brilliant student... This often happens... Especially with those who study Polish literature.'

★

My window in the Europa Hotel at Warsaw looked on to the tomb of the Unknown Soldier, guarded in the day by two infantry men, and whose flame shone through the night.

'Warsaw', said Yurek, 'is a place of memory.'

All over the town, on so many walls, at so many street corners, there were plaques to remind you that 'here thirty people were machine-gunned', 'here one hundred and twenty people were massacred'.

Yurek took me to the Lazarist Church of the Holy Cross, where resistance had been strong. To the university, where there was a memorial to all the poets who'd been shot down (as a student, he said, that memorial had obsessed him). To the Museum of the Earth, which had been a military hospital, and another strong resistance point, where, in a window encasement, he showed me a piece of marble with an unwonted stain on it: more spilled blood.

One night, at Pod Samuelem (Samuel's Place), a Jewish restaurant with about a hundred portraits of old long-bearded, glittery-eyed Jews pasted on the walls, he told me about his life in Olsztyn, a town up north, his home town, where he'd returned after his student days in Warsaw.

'I was morbid then', he said, 'fantastical.' One night he decided he must bear a cross through the streets of Olsztyn. So he went to an old Russian cemetery on the outskirts of town, where he found an abandoned crucifix. This crucifix he dragged on his shoulder through the streets, his wife beside him crying her heart out. At that time, in total despair, he drank gallons of vodka. That meant darkness, but also, now and then, 'a diamond flash of light'. One evening, crazy with drink, he decided he had to murder someone. So he took a knife, went out into the streets, and hid at a corner. After a while, a young man turned up, the same age as himself, exactly what he wanted. He sprang out, brandishing his blade. Then came *the diamond flash.* He saw the whole scene, 'right into infinity', and ran off into the darkness.

In a park at midnight, we saw two girls, abysmally sloshed, drinking from a bottle of vodka and singing, in raucous tones, an American song. Below a bridge, three coloured jars with three candles in them were burning in memory of a twelve-year-old boy who'd recently been knifed on that spot by his pals. And outside a baroque church that contained the most baroque pillars I've ever seen ('They pay drunken Poles three kopeks an hour to whirl them round', said Yurek) we gave some coins to a little Rumanian gipsy beggar who looked like the daughter of misery and the wind.

We left for Olsztyn the next day, but not as early as we'd expected, because I'd wanted to hunt about in some old book-shops.

★

So there we were, moving across a wide expanse of fields that must at one time have been a wild, wan, glacier-scrubbed wilderness – nomad lands, crossed by all kinds of migrating peoples: Goths, Vandals, Huns, Avars, Scythians, Sarmatians, Magyars, Mongols, Tartars, Slavs... Crosses all along the road. Graveyards with myriads of red lights flickering on the tombs. A beetroot factory belching smoke into the pale purple sky.

Night falls early on the North European Plain.

We pulled into an inn, a *Gospoda*, called 'Moon of Mazura'. I ordered a beetroot soup, *barszcz*, with panned pork. Yurek ordered a thicker soup, *zurek,* with sausages, and panned pork. 'Soup, pork, and a little vodka, *kieliszek wodki* – typical Polish meal', said Yurek.

The hallway to the inn, which housed, under neon light, a Bar and a Sex Shop, smelled pungently of disinfectant. Dark-green velvety drapes, heavy and glossy, covered the windows. A candelabrum with electric bulbs in the shape of candles hung from the ceiling.

'The crosses?', Yurek was explaining, 'that's because of all the accidents. The roads are narrow, cars go faster and faster, and a lot of Poles drive drunk.' Just the week before, the Mongol ambassador had got himself killed: 'He should have stuck to horses.' As to the lights in the cemeteries, that's because it was the Day of the Dead. 'There's a lot of deathness in Poland.' Recently there had been a spate of murders – for no reason at all, out of sheer boredom. But that was nothing to what it was like in Russia. Up near Kaliningrad he'd seen three men walking along the river with a dog. Suddenly there was a *plonk* in the water, the dog started howling, and now there were two men only. 'He's drowning', shouted Yurek from the bridge. The two men just shrugged and went on with their walk. The dog stayed on the spot and kept howling.

We got back on the road. The sky was clear, the Great Bear plain in the sky.

'Did you know there was a Pole without a soul sitting on the moon?', said Yurek.

'No.'

'He sold his soul for a pot of gold to the Devil. The Devil said he'd come to claim it in Rome. The man thought he'd driven a good bargain, with no risk – there was no chance of his ever going to Rome. Then one night he was sitting in an inn when the Devil turned up. 'But this isn't Rome!', cried the man. The Devil grinned and pointed with a rigid finger to the name of the inn: Gospoda Roma, grabbed his soul and despatched him up to the moon.'

'Fantastical folklore', said Yurek, 'Polish paranoia.'

In Warsaw, I'd wondered what kind of nightmare I was letting myself into. Now I was right in the middle of things, nightmare I knew there was – all the horror of European history – but in that nightmare, there was a weird, metaphysical humour, and, within that weird humour, there were strange erratic lights.

It must have been about eleven o'clock when we got into Olsztyn.

Grey frost, a yellow street lamp, and a drab block of a building.

Inside, in a little cubicle off the hallway, a woman wrapped in a blanket, huddled before a stove.

Followed a long discussion in Polish. Apparently there was a problem.

It turned out this building *had* been part of the hotel we were looking for, but was now a students' hostel. The entrance to the hotel was round the corner.

I checked in at the Hotel Mazurski, sliding my passport

under an iron grating and, bidding goodnight to Yurek who was going to join his family on the outskirts of town, in Jakob's Quarter, went up to my room. It was cold and bare, but had an elaborate, multi-bulbed candelabrum.

★

I woke around seven to the noise of a cement mixer in the yard and went downstairs to the restaurant for breakfast.

The restaurant was as big as a ballroom, with brown pillars gilt at the top, and goldenbrown velvety drapes at the windows. Yurek told me later it had been a place of communistic grandeur and that a lot of official functions had been held there. The menu was in Polish, German and English. I ordered scrambled eggs and coffee. The only other people waiting for breakfast were a German couple the waiter obviously know – he gave the woman an oldworld kiss on the hand. The eggs were greasy. The street outside looked dismally frozen.

After breakfast, I went for a walk: Mickiewicza Street, then Kosciuszki Street... Past buildings with mouldering mustard-yellow, palegreen façades and baroque scrolls in stucco round the windows (*Erbaut 1906*). Past rowan trees heavy with dark-red berries. Past the Bank of Dantzig. Past graffiti: *Skin's – Punx not Dead.*

I was back in the hotel about 9:45. Yurek called for me at 10.

We went up to the Old Town, the *Stare Miasto.*

It was in the castle there, working as an administrator, concerned with the allocation of deserted fields and the price of bread, that Copernicus (Nikolaj Kopernik) did his work on 'the revolutions of the celestial orbs'. On the wall above the entrance to the chamber where he lived you can still see the astronomical table he drew to mark the position of the sun at the moment of the equinox. His method was to put a dish filled with water on the window sill of his room and mark the points of the reflection in red, joining them to form hyperboles, and marking the equinoctial line in blue: *Ita profecto tanquam in solio regali sol residens circum agentes gubernat astrorum familiam* ('And so the sun as if sitting on a royal throne manages the family of planets busying around.')

Yurek said so much had been destroyed in Olsztyn: 'Russians smashed the town four weeks *after* the victory' – it was a

Russian ex-soldier in Kaliningrad, one of the first to arrive in Olsztyn, who had told him that.

We then went into the Church of St Jakuba. In a corner of the building, lit by a stag's head candelabrum, Yurek said: 'Here I had many visions.'

In the afternoon, we made for the lake and forest country to the north-west of the town. Wet, mossy woodland. The last yellow leaves of the birches trembling in the wind. Little *kavkas* perched quiet on the wintering trees. Two swans flying over Lake Ukiel.

We stopped in a village that had become a place of religious pilgrimage ever since two girls had seen the Mother of God, Matka Boza, sitting at the top of a tree babbling away in Polish. And at another, deserted, because all the inhabitants had moved to Germany. Yurek told me he often came cycling on those forest roads, and would go strolling through the woods. Every now and then he'd come across a grave marked 'unknown soldier here'.

That evening, at dinner in a restaurant at Olsztyn, I asked Yurek, while being pretty sure of the answer, if the area was polluted. He said he wasn't sure, but probably. At the time of Tchernobyl, he'd noticed that the sun had a funny colour, in fact the whole sky. But there was no information. Two days later, the population was told to drink iodine. 'Iodine and vodka – the new East-European cocktail.'

The restaurant we were in was a new place, frequented mostly by businessmen. In the days of Communism, it had been a special school for the children of the militia: 'The militia – not the police', said Yurek. 'Police was a bourgeois word. The militia were supposed to be for the people.' The militia always went about in pairs. That was because one could read and the other could write.

A couple of days later, we left for Poznan, where Yurek had some business with a mysterious Lithuanian.

★

Olsztyn station in the morning. A sleety rain falling. On the same platform (*peron*) as ourselves, an old couple carrying a wreath.

Travelling west. Moorland, lakeland, marshland. Yellow

reeds. Birches in the rain. A little stag at the edge of a pine-wood. A pheasant in a field.

Crossing the Vistula in the mist.

'That's where the Polish Army saw Our Lady in the sky', said Yurek. 'Miracle on the Vistula, the history books call it.'

We walked from the station at Poznan, past stands selling *Duze Hot Dogi* (big hot dogs), a Hamburgery, a New York City Pizza place, and settled in at the Mickiewicz Hotel on St Martin Street, which a few years ago was Red Army Street.

I stood at the window of my room listening to the sirens of police cars and the whines of trams, then went down to the hall where I'd arranged to meet Yurek. I was looking at a portrait of Mickiewicz accompanied by a couple of lines of quotation from one of his poems when Yurek said over my shoulder: 'For the Poles, Adam Mickiewicz and Jesus Christ are one and the same person.'

Outside, making for the National Gallery, we passed by a Strip Tease Peep Show, a Chinska Restauracja and a couple of chimneysweeps in top hats, ropes looped over their shoulders. What Yurek wanted to show me in the Gallery was its collec-tion of coffin portraits called 'Sarmatian painting' – 'All those little nobles liked to think of themselves as the Sarmats of Rome.' And there they were: short hair, long moustaches, in oriental clothes. It was another little flash of definition on those windswept, undefined plains.

The Old Town of Poznan is beautiful, but, given the general context, it seems a bit theatrical, like a stage set.

There was something theatrical, too, about the poetry reading Yurek had an invitation to and which he said we might as well look in at. This was to celebrate the '25 years writing' of a poet called Janusz, who put on a big act with gestures and expressions moving between deep Doubt if not Despair and totally inspired Resurrection. 'Janusz', said someone in the audience after the reading, 'you may be a good poet but you have no sense of humour.' 'The hand of God is upon me', replied Janusz. It ended with everyone singing '*Stolat, stolat*' (may you live a hundred years).

That night we had dinner in a restaurant in a cellar. 'After the War', said Yurek as we went down the stairs, 'that's all we had in Poland – cellars.' The walls of this one were festooned with all kinds of stuff: musical instruments, old dresses, photographs, farm tools, battle axes, copper basins. Above my head I had two crossed sabres, on the blade of one 'Long live the Hussars', on that of the other 'Glory to God Alone'.

'Polish Postmodernism', was Yurek's laconic comment.

He got on then to talking about what he called the 'Polish depression'. It was a long story, from the iron grip of the Teutonic Order, the 'Black Crusaders', on. He mentioned the deportations of 1655, those of 1864, and those of 1940. Twenty people of his own family had been deported, and others had been machine-gunned on the spot. Most were sent to Siberia, but his mother had spent six years in the Tien Shan. Anybody that offered any kind of resistance was put down. In 1940 the Russians had shot 20,000 Polish officers, most of whom weren't professional Army men, but intellectuals, artists in uniform. 'You know', he said, 'when I hear Russian music I could cry – but I hate Russia.' The first insurrection against the Communist regime had taken place in Poznan, in 1956 – Budapest's big rising had at first been only a manifestation of solidarity with Poznan.

As to Lech Walesa, the man the West thought was Poland's new salvation, Yurek had little time for him. Walesa had introduced anti-intellectualism into Poland: 'He goes about with the image of Our Lady in his buttonhole.' 'We're tired, sick tired of our history and our religiosity', Yurek concluded, 'but what have we got in its place? Just: get rich quick. The old question was always: Are you a patriot and a believer? Now it's: How much money you got?'

It was to get out of all that depressing history and its aftermath that I asked Yurek if he know the town of Kolno.

'Very well. That's where my people come from. That's where my grandparents lived.'

Not that he had very fond memories of it. On the wall of the room he occupied there when he was a child hung a painting, *Death* (an old man and a woman with a scythe) by Malczewski, and that had marked him for life. Then, when his grandfather died, he was invited to be one of the coffin-bearers, which was an honour. But if the other three bearers were strong peasants, he was weak at the time, very weak, he hardly ate anything, he only drank vodka, and he'd collapsed at the entrance to the graveyard, which was shame on his head.

Why the devil, he asked, was I interested in Kolno?

I told him about a very rare book ('*savant ouvrage, devenu rarissime*', as the catalogues put it) I'd found in Brussels, about transatlantic travel before Columbus, the *Géographie du Moyen Age* by Joachim Lelewel, the Polish historian who'd been removed by the Tsarist authorities from the Chair of History at Wilno, and had lived in exile in Belgium. In that book, Lelewel talks about one Johannes Scolnius, that is, John of Kolno, a Polish sea-pilot. He'd led a ship fitted out by Kristiern II of Denmark who wanted to find out exactly what had happened to the Greenland colony. That was in 1466. John of Kolno had dropped in on Greenland and then gone on further west to Labrador and into those straits that the Portuguese Cortereal was to call the Straits of Anian, thought at one time to be a passage to Cathay.

'It's just a crazy story', said Yurek.

'But who would want to invent a Polish pilot from Kolno?'

'A Polish patriot.'

'But Gomara in his *Historia de las Indias* mentions him, and Cornelius Wytfilet in his *Extensions of Ptolemy*, written in Louvain at the end of the sixteenth century – long before Lelewel picked up the track.'

'Hmmm.'

I called over the Sarmatian waitress and asked for another couple of vodkas:

'To John of Kolno!'

★

It was maybe the mention of Johannes Scolnius, as well as the desire to get out of the sea of vodka-soaked history that made me think more and more of going up to the Baltic coast. Yurek said he couldn't come with me, because he had business to attend to in Olsztyn, but, yes, he was sure I would get a lot from such a trip.

It was a drizzly morning at Olsztyn central station when I boarded the little yellow train for Danzig.

Up along cold marches, beside lakes left by glaciers.

I was remembering old geographies.

Describing the shores of what he calls 'the Swabian Sea', Tacitus in the *Germania* says that 'at this point ceases our knowledge of the world'. Ptolemy for his part calls the Baltic 'the Sarmatian Sea'. And Olaus Magnus' map of 1539 indicates 'The Amber Beach' – that's where the Amber Road started that went down from the Baltic to the Balkans.

Known as 'Poland's porthole', Danzig (Gdansk – from *ku*, 'towards', *dana*, 'the sea') was a little Pomeranian fishing village till, one night of 1308, the Teutonic Knights massacred all the Slavs, after which it became German. But it was crammed also with Dutchmen and Scotsmen doing a roaring trade in corn, timber, fish, furs and skins. The poet Jan Dantiscus (sixteenth century), son of a brewer and cosmopolitan cleric (he travelled in Greece, Palestine and Arabia), called it the place of three monsters: *impietas, fastus, luxus*. Over the years it was to move between Prussia and Poland, with now and then a republican status of its own.

When the Prussians attacked the town in 1793, the family of the philosopher Schopenhauer left, as he says in his *Curriculum Vitae* preserved at the University of Berlin: 'When In 1793, the King of Prussia annexed the town of Danzig, my father, who loved liberty as much as his native town, could not bear the fall of the old republic. He left Danzig with his wife and child, making for Hamburg. Which means that I have been homeless, *heimatlos*, from the age of five. Since then, I have never acquired another nationality.'

In later life, Schopenhauer was to present himself always as 'Doctor of Philosophy, from Danzig'.

From a room in the Long Street I wandered around the red brick Gothic town for a couple of days, before moving twenty miles along the coast to Sopot, a resort once famous and much frequented, but which has now come down a bit in the world.

There was a frosty greyness that mid-November on the Baltic coast.

I had a room at the top of the Danzig Hotel in Sopot, with a window that looked out over the sea.

The place was more or less deserted, which suited me perfectly. I spent most of my time at the window of my room, or walking along the sands. There was one woman who seemed to be doing something of the same as myself. I'd see her now and then picking up pebbles.

Passing by the breakfast table of this Polish woman one morning, I noticed that she was reading Ouspensky's *Fragments of an Unknown Teaching*. Beside the book was a little scattering of pebbles, among which I noticed one that looked like amber.

That gave me an idea.

I'd assumed that, all the beaches along this coast having been combed and recombed over the centuries for amber, there was nothing left. But it seemed that at least some insignificant pieces (insignificant from a jeweller's point of view) could still be found. I started looking for them systematically, and soon, had six chunky little bits of yellowy-brown, solid, weathered resin that delighted my mind.

When I wasn't on the beach looking for more amber, I'd be in my room reading a book I'd picked up in Warsaw, the fifteenth-century *Chronicles of Poland* written in Latin by Johannes Dlugoss: '*Ianussius Masovie dux et dominus Cirnensis de consensu Alberti Iastrambiecz episcopi Posnaniensis in ecclesia parochali sancti Ionnis in Warschovia fundat collegiatam ecclesiam.*'

Reading Latin at the edge of the world, picking up stones from a deserted beach, looking out from my window on a grey empty seascape...

After a week or so, the frosty greyness turned to snow, with thin flakes drifting over the sea, getting thicker and thicker. It was becoming more and more difficult to discern the gulls. But I could hear them out there, crying, faintly.

The Cry of the Loon on the Kennebec

That September, in the company of three Quebeckers, Gabriel Bellechasse, Sylvain Jolicoeur and Arsène Tremblay, I left the city of Montreal in Canada for the forest and the coast of Maine.

It was a beautiful clearblue morning as we rolled out south by the Champlain Bridge.

Arsène's car was the one we were travelling in and we were making in the first place for an outlying garage where Sylvain's car, meant to be the trip's car, was being repaired. When we got there, it was to learn that Sylvain's car wasn't ready, but that another one was at our disposal. This car looked OK and it was bigger, so we accepted the garage-man's proposition and got out on the road again.

Thirty kilometres later the thing started steaming like hell. We pulled in to a roadside restaurant (big shack of a place, arc-lamps, dust blowing) beside a couple of mammoth trucks: one, a Wausau Carrier, the other an SGT marked Canada-US-Mexico. Sylvain and I went in to the restaurant to get some water. That's when we realised it wasn't a restaurant, but a truckers' relief-joint, with a bar on one side, and on the other a darkened barn with thick smoke, thumping music, a crude floor-show, and a pervasive smell of disinfectant. To get in, you had to pay two dollars, and, once in, the topless girl André explained his problem to couldn't believe ('*Sans farce!*', she cried – 'No kiddin'!') he was just in there for a pail of water.

With a gallon in the dripping radiator, we crawled back to the garage.

There, Arsène was all for taking *his* car, but the garage-man said the little mishap was no big deal, just an oversight, and that he would have the big car 100 per cent perfect in no time. Maybe we should take two cars, just in case, said Arsène: '*On m'a élevé à toujours envisager le pire*' ('I was raised to be always ready for the worst'). But the garage-man sounded convinced, the other car was a lot roomier, and it would be better fun maybe to stay grouped.

So we started out again, with Arsène commenting: '*C'est un vrai voyage – dans un vrai voyage il faut passer par tous les stades de l'inquiétude'* ('This is a real journey – on a real journey, you have to go through all the stages of anxiety').

It was already obvious that Arsène was going to be the philosopher of this trip.

★

Hardly had we got under way again when our existential philosopher started worrying about the frontier. *'Je ne veux pas faire de la paranoia, mais ces gens-là n'aiment pas les étrangers'* ('I don't want to be paranoiac, but those people just don't like foreigners'). Once he and a couple of pals were at the US border and they were asked for what reason they wanted to visit the USA: 'We are going to buy Cheddar cheese', said Arsène, which was absolutely true, but he saw right away that he had awakened deep mistrust. Another time, the customs-man had said: 'Any one of you have more than $10,000 in your pocket?' 'Unfortunately no', said Arsène, which was just saying how he felt. 'Get out of the car!', said the fellow. Not only did those people not like foreigners, they had no sense of humour. You could never know what they might be up to next: *'La nature humaine est sans fond'* ('Human nature is fathomless').

We were travelling south on Route 147 and had passed by those South-Quebec places such as Scotstown and Stornoway (André's comment: 'That was the tactics – to encircle the French'). Evening was colouring the streams with beautiful lights. *'Kolis, c'est beau ça'*, cried Arsène, *'c'est beau en étole!'* ('Chalice, that's beautiful, beautiful as a priest's stole!').

It was decided, democratically, to stop in at a supermarket to lay in provisions, since we didn't know what we were going to find at the forest-place where we were going to stay. My companions piled up an improbable amount of heterogeneous grub, including a tribal size packet of potato crisps. Whatever we did in Maine, we would not starve.

Arsène suggested we should also use the opportunity to check the car-lights, each and every one of them, so the border-officers would find no fault. We were to make sure also, he insisted, to provide the squarest, straightest, most solemn answers to any possible query or remark.

By now we were close to Coburn Gap. A half-moon was leaping among the clouds like the ghost of some ghost dance

Indian. Mount Magantic rose on the skyline: *'Ce sont les endroits perdus du Québec'* ('These are the lost places of Quebec'), said Gabriel. At Notre-Dame-des-Bois, a fluorescent cross on the hill marked the last French village. Beyond that, it was pagan Anglo-Saxon darkness.

At the frontier, a notice stated that all vehicles must pull up for inspection, and that you must 'stop engine, stay in vehicle, wait for officer'. That, very scrupulously, is what we did, with Arsène whistling a carefree little tune.

'Where do you folks live?'

'Montreal.'

'Canadian citizens?'

'Yes.'

'Where are you going?'

'To Maine.'

'Purpose?'

'Tourism.'

'How long are you going to stay in the US?'

'A few days.'

'Anything to declare?'

'No, nothing.'

'OK, go ahead.'

'Batêche, je me sens rudement soulagé' ('Boy, am I relieved'), sighed Arsène.

We went on then through the forest via Carabassett, Kingfield, New Portland, North Anson, and moved up the Kennebec River by Solon, Bingham, Moscow, Caratunk, to the Forks, at the junction of the Kennebec with the Dead.

★

Checked in at the Northern Outdoors Centre (big dead moose-heads looking down dolefully over the desk), we made for the cabin where Rick Rodrick was waiting for us.

Rick Rodrick was an American who'd thought he was of Scots descent till he'd recently discovered his roots were probably Basque. That gave him a dual identity problem, which he was working double time on. He was also engaged in a research project in ethnic studies at the University of Quebec concerned in particular with the old Canada roads from Quebec to Maine via the Kennebec and the Chaudière.

Since it was already late ('*Je suis tanné*' – 'I'm dead beat', said Arsène), and we intended to have a full day on the morrow, we decided to turn in. André and Gabriel were to be bunking on the ground floor with Rick; Arsène and I were to be on the top deck. It was the appropriate moment for Arsène to lay forth his philosophy about nocturnal nasal vibrations: 'If you hear the other guy snoring, you're not snoring. If you don't hear him, it's you that's doing the snoring.'

I feared the worst, and my fears proved to be well founded.

Up at the crack of dawn, I crept out of the sonorous cabin, made my way through the camp-ground and into the forest. Big silence: only one bird going *juck juck juck – juck juck*. Through the trees, red and yellow reflections on the river water. I had my map with me: up to the north-west, Moosehead Lake and Mt Katahdin; down to the south-east, the coast of Maine and the Atlantic ocean; between them, the Kennebec and the Penobscot.

With my back to a pine tree, I must have snoozed off for a while. When I woke, it was to the distant sound of bagpipe music. Back at the Northern Outdoors, I saw that this was Rick exercising one of his identities. People were coming out of their cabins to listen to him. Some obviously wished he would drop dead.

After breakfast, we crossed the Kennebec on a rubber dinghy, out to spend the day on the hunt for traces of habitation on the Canada road. Rick had a gun with him, his grandfather's, 'a Fox Stevens factory second' – just in case a moose decided to come charging at us. That had happened to him once, over in Alaska. This big moose was staring at him from about twenty paces. With his pan-Caledonian repertoire, and thinking he could maybe charm the beast like some Celtic Orpheus, he started singing *Men of Harlech* at the top of his lungs. No doubt taking this as a challenge to its dignity, the moose charged, and Richard the Lionheart had to shoot it with his ancestral 12-bore peashooter.

On the other side of the river we met a surveyor engaged in marking boundary lines for the National Park: 'Bustin' your butt for thirteen hours a day.' One of his mates was down with 'beaver fever' from having drunk still water. As for the trails, somebody, he said, must have let a pig loose one day and just followed it. On some days in some places, he'd been eaten alive by all kinds of flies, *brûlots, mouches à chevreuil, frappe-à-bord*, no see'em... Yes (in answer to Rick's query), he had seen some signs of a cabin over there by the gulch.

We wandered about that area and came first across two gravestones. According to Rick, people would bring their gravestones with them into the wilderness, all written up except for the date. Thereafter we found the remains of a drystone wall, an old pan, bits of a stove. Rick noted it all down carefully on his tablets and pinpointed the site with his satellite-connected GPS equipment.

After a couple of hours, I was thoroughly fed up scrabbling about for pots and pans, knives and forks, and said I was going to take a walk up the Appalachian Trail which I'd noticed crossed the Kennebec just a bit lower down on its way to Katahdin: rendezvous by the riverside at sundown.

I'd hardly gone a couple of miles up the trail when a guy with a long red beard came towards me, wearing boots and leggings, all besplatched with mud, walking fast with two sticks. Obviously no time to spare, but he did say: 'Hi.' Just for the hell of it, I answered back in French: '*Salut.*' A few miles later, another guy came along. He was sporting a yellow beard but looked so beat he must have come all the way from Alabama, and was totally aphonic.

As I walked farther up the Appalachian, I was thinking of American trails in general, and in particular of the great Travellers' Highway, three thousand miles long, that went from Montreal via Grand Portage, Lake of the Woods, Lake Winnipeg, Flin Flon, Ile-à-la-Crosse, Fort McMurray, right up to Fort Chipewyan on Lake Athabasca. The travellers on the highway would be either *voyageurs*, hired to paddle the canoes (the Montreal canoe, 36 feet long, twelve men; the Northern canoe, 25 feet long, eight men), or freelance trappers and traders, *coureurs de bois*. Some of them were pretty rough: not owning even plates, they'd get the camp cook to ladle their soup into hollows in the rocks and lap it up like dogs. And they were generally known as miscreants. 'When a Christian starts to travel', said an eighteenth-century sermon-in-verse, 'he goes straight to the devil.' The authorities loathed them. But they were the real discoverers of America. Their motto: 'Carry, paddle, walk and sing.'

There were a lot of Scotsmen on these trails also, with bits of ragged tartan on their backs and a wild sense of space in their history-stricken eyes.

Beyond the trails, I was thinking of the landscape itself: how the Caledonian Chain in Scotland belonged to that series of circumarctic orogeneses that comprised also Greenland, the Canadian shield and the Appalachians, and how the Great Glen of Scotland corresponded exactly to the Cabot Fault in the Canadian Maritimes...

It was Autumn on the Appalachian Trail: ruddy reds, smoky blues. And there, as I turned a corner, I saw a black bear scuttling away through a thicket. A mile or two further on, it was a little chipmunk, which the Quebeckers call *le petit Suisse*. By late afternoon, I was lying on the banks of the river listening to the crickets near at hand, and, in the distance, the cry of a loon.

★

That evening, around a bottle of Kentucky bourbon, the talk in the cabin was about the condition of Quebec.

All of my companions were, in one way or the other, part of the Quebecontestation. Sylvain was geo-cultural, Rick was politico-historical, Gabriel was nostalgic for what he called 'the little people' and for all the 'little Canadas' that can be found all over America ('*Partout où il y a des trous de monde pauvre, il y a des francophones*' – 'every time you come across some poor hole on this continent, you'll hear folk talking French'), as for Arsène, he was a worried man, looking into the dark for an image, or a cluster of images, he could feel at home with.

'Right from the beginning', said Sylvain, 'what France wanted to create in New France was a replica, a lost bastion of the feudal and papal state that was falling apart in the home country.' That was finished, of course. But nowadays all France looked for from Quebec was a folkloric variety show: '*Les Québécois sont arrivés, gais, gais...*' As for the Anglo-Canadians, they'd been content to have Quebec as a kind of ethnic ghetto, or a luxury reserve, something like Louisiana, till the big business multinationals came along and turned Montreal into another New York. Wheeling-dealing Montreal, and, back of it, Nowhere North America... Quebec had never been able to evolve in an original way. The people didn't even like the part of the planet they inhabited, there was a kind of geographical and climatic racism in the air. Most of them loathed the winter, for example – a local poeticule who sang songs had said he found the blue of the winter sky *aggressive*. Then there was the image the Franco had in the eyes of the rest of America: vaguely picturesque and charming, but feckless. That was partly true, but it was because the people hadn't had a chance. And it certainly wasn't always true. Those who had made some move into new space were actively put down. Take the example of Capitaine Bernier who was up in the Arctic, trading with the Inuit, might even have reached the North Pole, when he received orders to turn back: it was inconceivable, totally unacceptable, that a lousy French Canadian reach the Pole before the bold and enterprising Anglo-Saxons.

'Another example of that', broke in Rick, 'is Tom Plant. He was born here in Maine, of a family French on both sides (his father's name was Antoine Plante) that had travelled through the woods in the twenties and thirties of the nineteenth century. Tom was raised on what was called "French Hill", at Bath, just down the road. Leaving school at fourteen, he made a living as boilermaker and ice cutter before moving off to Lynn, Massachusetts, to work in the shoe-making industry, finally founding his own company, which became the largest shoe factory in the whole damn world. But this isn't part of the folklore, this isn't part of the image. We're awash in a sea of lies.'

'*Tonnerre de Brest, c'est vrai ça!*' ('Thunder of Brest, that's true!'), cried Arsène.

'What had always been brushed away under the carpet', went on Sylvain, 'was the half-breed thing. Louis Riel had been written off as a madman. There was a fine old half-breed ethic that had been obliterated. Every attempt had been made to break the link between the Canadian and the *Sauvage...*'

All in all, Quebec was on its own. Nothing to hope for from Canada, nothing to hope for from France. The only real model possible was the St Lawrence, moving on its deepflowing way through uncoded space.

Sylvain's father had been a pilot on the St Lawrence. And he had told me there were Indians in his family. He was on a big autochthonous trip at that moment, attending Half-Breed conventions, attending First Nations ceremonies and rituals from Montreal to Montana. Not that he was of the 'Wanabee' tribe – those who 'want to be' Indians. He liked to think of himself rather as a Malecit, half-Indian, half-Malouin, living out his life on the banks of the big river.

It was with all this in mind, and also because I knew he was a good man with a canoe, that I'd suggested to him that, on the next day, while our three companions continued their pot-and-pan investigations on the Canada Road, we'd take a trip down the river to Solon. I'd heard (in fact, read in an old guide-book) that there were Indian pictographs at a place down the Kennebec, and had inquired at Northern Outdoors. They'd heard of them, vaguely. But there was somebody who might be able to give me more information, a local antiquarian, a retired schoolteacher down in Solon, Miss Fanny Oates.

On a fine sunny September morning, we set out early, with Sylvain at the prow. The 'long water' was soon about sixty yards wide, with a strong current. We passed a boat fishing for bass, learning that formerly there were salmon and sturgeon in the Kennebec, but no longer. It was pleasant canoeing, mile after mile, with the Autumn woods on either side.

'The village in which I live', wrote the Jesuit priest Sebastian Rasles, missionary to the Abenaki in the early eighteenth century, 'is called Narantsouak. The river which flows through my mission is the largest of all those which water the terri-tories of the Indians. It should be marked upon the maps by the name of Kinibiki.'

Miss Fanny Oates knew all about Sebastian Rasles, and about Benedict Arnold, who left from 'the great Carrying Place' on the Kennebec for his journey up through the wilder-ness to Quebec. Known locally as the incarnate memory of the Kennebec Valley, she was writing a novel, *An Abode in the Wilderness*, of which she read us the first pages: 'Winter was coming on, with storms of sleet and snow sweeping down upon the little colony. Jeannie McCracken had just given birth to her first baby, Ewan...' She was also compiling an anthology of *Valley Verse*, which contained, among other beauties, this piece 'written by me in 1792, with Indian paint':

> *Benjamin Thompson is my name,*
> *And English is my nation,*
> *Seven-Mile Brook is my dwelling place*
> *And Christ is my salvation*

As to the pictographs, yes, she knew of them, but 'a red-haired Indian from Quebec' had told her they weren't a message, just doodling. Just doodling or no, I was still keen to see them. She gave us directions how to get to the place.

It took us over an hour, pushing our way through the thorny thickets and scrambling along the riverbank, before we found this rock jutting out into the waters. It was smooth stone, and there were many drawings, but much eroded – a little water splashed over them, however, brought out the lines. There were, so far as I could make out, dancing figures, a schooner, a cross, a bear, bird-men, a canoe, a wolf...

Just doodles?

★

Next morning, leaving Rick up there at the Forks to get on with his Canada Road research and his identity problem, the four of us continued our Maine trip, going down Route 201.

Route 201, 'the backbone of Maine', runs from the Canadian border above Jackman all the way to the coast at Topsham. From it, on smaller sections, you can go to Athens and China.

Huge logging trucks. Breaks with dead horned animals splayed on their bonnets...

We passed through Caratunk and Moscow before stopping at a diner for a 'Breakfast Special' that consisted of eggs, bacon, sausages, pancakes (with maple syrup) and home fries – all on the same plate. '*Kolis, c'est chaud, ça*', cried Arsène as he touched a burning forkful to his mouth, adding later, as an afterthought, that if we weren't going to get 'as fat as the Yankees' we'd have to be satisfied now and then with a *'repas granola'*.

Houses of wood and red brick. American flags displayed in the gardens. In the garage, a canoe hanging above the car. Shops selling moose antlers, deer hides, and kitschy little things made of bark and moss. I went into a place called the *Now and*

Then Shop where an old pair of snowshoes lay alongside a dusty Frank Sinatra record and a battered Bible.

Back country America. A bit sad. But infinitely preferable to the glossy, noisy, vulgar image prevalent everywhere.

We passed thereafter through Solon (*Trapper Muzzle-loading Supplies, Flytying Angling Supplies*) and at Skowhegan (*The Kingdom Hall of Jehovah's Witness*) switched from 201 on to East 2.

Thereafter it was Canaan, Palmyra, Newport, Etna, Damascus, Carmel, Hermon, and the crossing of the Penobscot, when we got on to South 15, going down via Orrington, Bucksport (*Live Lobster, Clams, New Taters*) to Castine.

At Castine, there's a notice indicating 'the site of an ancient Etchemin Camping Place, Betsabé's permanent camp of 80 wig-wams and 300 [here a word had been obliterated and "Native Americans" put in its place]'. Another notice informs you that 'in 1692 James Giles, a boy, and an Englishman, taken at Gasco, held in slavery by Madockawando for attempting to escape, were tortured by fire, compelled to eat their noses and ears and then burned to death at the stake.'

The town of Castine takes its name from one Jean Vincent d'Abbadie de Saint-Castin, who was born in 1652, near Oloron, in the Atlantic-Pyrenees. His relations with the Indians were apparently a lot more congenial than those just described. In 1687, Minnerval, Governor of Acadia (that is, Maine and the Maritimes: 'New France') wrote this: 'The Sieur de St-Castin is absolute master of the savages, and of all of their business, being in the forest with them since 1665, and having with him two daughters of the chief of these savages, Madockawando, by whom he has had many children.' Two of his half-breed sons were to run the outpost at the mouth of the Penobscot, called Pentagoet, after his return to France in 1701.

We found rooms at the Village Inn, just next door to Bah's Bake House, which advertised itself as 'bakery extraordinaire'. Pretexting an attack of the 'flu, in fact wanting to protect myself from the resonant Arsène, I said I'd like a room of my own. Sylvain and Gabriel also seemed to be wary, so they decided to bunk together in another room, leaving Arsène all alone with his philosophy.

We then went out for an exploratory stroll, and came across the Harbour Tavern.

'No Fighting before 11:30 p.m.'

'Free Beer Tomorrow.'

The Harbour Tavern was a snug little hole decorated with stiff taxidermied fish and a wooden mermaid sporting a long winding tail. Its shelves were well packed with One-Eyed Jack, Carrabassett Ale, Allagash White.

'*Je paie la traite!*', cried Arsène. So we all had a mug of Carrabassett ('handbrewed in the Mountains of Maine'), which we followed up at my suggestion with a Katahdin Red, drunk to the health of Henry Thoreau.

After drinking health to Henry Thoreau, Henry Miller, Jack Kerouac and a few other American loners like them, we went back up to the Village Inn for dinner: black bean soup, fish cake and coleslaw. The waitress was a cute-looking gal from Oregon. She'd come to Maine in order to be with her boy-friend, who was in the local naval academy, but she found the life dull and slow: 'What brought you guys down here?', she enquired. 'You', said Sylvain, coming on the Frenchie.

After dinner, my companions were all for going back to the Harbour Tavern, to drink some more healths. But I had other plans.

★

Up in my room (walls of dark wooden laths, with an oaken table, an Adirondack chair, a bed covered with a paleblue and white patchwork quilt), I pinned to a wall, according to my old habit, the big map of the Coast of Maine put out by the NOAA (National Oceanic and Atmospheric Administration), and took two books out from my travelling bag. One was Vol. 1 of the six-volume edition of Champlain's *Voyages* published by the Champlain Society of Toronto in 1922, the other the Portfolio of Plates and Maps accompanying that edition, which I'd picked up, at an all-American Book Fair (my bookseller was from St Louis), in Montreal.

I was all ready for a long night session.

On 2 September, Champlain set out from Ste Croix, the French island settlement in Passamaquoddy Bay, in order to 'explore along the coast of Norumbega', Norumbega being the area of the Penobscot. Bad weather followed by thick fog held him up for a few days. Then, 'continuing our course along the coast we made this day some twenty-five leagues, and passed a great number of islands, sand-banks, shoals and rocks, which in some places project more than four leagues out to sea.'

On Champlain's map of 1607, I see islands marked Isle Haute (High Island), Monts Déserts (Desert Heights), Isle-aux-Perdrix (Partridge Island), Isle-aux-Perroquets (Puffin Island), Isle-aux-Corneilles (Raven Island), and groups of islands given collective names, such as Isles Rangées (the Ordered Islands), Orsènes Isles (the Outer Islands), Isles Perdues (the Sunken Islands). Also marked, the River Norumbegue and the outpost of Pentegoët, which may be a French transcription of the Indian 'penobscot', but which also sounds vaguely Breton, as if it were something like 'head of the woods' – on some maps, I've seen the place marked also Pentecost. On the map of 1616, Pentegoët is Pemetgoit, on the Rivière de Quinibequy. On the *Carte Géographique de la Nouvelle France*, which takes in more ground, the north bank of the St Lawrence bears this note: '*L'auteur n'a point encore recongny cette coste*' ('The author has not yet reconnoitred this coast.'), but some places are marked in, such as Baye Sauvage and Croix Blanche. As to the Isles Orsènes, they seem to have become the Isles Jetées (the Outcast Isles). On the *Carte de la Nouvelle France Augmentée* of 1632, Pemetgoit is clearly marked, and the Isles Horsaines, as well as the Isle-aux-Tangueux (Gannet Island) and the Isle-aux-Loups Marins (Sealion Island). And way up north of the St Lawrence shore, you read: 'Terres de la Brador – Esquimaux'.

Back to the text.

The next day, the sixth of the month, we made two leagues, and caught sight of smoke in a cove which was at the foot of the mountains above-mentioned; and we saw two canoes paddled by Indians, who came to observe us at a distance of a musket-shot. I sent out two Indians in a canoe to assure them of our friendship, but the fear they had of us made them turn back. The next morning they returned, and came alongside our pinnace, and held converse with our Indians. I had some biscuit, tobacco and sundry other trifles given to them. These Indians had come to hunt beaver, and to catch fish, some of which they gave us. Having made friends with them, they guided us into their river Peimtegouet, as they call it, where, they told us, lived their chief named Bessabez, headman of that river. I believe that this river is the one which several pilots and historians call Norumbega, and which most of them have described as large and spacious, with a number of islands...

From the text then, I went back to the big NOAA map of the gulf of Maine that I'd bought at Newport, a beautiful thing, fawn and pale blue, with all its exactitudes.

There's Mount Desert Island, with its outliers, Great Goat Island, Placentia Island, Black Island. There's Isle Haute, now, curiously 'Isle au Haut', there's Deer Island and its bewildering archipelago: Spruce Island, Devil Island, McGlathery Island, Wreck Island...

I kept on reading and looking at maps till about three in the morning.

Outside, the wind was rising and rain had begun to fall.

★

'We're gonna have us a wang dang doodle all night long!'

This was a guy laying out to three friends of his at a round table in the eatery his plans for imminent rejoycings. At another table, an enormously obese man and a woman with her mouth twisted from a stroke were talking about cranberry-picking. It was morning at the Village Inn. I was munching a muffin that tasted of baking powder and drinking a coffee that tasted of lysol. The morning was rainy, all grey, blue and white. I had a blurred image through the window of the *Patriot State* – the ship of the all-American Maine Maritime Academy.

'Yessir, we're gonna have us a wang dang doodle!'

My companions were slow coming down from their roosts, but we finally got out on the road.

Rocky promontories, islands, piney coves, crows, white board houses, mist, red-orange sun.

West Brooksville, North Brooksville, Brooksville...

At Stonington, we went into a bookshop and after browsing about for a while got into conversation with the owners, a couple of retired teachers. To a polite question put by the wife as to what we were doing in Maine, Sylvain responded wildly: 'We have come to recover our lost lands! We speak the original language of Maine!' The woman gave him a look as if he was

75

about to pull out a tomahawk, then another as if he was completely off his head.

We got back on the road.

Blue Hill, East Blue Hill...

Just outside Sullivan, a black bear crossed the road. It was disappearing into a wood when Sylvain called out: '*Salut, frère!*' and the bear turned round.

'*C'est le seul ours francophone du voisinage*' ('That's the only French-speakin' bear in the neighbourhood'), murmured Sylvain.

Ashville, West Gouldsboro, Prospect Harbor.

At the Fisherman's Friend, Prospect Harbor, looking over to Petit Manan Point, we ate a big bowl of delicious clam chowder followed up by some good old blueberry pie and coffee.

Gouldsboro, Millbridge, Harrington, Columbia Falls...

Then down, via Indian River, to Jonesport.

There we took rooms at the West Bay Hotel.

'Summer season's over', said the owner. 'Still some folks around, but not many. Mainly empty nesters.'

The West Bay Hotel was also an Old Curiosity Shoppe. Where we talked, we were surrounded by a diving suit, a pair of oars, an anchor, a table piled with books and cases full of scrimshaw. 'I go antiquin',' continued the owner. 'All over the place – far as Florida.' He'd just take off whenever he got the inclination and bring back a lot of stuff. People liked it. They found it reassuring. He didn't make a fortune with it, but 'You earn a dollar, you lose a dollar – I break even.'

He used to work in Detroit. Up there, 'I spent three-quarters of my time filling in forms.' So he thought, if he was going to be really constructive with his life, he'd come right down east and do nothin'.

No, he didn't serve meals, but there was a diner down the street.

So we went to the diner, got something (totally undefinable) to eat, and turned in. On the wall in front of me, I had a Japanese flag, a harpoon, and the ceremonial banner of the Knights of Pytheas.

Up early the next morning, I went over the Moosebec Bridge to Beals Island.

Two or three goodlooking white pinnaces anchored in the bay.

Past the clam hatchery, dark rock, pinewood.

When I came back from the tip of the island that looks over to Great Wass (Champlain's 'Crow Island'), I met the last visitor of the season, from Vermont: a woman, about thirty-five years old, standing on the veranda of a cabin with a mug of coffee in her hand and a vague, empty look in her eyes.

★

By mid-morning, we had passed Machias, Whiting, Lubec, and there really was a strong atmosphere of being way 'down east': more white board houses with paint flaking off them, more barns squee-gee, sagging, or caving in.

At Pleasant Point, on Passamaquoddy Bay, we came across, by the roadside, a big ramshackle building that bore a handbill saying it was the Indian Township Thrift Shop (Recycling Center, open on Saturdays). Sylvain said this was the township of the Passamaquoddy Tribe and suggested we pay a visit. Nobody had any objection, and Gabriel thought he might find there an Indian basket as a present for his little daughter.

A huddle of white-painted shacks surrounded by trees. Cars parked. Canoes on trolleys.

One big shack near the entrance, built of shingles, containing two establishments: Indian Handicrafts, and Molly's Take Out Shop.

A brown dog with a red collar at rest on the veranda.

Inside, a handful of Indians drinking coffee or coke.

Among them, the tribal governor, whom Sylvain engaged in conversation. As I looked through an Indian calendar (*Opol ah-somuwehs*, 'whirling wind month'; *piyatokonis*, 'when the spruce tips fall'; *sigon*, 'Spring moon'; *ponatom*, 'egg-laying month'...), I heard the name mentioned, a strange name, of one Ovide Mercredi ('Ovid Wednesday').

Finally, 'have a good ride', says the chief to us all.

Outside, I asked Sylvain who Ovide Mercredi was. President of the Assembly of the First Nations, he told me. And added: 'He's a compatriot of yours. That 'Mercredi' was originally McCreadie.'

Robbinston, Red Beach, Calais, Princeton, Waite, Topsfield, Brookton, Eaton, Danforth, Weston, Orient, Houlton, Monticello, Bridgewater, Blaine, Presque Isle...

Forest, forest, forest. Blue hills on the horizon.

WELCOME TO CARIBOU.

Judging by the names on the store fronts, the population of Caribou seemed to be a mixture of Anglo-Saxon, French and Scandinavian (I learned later that, in the mid-nineteenth century, when America was going West, in order to get settlers for that tough north-east corner, the Commissioner of Immigration for the Maine legislature had invited in Swedes from Gothenberg). Since Gabriel hadn't found the basket he wanted on Passamaquoddy Bay, and since Arsène had by now decided he wanted one for his girlfriend, his 'blonde', we went into Roux's grocery store, which stood next to Olson's newsagents and Russell's insurance agency, to enquire where at Caribou we might find Indian baskets. The man behind the counter said the best place, the biggest choice, was at Washburn, down on 164 – Harold's Barber Shop.

So down we went on 164 to Washburn, and there was Harold's Barber Shop, just next to Johnny's Redemption Center, with Indian baskets galore piled up on the sidewalk.

Harold's Barber Shop was like something out of a film of the 1930s. The chair was an heirloom, thick and massive. The electric clippers hanging beside it were antiquated. On the walls were would-be humorous messages: 'Lose weight quick – get a haircut'; 'From Hair to Eternity'; 'This house is guarded by shotgun three nights per week – you guess which three'.

'Want baskets? Sure, take your pick. Got more in the storeroom.'

These were Micmac baskets: 'Our traditional wood splint baskets are made by Micmac tribespeople living in Aroostook County Maine. On regular hunting and gathering journeys our fore-fathers and mothers carried their belongings in similar baskets. Today using old methods, we pound trunks of ash until they separate into thin layers by year rings. Then we splice the layers into strips which we weave into various basket designs: potato, picnic, laundry, pack, hamper, fishing, fancy...'

Gabriel and Arsène found what they wanted. As they were paying, Harold told us about life in Washburn: 'When the aircraft base closed down, that hurt awful. Nothin' here now but taters an' lumber. Stores and restaurants closin' down all the time.'

It was the end of the Cold War in Washburn.

But just wait. They'll find another one.

Back up in Caribou, we went into another diner for something to eat. Hearing us talk French, a woman came over and started talking French too, with a strange old accent ('droite' came out as *drwett*). Sylvain was delighted. Especially when another woman came out from the kitchen and started talking French as well. 'I didn't know you talked French!', said her friend. 'You never asked me. I didn't know *you* talked French.' Sylvain was in his element. '*Partout en Amérique tu tombes sur de vieux Français*', said the first woman in conclusion ('Everywhere in America you come across old French folk').

While this talk in French was going on, a good-looking, grey-haired elderly Yankee came in, ordered a take-away sandwich at the counter and left saying:

'Fall's here. Looks like snow.'

★

'From Key West to Fort Kent' – that's the usual phrase for indicating the whole stretch of North America.

We were on the Fort Kent Road now, having come out of Caribou on 161 by New Sweden, Jentland, Guerette and Daigle.

Old Fashioned Revival Center.

New Life Baptist Church.

An old man gleaning potatoes in a field.

If there were French names at Caribou, there were even more at Fort Kent: Deschaine, Caron, Voisine...

Northern Timber Trucking.

Northland Frozen Foods.

A few miles beyond Caron Brook, we crossed the New Brunswick-Quebec line.

'What time is it?', asked Arsène.

'Three o'clock,' said Sylvain.

'*Une heure plus tard dans les Maritimes,*' added Gabriel. ('One hour later in the Maritimes').

QUEBEC VOUS SOUHAITE LA BIENVENUE

'Yeah!', cried Arsène,, and blew the horn.

Les Étroits.

St Marc du Lac Long.

Rivière-Bleue.

At Rivière-Bleue, Arsène had relatives, and he wanted to pay them a visit. Sylvain and Gabriel decided to go with him. I said I'd wait for them – in that bar over there.

★

A big pool table. A video-machine. Four guys hunched at the counter drinking beer.

I sat down at a table in the far corner.

Feeling the 'flu I mentioned earlier beginning to get some definition, I decided it might be beneficial as well as pleasant to drink a toddy. So when the girl came over, I asked her to bring me a glass of whisky, with some hot water and sugar on the side.

When she came back ten minutes later, she told me she'd already put the sugar in the whisky.

'Oh, okay – thanks.'

So I poured in the hot water, whirled the glass around a bit, put the toddy to my lips and tasted.

That sugar she'd put in was salt.

I like salt with tequila, and I know it was an old Quebec practice to put salt in beer, but, dammit to hell, this was *whisky*.

I called the girl over and we straightened it all out.

So there I sat, in a bar at Blue River, in the Témiscouata country, the backlands of Rivière-du-Loup, drinking hot whisky, at the window behind me the light of a late Autumn afternoon in the cosmos.

It was pleasant, planetarily pleasant.

All on my lonesome in Nowhere North America...

My companions turned up about five-thirty, determined to get to Quebec City and Montreal that night.

★

The border is at Estcourt Station.

Estcourt Station is a row of houses called le Rang de la Frontière, a wooden bridge known as Le Pont des Contre-bandiers, and a store bearing the name Magasin Général Américain. We stopped just long enough to take a quick look around, buy chewing-gum at the store, and got on the road again.

A lake lit by golden light.

I could no longer make out the names of the villages. We were just moving on and on through the darkness.

Till the St Lawrence came in sight.

'*Tabernak, en voilà un fleuve!*' ('Tabernacle, there's a river for you'), cried Arsène.

Then it was the neat little villages along the river: St-Jean-Port-Joli, Bellechasse, and finally, Quebec City.

We went to Gabriel's place where I was going to be staying a few days, had a cup of coffee and a sandwich, then Sylvain and Arsène left for Montreal.

★

I sat on the terrace of the Château Frontenac in Quebec City, drinking a *de luxe* Canadian whisky... I walked along the Rue Jean-Bourdon, '*arpenteur et cartographe*'... At the Petit Coin Breton, I ate a Breton *crêpe* they called a 'Trébeurden'.

One morning, I followed the wooden walk that skirts the St Lawrence and from there ascended to the Plain of Abraham. Up there, I met an old man who told me that if the Quebeckers had only been allowed to fight '*à la canadienne*' (using guerrilla tactics and Indian ways) instead of '*à la mode parfumée*' (according to the strict etiquette of the military book), the British wouldn't have won the war and Canada would be French.

The white geese were flying over the St Lawrence, making for the south. In the backyard of the house, the little brown and silvergrey squirrels were foraging round and round, getting in supplies for the Winter.

Around Corsica

'You're not a real Scotsman', he said.

'How come?', said I.

'You're not wearing a kilt.'

'Oh, I see. And I don't have a bushel of red hair on my head either, do I? And I'm not playing the bagpipes.'

'You get my meaning entirely', he said, smiling.

'Let's say I'm an evolving Scot', I said.

'That's an interesting idea', said he.

'You might also say that I'm para-autochthonous. Engaged in a delocalized process.'

'That's more than interesting, it's intriguing.'

There was a short pause while we both took a sip of Nicrosi from our glasses, looking up complacently and connivingly into the empty blue of the sky.

'While we're on all this identity stuff', I then resumed. 'You're not a real Corsican.'

'No?'

'No. You're not wearing a red woollen bonnet, you're not cradling a rifle in your arms, and you don't have a *pistola* stuck in your belt. In short, you don't look at all like a bandit. No novelist would look twice at you.'

'But I *am* a bandit', he said.

'You don't say', I said.

'Yes, I do say. And there are a hundred bandits all around us, all quietly sipping their *apéritif,* but with their minds up to all kinds of dreaming and scheming.'

'*Bandits d'honneur?*'

'Honourable bandits, business bandits, political bandits. We've got all the categories here in Corsica. And inside each category, you've got the big ones, the middle ones and the small ones. The biggest bandit of them all was Napoleon. He was the imperial bandit. He was out to get rid of all the rest.'

'But you don't look a bit like Pascal Gallocchio, Théodore Poli, or André Spada alias "the wild boar".'

'I see you know your stuff.'

'I do my best. I pick up information here and there.'

'Interesting. Nobody does anything like that here. We just

hang about, play a crafty little trick or two on the other fellow, drink our *apéritifs*, then we kick the bucket and the local rag says what great guys we were.'

★

It was five o'clock of the evening, at the back end of October, in the good city of Ajaccio.

Autumn in Corsica: the sky absolutely blue, every outline neatly edged and, although the leaves of the trees were turning yellow-red and the starlings were wheeling over the town, making at nightfall an unholy late-final racket in the branches of the plane-trees, it was still very pleasantly warm.

I'd got into Ajaccio two days before, via Paris. Since air-traffic was congested in south-eastern France, the Air Inter plane, deviated from the normal route, had made its way down to Corsica, and it was a route that pleased me better, via the Swiss Alps, Turin and Genoa.

Paris had been wrapped in a dreary, drizzly grey. But the farther south we got, the more the world opened up.

At Ajaccio, I went straight to the Hotel Napoléon. My room looked out on to the mustard-coloured wall of the building opposite and a little grove of orange trees. Down in the hall, there was a black bust of the Man Himself and a large coloured map of Corsica. Need I say I spent more time with the map than with the bust?

My plan was to move right round the coast, making incursions here and there into the interior of the country but, to begin with, I wanted to have a look at Ajaccio and try to get the feel of it.

So I strolled down that thoroughfare known as the Cours Napoléon. I sat in opulent, copper-and-leather cafés looking out on to royally soaring palms, I continued along the quays: the Quai Napoléon, the Quai de la République, the Quai de l'Herminier, passing the monument to the Resistance on the Waterfront – *À ceux qui ont donné leur vie pour une Corse libre et française* ('To those who gave their lives for a free and French Corsica'). I drank glasses of pungent Corsican wine (Fiumiccicoli, Polidore, Fiumucini...) in those waterfront dives you have to step down into, listening to conversations: 'Hey, Pascal, business going well? – It's not going at all – Not going?

Well, get it going.' I even paid a lightning visit to the Bonaparte house, where I saw a narrow little bed the young Napo had napped in.

In one of those waterfront cellars, I met a fellow about thirty years old who said he had been waiting for me. His 'Guide' (a spiritual guide, who existed only in his mind, he explained) had informed him that one Autumn, in a dark place by the sea, he would meet up with a foreigner and that this foreigner would give him a sign. He asked me a lot of questions, and when it finally came out that I had been born in Scotland, he said *that* was it: he knew now he must go to Scotland, and to the exact spot where I had first seen the light of day. I suggested he maybe shouldn't rush things, and should check with his Guide before making any rash decisions. He said he was sure, dead sure – wasn't Scotland a country of initiates? I said, well, maybe it was, kind of, a long time ago, but... Brushing aside my post-druidical scepticism, he was already telling me that Corsica too was a land of initiates. Take Napoleon for instance. Had I noticed that, as Bonaparte, he always kept his left hand under his coat, whereas as Emperor, it was his right? I admitted that detail had escaped my attention. It had esoteric significance, declared my companion. And did I know about Napoleon's one true love? 'Josephine?' I said, diffidently, knowing well I would be hopelessly wide of the mark, but wanting to make him feel I was participating. 'No, no, no', he said impatiently. 'Daria – a girl he met at St-Jean-d'Acre. Daria – *aria* – air, you see?' I said I was still a novice in high-level Napoleonica. So he explained that Napoleon was essentially a mind looking for space and air – hence too his obsession with eagles, see? 'That's interesting', I said. 'Are there eagles in Scotland?' he asked. 'Some', I said cautiously. 'That settles it', he said.

He probably made a beeline for Glasgow airport the very next day, while I got ready for my trip round Corsica.

★

Possibly the best known island-book, at least in modern times, is *Robinson Crusoe*, that novel by Daniel Defoe (His Britannic Majesty's spy in Scotland), based on the experience of a Scottish seaman, Alexander Selkirk, of Largo in the East Neuk of Fife, abandoned on Juan Fernandez, where he lived for five years, from 1704 to 1709.

I read the novel as a youngster, but I've long since preferred the brute document. Here, summarized, is the account of Wood Roggers, the man who picked up Selkirk from the island:

He had been put ashore with his clothes, his bed, a gun, a few pounds of powder, bullets, some tobacco, an axe, a knife, a cooking pot, a Bible, and his navigation instruments. For the first eight months he found it hard to overcome his melancholy. He built himself two huts made of tree-branches, situated at some distance the one from the other. He roofed them with reeds and lined them with goatskins. When his powder began to run out, he found a way of making fire with two pieces of spicy wood he would rub together on his knee. The smaller of the two huts he used as a kitchen. In the bigger one, he slept, sang psalms and prayed to God. He'd never been such a good Christian. At the start, because of his sadness and the lack of bread and salt, he ate only when he absolutely had to, just as he retired to rest only when he couldn't stay awake any more. The spice-wood he used for cooking his food also provided light and its aroma revived his spirits. He killed up to five hundred goats. Once his powder had run out, he'd chase them on foot. This exercise made him so agile that he could run through the woods, along the rocky shore and up and down the hills at an amazing rate. Gradually he got used to eating without salt. In the right season, he'd gather in a kind of turnip, which others had sown and which covered several acres of ground. He found good cabbage too growing on trees, and would season them with Jamaica pepper. There was another kind of pepper too, a black pepper, *malachita*, excellent for stomach troubles. At first, wild cats and rats that had multiplied from a few survivors of shipwrecks were at war with him. The rats would gnaw at his clothes and even his toes during his sleep. To keep them at bay, he tamed the cats, offering them a share in his goat-meat. The cats were so grateful they gathered around his hut in bands. He even got some of them to dance with him. When his clothes ran out, he made himself a jerkin and a bonnet of goatskin, and shirts out of the piece of sailcloth he'd been left with. When his knife became worn, he made himself new ones out of iron hoops he found on the beach. In time, he triumphed over the horrors of solitude, and lived content.

It's all there in that blueprint – the rest is padding, and an encumbering of the mind.

As is probably obvious enough by this time, I prefer, by far, real islands to imaginary islands, just as I prefer prime documents to novelistic remakes. That's because the real is richer than the imagination. The real demands investigation and is an invitation to sensitive knowledge, whereas the imaginary is more often than not just a collection of stereotypes, a soup of clichés offering an infantile kind of satisfaction. Then, a relationship to the real and its resistance requires changes in thought, in ways of being, in ways of saying, it leads to a transformation of the self. Whereas imagination is nothing but compensation. There's even something horribly autistic about sitting in one spot and spinning out invention by the yard. How much more interesting an open and poetic process involving contemplation, study, movement, meditation and composition!

That said, even real islands have come in for a lot of imaginary projection. There are all kinds of reasons for that. You can conjure up marvels, eldorados and whatever if you want to attract people. To keep them away, you can make up monsters and horrors. And sometimes imagination comes into play simply because you haven't yet found the language of the new phenomena.

When Pytheas left the Greek colony of Marseilles in the fourth century BC, he was travelling north up across the wild and unknown Atlantic. When he came back, he talked about lungs of the sea, and about water that lipped the edge of the land and then in a few hours was miles away, and about great palaces of some shining, transparent substance that floated on the sea. A scientist like Strabo said he was a downright liar, that all that was *impossible*. Others appreciated him as a damn good yarn-spinner. It was going to take centuries to see into the reality Pytheas first glimpsed.

At one time, my own home-island, Britain, along with its distant archipelagoes, the Hebrides, the Orkneys, the Shetlands, was considered as the number 1 place for marvels. In a fine old fifteenth-century Mediterranean book, *An Account of the Navigation of Don Pedro Niño*, one finds this:

> The name England means *land of marvels* and the reason for that is the number of extraordinary things to be found in this country, some of them even now. When the inhabitants were savages, they were covered in fur like animals. There were also

serpents, terrible dragons, and a multitude of fierce beasts. Even today, there are birds called *vacares* which live on trees. It is said they are born in the following manner. These trees grow among the rocks, on the sea shore. They have great red flowers. When the flowers have faded, there is a cocoon, which develops gradually. As it grows, it bows low and as it hangs in this way you see limbs and a body. When it is ripe, it falls from the tree with a cry like a crow.

Father Labat, who spent years among the islands of the Caribbean, where he raised buildings, converted souls, worked out his own technique for making rum and wasn't averse to a tall tale (he believed in God, after all), trots out the same story a couple of centuries later: 'One must consider the puffin as a real fish or rather as an unfinished animal, a caprice of nature, born in the air, raised in the water. According to the eye-witness accounts of many *bona fide* observers and authors, it's the fruit of a certain tree to be found on the shores of Scotland, Ireland and the Orkneys.'

It was, again, going to take a good deal of time before all this was cleared up, and something both sensible and interesting could be said about the nature and habits of puffins.

And it's a pretty safe bet that there's an awful lot we still don't know, because the real is practically inexhaustible.

★

All this was going through my head one morning as I sat in the Grand Café de la Méditerranée, and was the background, or rather the underground, to another Corsican conversation, which went like this:

'We separated from the Continent about thirty million years ago', said my interlocutor. 'I'll admit that was a bit before our time, of course. But we Corsicans are still wondering about it. That's the main fact in our history. When we became an island...'

Jacques Biscaglia, for that was his name, was referring to that moment, in the Oligocene or thereabouts, when Corsica and Sardinia (at first, probably one big hunk) broke off from the Pyrenean-Alpine region and swung round for a while in an anti-clockwise direction till they acquired their present form and position.

'From that moment on, we were isolated, exposed, and on

the defensive. You name any marauding band you can think of: Vandals, Ostrogoths, Saracens, Turks, Moors; they've been here, and they've left traces. Invisible traces, maybe, but traces. If you understand that, you understand Corsica and its history. Funny thing – have you noticed how the island seems to be pointing an accusing finger at Genoa? That's because the Genoese overran us more systematically than the others. I mean, before the tourists, God bless them.'

He went on then to expatiate on the nature of insularity.

'All islanders are manic-depressives. Take the English, take the Japanese. Same with the Corsicans.' And he went on: 'Imagination ferments on an island...'

'But it doesn't have to be like that', I said, warming to the subject. 'It's like closed systems and open systems in thermodynamics. The difference between a thermos flask and the earth: the one has no exchange of energy with the outside, the other is all exchange.'

'So, what of it?'

'Well', I continued, 'an island is a little bit of the earth, a microcosm. And it will be bottled in or out-breathing, depending on whether it conceives of the surrounding sea as isolating barrier or as communication area. That again can depend on historical circumstance, so far as the community is concerned. But an individual mind can *always* keep the open view. See what I mean?'

'Uh-huh.'

'What I'm suggesting is that, for that mind, the island will be all benefit, as a comprehensible space, I mean one that can be grasped as a whole, as a living entity – which is hard to do with a whole continent. That mind will see the island also as a place of *concentration*. And since all islands share certain features, notably regarding their coastlines, it's easy to go there from the local to the global and get at a kind of cosmic conscience that is neither closed-up isolation nor abstract universality. OK?'

'You're an optimist,' he said, 'a utopian.'

'No', I said, 'Nothing so doomed to disaster. I'm just an arch-individualist, a possibilist, an abstractionist and a practitioner of geopoetics.'

'Just!', he said.

'In plain terms, I don't think history is fatal – at least for the individual. The individual is a kind of island, and an island can be a kind of individual. And anybody can try to be an individual – an open individual. Take the best writer ever to come out of Corsica: Paul Valéry. He calls himself an intellectual Robinson Crusoe, "giving shape, with adequate instruments, on the island of his will, to a body of radical truth".'

'Paul Valéry as a Corsican writer – that's a good one. And you said the word: ever to come *out* of Corsica. He got out. What's sure is that nobody who can be called "a Corsican writer" today evolves in anything like a space comparable to Valéry's.'

'That's because of historical circumstance. There's nothing essential about it.'

'So how do you change history?'

'I don't know: there's no simple formula. Maybe you don't have to change it at all, just think round it. Try to get at something else. As in literature. What an accumulation of narrative non-entity! But literature can be more than telling stories.'

'What then!'

'One of my compatriots, Robert Louis Stevenson, told stories all his life. Then one day, on a little island in the Hebrides, he had a revelation and began to have qualms. He asked himself if maybe the writer didn't *deform* the island when he integrated it into a work of fiction: to be up to the *reality* of the island (*all* the reality) would take more than fiction. A kind of cosmo-poem, in fact. Stevenson overrode his own personal qualms, but the question remains... About Paul Valéry again, if he'd been able to stay in a place like Corsica instead of getting himself closed up in Paris (with a family into the bargain), he might have been less purely rationalist than he was.'

'Do you really think Valéry was a Corsican poet?'

'Sure', I said, laughing. 'A super-Corsican poet.'

★

On 21 January 1849, in the Hotel d'Europe, Ajaccio, one Esprit Requien made out his last will and testament. Item 4 went as follows:

> Having come to Corsica in order to draw up the flora and the conchological fauna of this island, if God doesn't grant me life to

bring these two studies to completion, I request my friend, Moquin-Tandon, professor of Botany at Toulouse, to be so good as to pursue this task. For this purpose, my executor and the administration of the Calvet Museum will put at his disposal not only all I've gathered in Corsica during this particular journey, but also all the Corsican material that lies in my herbarium and in my conchological collections.

I made the acquaintance of Esprit Requien years ago in Avignon, where he'd been responsible for the art gallery and the fine book collection of the Musée Calvet and where he was instrumental in the setting up of the Natural History museum that now bears his name. But it was only when I picked up in an antiquarian bookshop in Ajaccio a copy of his little booklet *Catalogue des coquilles de la Corse* (Avignon, 1848), alongside his *Catalogue des végétaux ligneux qui croissent naturellement en Corse ou qui y sont généralement cultivés* (Ajaccio, 1852) that I realized he had also done a lot of work on Corsica.

Requien came to Corsica in 1847 for several reasons: get away from local bickerings and small-minded municipal politics in Avignon; recover his health; live more cheaply, since he'd spent practically all the fortune he possessed in fine books and collections; pursue his naturalist's work in a different area, and one which he knew, not only through his studies, but because of an earlier trip to Corsica he'd made with his friend Urbain Audibert de Tarascon, in 1821, to be exceptionally interesting.

It was with a good provision of thick herbarium paper in his luggage that he left Avignon on 12 April 1847, made for Marseilles where he stayed for a few days, and then from there embarked for Ajaccio where he arrived on the 24th.

Natural history he found in a very undeveloped state on the island. If people were interested at all in shells, it was only, he said, to turn them into artificial flowers or decorate boxes with them.

Requien travelled all over Corsica, exploring beaches and forests, from the region of Ajaccio to that of Bonifacio, from there to Bastia, from where, as a passenger on the *Paquebots Valéry*, which ensured the Bastia–Leghorn run, he went out to the island of Caproria.

Here's an excerpt from a letter he wrote concerning a botanical excursion to Monte Renoso:

> After spending three months in the hottest part of the island, at Ajaccio, Bonifacio, etc., I resolved to begin the exploration of the alpine region on a mountain never before mentioned by travelling botanists: Monte Renoso, which rises at the top of the Bastelica valley. We arrived at Cauro around 8 in the morning. After a light meal, we left the royal road of Sartène and entered the valley of the Prunelli. An hour later, it was Bastelica, the beginning of the mountain area being clearly visible in the vegetation.

In Corsica, Requien was in his element.

One of Requien's correspondents was Prosper Mérimée, Inspector of Ancient Monuments for the French government, also a novelist. Mérimée had spent some time in Corsica, but he wasn't much interested in natural history, to say the least. It was more the ethnological he was into, or rather what you might call the ethno-picturesque.

In a letter to Requien of 30 September 1839, Mérimée wrote this, which makes his position crystal-clear while, at the same time, showing him up for the little literatus he was:

> I'm not going to talk about the *maki*. They smell all right, but they rip your clothes to shreds. I'm not going to talk about the glens and the mountains. They're all the same, horribly monotonous. The same goes for the forests. No, what interests me is HUMAN nature. There are some very strange specimens of the genus Man here in Corsica. I can't hear enough stories about the *vendetta*. I spent several days in Sartène, *sciopettata* town, at the house of a famous gentleman, M. Jérôme R., who in one day shot down in cold blood a couple of his enemies. Since then, he's killed another one. Every time, he got a unanimous acquittal from the jury. I've seen another local heroine, Mme Colomba, famous for her excellence in the manufacture of cartridges which she is always ready to dispatch into the constitution of those unfortunate enough to meet with her disfavour. This illustrious lady, who is sixty-five years old, took a real liking to me. When we parted, we kissed Corsican fashion, that is full flush on the mouth...

When Requien travelled in Corsica, it was as correspondent for the Ministry of Education, a post that Mérimée, well in with all the Ministries, had no doubt helped to get for him. Which is why he felt justified in asking Requien to do a few archaeological chores, as in this letter of 7 September 1847:

You have the *Stazzona del diavolo* in the valley of the Gauria ...
There are a good number of *Stantare* on the Sartène road ... and
statues at Baril Veccio ... If you pass by there, try to make a
sketch and take some measurements ... Try to find out about a
strange stone, which I think is Punic...

★

It was on the way to Sartène I now found myself, following the
coast road, with an eye open for standing stones, while more
interested in unhandled ones. The Gulf of Ajaccio was beautiful in the morning light, and on a rock a cormorant was
spreading its wings to dry.

This is the granite side of the island, what used to be known
– from the Genoese administration point of view – as the
Banda di fuori ('the outer section'). And the granite comes in all
colours: red, grey, rosy, blue, with upper surface flaking off in
patches, and the erosion of the softer minerals leaving round
holes and curving hollows. Most people see granite as polished
and monumental, but left to itself it lives its own life, and that
lithic life is more complex than one might think. Which is why
a great poetic mind like that of Goethe felt the need to write
several essays on it.

Many, says Goethe in these essays, will find it hard to
understand how someone like himself, who had devoted his
mind for so long to the study of human passions, should
suddenly switch to the passionate study of granite. That's because,
he continues, their understanding remains within narrow limits
and on a superficial basis, and because they have no sense of
the whole interconnected field. By interesting himself in granite,
Goethe felt that he was entering into a 'higher consideration of
nature', and at the same time giving a more fundamental ground
to his own existence. Granite appeared to him as the very
foundation of the world. 'Every road into unknown mountains
confirms the experience: that the highest and the deepest is
always granite.' Then, he's fascinated by its composition. Made
up of various components (quartz, feldspar, mica, etc.), it nonetheless constitutes a unity. How does a mass of heterogeneous
materials crystallize into individuality? And the answer is: by a
dynamic process comprising both turbulence and tranquillity.
Here what started out as 'an interest in geology' opens out on to

a whole theory of development, both on the panoramic cosmic scale, and on that of an individual existence. And implicit throughout, there is a poetics, that of a highly complex simplicity. I don't hesitate to say that I'd give all of the *Sorrows of Young Werther*, and probably *Faust* too into the bargain, for such gropings after a theory and a poetics as you find in those Goethean essays on granite.

Anyway, there I was, that windy Autumn morning, on the granite road to Sartène and places farther south.

At Filitosa, walking among the stones, I realised that Corsica must have been an important stage on the megalithic road that went (at least for our part – you can trace it back to the Caucasus and beyond) from the sunbeaten far-eastern end of the Mediterranean up to the grey and windy Orkneys. There are stones there that were maybe originally intended just to mark out a territory. Others maybe served as sundials. Maybe later on standing stones were a male assertion (phallic fellowship) over some great Mother religion. And some of the stones at Filitosa are obviously tied in to a warrior cult: they are sculpted in the shape of stern, surly characters bearing swords, which has perhaps something to do with the Peoples of the Sea, those Philistines who gave their name to Palestine, those Shardana who gave their name to Sardinia.

So, there are stones standing erect as markers or symbols, and they are interesting enough. But the stone which attracted me most had no purpose. It was a natural rock in the shape of a bird, and it threw me back farther in space and time. Maybe it was that rock made people choose Filitosa in the first place as a good spot to live in: already 'totemized'.

I didn't find any stelae. I'd have liked to find one, in a language difficult to decipher, that might have gone a little like this:

> *I came on a blue wind*
> *looked around*
> *saw a world of stone*
>
> *I raised this*
> *not to stand against time*
> *just to mark the passing*
>
> *of a man without a name.*

After the grey granite country, to come upon the cliffs of Bonifacio is to be dazzled by absolute whiteness.

Envision for a moment an ancient sea, warm and wild, pounding shells and piling up chalk-deposits, millennium after millennium. The result is a limestone plateau, its sediments a hundred metres thick, stretching over thirty kilometres between the Sartène granite massif to the west and another granite mass in the east going from Cala Fiumara to Punta Coppiciola.

The city itself goes back to a castle a Crusader built on the headland after his return from the wars. When the Republic of Genoa took it over, none of its citizens was willing to emigrate to such a godforsaken spot, situated as it was between a pirate-ridden sea on the one hand and a backcountry infested with barbarous sheepmen on the other. The Republic finally colonized the place with serfs, offering them danger money and, later on, when things got under way, tax exemption. Those ex-serfs turned Bonifacio into a thriving city.

Not, I imagine, without difficulty. When it wasn't attacks and depredations, it was the plague. For the constant threat of attack, you need only look at the very steep and narrow staircases in the houses. At the beginning, there were no staircases at all – only ladders that you could pull up, keeping twenty feet of empty space between you and your assailants. As to the plague, a chapel dedicated to St Roch at the entrance to the city has this:

> *Sancte Roche*
> *bonifacii civitas*
> *ab omni contagione*
> *animae et corporis*
> *fiat secura*

'Oh, Saint Roch, let the city of Bonifacio be free from all plagues of body and soul.'

Entrance is by a heavy gate studded with massive nails followed by a tortuous passageway.

I was hardly out of the passageway when I saw three graffiti. One of them was racist: '*I Araba fora!*' ('Arabs, out!'). Another was schoolboyish: '*Le maître est con comme une pute*' ('The schoolmaster is as dumb as a whore'). The third was both illiterate and illuminated: '*Le Maître du Mond et de la Galaxi*'

('The Master of the Wurld and of the Galaksy').

Walking through the streets, I came upon church after church: St John the Baptist, Sainte Marie Majeure... In one, full of red burning lamps, there was an eighteenth-century plaque to *Il Glorioso Giovanni Nepocumeno Protomartire del Sacramentale Sigillo Gran Taumaturgo*. If Bonifacio was a merchant town, it also, apparently, had a mystical margin to it.

The public buildings weren't, of course, all churches. Other buildings I met up with showed another aspect of Bonifacio as Foreign Legion recruitment office and as base for commando operations: *L'Amicale des Anciens Légionnaires, la Maison des Anciens Combattants, l'Union Nationale des Parachutistes.*

I stood on the high ramparts of the city, looking out over the straits and along the white cliffs, and then went down to the harbour.

An excursion boat was tied up there – *Fleur de Corse* – and the Captain was bawling out an invitation:

'Roll up, ladies and gentlemen, roll up and all aboard. We'll be moving out in a quarter-hour.'

It was twenty to three.

'A real quarter-hour?' I said.

'Well, a Bonifacian quarter-hour!' he answered.

I asked where we'd be going.

'Today, it'll be the Balearic Isles, the Canaries and Guade-loupe...'

'That all?'

'No. There will also be the cliffs and the grottos of Bonifacio and the King of Aragon's Staircase. That suit you?'

'Suits me fine.'

I turned up at five to three.

An elderly German lady was getting aboard at the same time as myself.

'I hope Madame is not liable to seasickness. We have waves twenty-five feet high here, and going twenty-five feet down.'

'Really?'

'No, no, my dear lady, I'm just joking. It's a tempest of utter tranquillity we'll be moving through today!'

We left at twelve minutes past three. The Captain gave me a wink:

'I told you: a Bonifacian quarter-hour.'

He then took the wheel and a younger man took over the spiel.

As we passed by one bulging section of the cliff, this joker informed us that the site had been used for the shooting of the film *Les Canons de Navarone*, adding: 'Don't get it confused with *Les Caleçons de la Baronne* – that's another kind of film.'

Inside the beautiful grotto known as Le Chapeau de Napoléon because the outlines of its entrance evoke the shape of the Man's hat, he wound up his statistical account of the stalactites and stalagmites with this: 'You see that, well furnished, Napoleon's Hat would make a *bon apparte*' ('a fine apartment').

The German lady didn't get the joke.

'Don't worry, lady', said our jovial guide. 'All my patter is for the Parisians.'

Then, turning to me:

'I hope you're not a Parisian, monsieur.'

'No, I'm a Breton.'

'Ah! A Breton and a Corsican, that's the same thing.'

Back on land, I decided to go and have a look at the Graveyard by the Sea.

Like many another in Corsica, it's a city in itself, with ninetomb, twelve-tomb family chambers as big as chapels. On one I read this:

> *Terra tenet corpus*
> *nomen lapis*
> *animam coelum*

'The earth has the body, stone has the name, heaven has the soul.'

It was near nightfall. The red orb of the sun, very low on the horizon, was huge in the grey evening mist.

★

'*On a l'impression ici d'être le cul des Zouaves.*'

This was a girl talking, originally from Paris, but who had been living on Corsica for the past ten years, working here and there in hotels.

The reason she likened the south of Corsica to the arse of a soldier in the Africa Corps was that she felt the whole territory to be a cultural backwater. I suggested that backwaters were better than fairgrounds. She didn't look very convinced.

The Cala Rossa is a quiet residence on the shore down from Porto Vecchio.

I had a room looking down on to a garden full of vigorously green maritime pines. Now and then there'd be a shower of rain, especially in the mornings, and the mountains would appear a uniform soft blue. When the rain stopped and the sun came through, they were a paler blue with outcroppings of greywhite, and through the rain dripping from the pines I'd hear birdsong again. It was in that room I spent most of my time, reading texts in Latin and a book of sixteenth-century cosmography I'd bought at a bookshop called La Marge, in Ajaccio. Despite appearances, there is a kind of logic in this, because, situated away at the extreme west of the known world, Corsica occupied in classical times the same kind of situation as the Isles of America were to occupy about twenty centuries later. Young fellows in Tyre, Carthage, Athens and Rome probably dreamt of Corsica the way young Europeans later were to dream of Martinique, Guadeloupe, Hispaniola. The Baleares were a bit farther west still, but they were the Balistic isles, full of dead-eyed stone-slingers, and it was probably considered advisable to steer clear of them.

So, those late days of October, I spent most of my time in my room. But I also went for walks along the eastern shore. And made a few excursions farther afield.

One day in Porto Vecchio, in a café close to the old tree on the Church Square, I got into talk with a man who had been raised in Algeria. He told me that the three blows Corsica had suffered from most in recent times were: first, the draining of its most enterprising men into the French administration system, as gendarmes, customs officials, superintendents of this or that, on the Continent or in the colonies; second, the 14–18 War, which had left the island full of widows; third, the massive arrival in the early sixties of French repatriates from Algeria, among them ex-Corsicans like himself, who'd come in with more money, bigger land projects, leaving the home Corsicans feeling that they were being pushed aside – it wasn't always true, but that was the *feeling*. He wasn't a big land-owner himself, he said – far from it. He lived in Ajaccio, and he'd opened up a café on the Route des Sanguinaires called The Bloody End. Cute, eh? All in all, he had a pretty good time with a bunch of pals. They gave themselves Amerindian names: the Apache, the Sioux, the Comanche, the Cherokee. He was the Blackfoot, naturally. He was thinking of opening up a new café in Porto Vecchio, or maybe in Bastia, that he'd call the California, maybe the Colorado – that was better, no? You had to try and move with the times, you couldn't just go on singing Corsican shepherd's songs for all eternity...

I also went up into the mountains, on the Zonza road, passing through the dwarf oak country, till I got to the magnificent pine forest of Ospedale. Apart from contemplating the landscapes, I wanted to get hold of a piece of that stone called *diorite orbiculaire* that can be found around Sainte-Lucie-de-Tallano – not a big hunk such as they used to turn into clocks (and maybe, *horribile dictu*, still do), just a handy little piece to accompany the bits of stone from round the world that I have in my house in Brittany. I didn't find any lying around, but at Sainte-Lucie I saw an old house bearing a sign, *Pierre corse – Korschischer Stein*, and was able to acquire a bit there. It's a beautiful grey-greenish stone, with eye-patterns. I then went on to the Col de Bavella (*Bucca di Blavedda*, in Corsican). All along the road, piles of grey and red rock chaos, pine trees with red and grey flaked bark and everywhere the red and orange fruit of the arbutus. At Bavella, the gullies were full of cloud, like smoking cauldrons, the pines all had amazing gestures, and the cry of a crow – *kraa, kraa, kraa* – echoed among the rocks.

At sea-level, I walked round Rondinara, along little banks and cliffs of dried seagrass, the terrain strewn with balls of the same posidonia, and watched, at Pinarello, the head of a great wild-eyed tuna fish lolling at the edge of the tide.

I've been talking about quiet days. But I'd hardly left the Porto Vecchio area when I read in the newspaper that, the afternoon of the day I'd been to Pinarello, the mayor of Zonza had been shot at from a car in the streets of the village and had only narrowly escaped death. *Corse Matin* printed this commentary:

> I'm well aware a lot of people would like to see me out of the way. But I can't believe that my fellow-citizens would go the

length of murder. Local quarrels can't take on such a dimension. Between the destruction of property and human life, there's a margin. If this isn't so, then I'm really out of touch with the contemporary situation. I'm deep in my memories of an older Corsica, a Corsica that had other values. Today the situation is unreal. Nobody knows who is who, who does what. And yet I'm convinced that what most people want is peace and quiet.

But I wouldn't want to end this section on a gunshot note.

Rather with this.

Walking among the red rocks on the shore one day, I saw a shoal of very small green fish, millions of them, totally unaware of 'the Corsican problem', maybe getting ready for some great migration round the globe.

★

I'm sitting on the terrace of a café on Place Paoli in Corte. This is the rocky heart of the country, which is the symbolical reason why, on becoming head of the independent Corsican nation, Pascal Paoli chose it as his capital – the other reason being that in the early days the Genoese still held all the ports.

With its castle on the crag, it feels like a little Edinburgh.

I've been walking through the streets and backstreets. Reading the nationalist graffiti: *Corsica Nostra*; *Testa mora é fiore rossu*; *Sozzi – Gloria a té*; *Corsica Ribedda*; *Sozzi Muzy morti per a Corsica*; *Petru semple vivu*; *La Gjuvellina Paolina – strada diritta e core in fronte*.

Once you're off the main street, you're walking on old cobbley alleys in front of flaking façades and ruined walls overgrown with weeds. One austere, sturdy building with a huge wooden door and barred windows turns out to be the old National Palace: 'From 1755 to 1769, this palace was the seat of the national Corsican parliament and the residence of Pascal Paoli.' That was a brave moment, that of the Corsican nation, which lasted forty years, from the storming of the Genoese governor's residence at Bastia in 1729 up to the annexation of Corsica by France. After that, Corsica got involved in battles that weren't necessarily its own, battles in which Corsicans often found themselves in the front line. Witness the names of squares and streets here in Corte such as 'Place du Poilu', 'Rue du 1er Bataillon de Choc'. The same thing happened to Scots in the imperial British context. Not that the predominant nation always did this deliberately (though it happened), it's just that, psychologically, when you belong to an oppressed and caricatured country, you want to show that you're in some way better than the next man – even if it only means going out of your way to get yourself killed before him.

In a shop, I overheard the tail-end of a conversation about the Corsican problem between a woman customer and a shopkeeper that went like this:

Woman: 'Nothing's done to get us out of the rut. The State sleeps from morning to night. Same on the left as on the right.'

Shopkeeper: 'Oh, it's more complicated than that. The problem isn't there.'

Woman: 'Where is it then?'

Shopkeeper: 'I don't know. Maybe that's the problem.'

Then, without a moment's transition, the shopkeeper turned to me and, in a touristically convivial tone, said: 'Great weather, eh? Sun shining and all. Pure paradise.'

Corsica could be 'paradise' all right, but there is a persistent, nagging *problem*, a historical cancer.

The fact is that to revolt in the name of liberty and fight for independence is one thing, but to know what to do with your liberty and independence once you've got them is another.

For long after their declaration of independence, the Corsicans weren't at all sure what to do. So much so that when a German baron by the name of Theodor von Neuhof turned up on the coast on a British sloop out from Tunis waving a picturesque flag and declaring his willingness to be their king, they were, incredible as it sounds, ready to accept the proposition. When Pascal Paoli came along, he had several ideas in mind and had a firmer grasp of things. But he was still far from sure. Which is why he decided to seek the advice of Jean-Jacques Rousseau.

Rousseau had already expressed interest in Corsica. In his book *The Social Contract*, he had written this: 'If there's still a country in Europe capable of legislation, it's the island of Corsica. The courage and determination with which these brave folk were able to recover and defend their liberty deserve some wise man coming along to teach them how to preserve it.

I have a feeling that one day this little island will astonish Europe.'

In Paoli's search for a political-economic-cultural consultant, Rousseau was, then, an obvious choice.

Contact was established in the Autumn of 1764. On 31 August, a captain of the 'Royal Corsican', a French regiment, Matteo Buttafoco, addressed a letter to Monsieur Jean-Jacques Rousseau, 'citizen and writer of Geneva', who had taken refuge in Môtiers, in the principality of Neuchâtel (then under Prussian jurisdiction, and whose governor, George Keith, 'hereditary marshal of Scotland', a Jacobite exile, was a friend of Rousseau's), where he was composing, among other texts, his *Letters from the Mountain*, a polemical pamphlet in which he was protesting against the damning of his books by the Council of his native city.

'Sir, will you permit a Corsican full of admiration for your work to make an incursion into your retreat?' – so commenced the letter.

Buttafoco had been mandated by Pascal Paoli to get in touch with the Swiss-born nomadic European intellectual and ask for his help on two counts: advice on the drawing up of a constitution, and the writing of a text (a history of the island) that would change the image Corsica held in the eyes of Europe.

Rousseau was attracted by the proposition, saying that the very idea 'raised his soul'.

But... There were going to be quite a few buts.

First of all, Rousseau wasn't going to just write this thing off the top of his head. It would take 'a lot of study and reflexion' and he'd be needing documentation, loads of it. A good map to start with, if possible in colour, giving all the place-names. Then, a detailed description of the island: its natural history, its products, etc. What about the towns and parishes, and the psychology of the people? And what exactly had been done by way of legislation up to now?

Buttafoco started to get material together and sent it to Switzerland, with Rousseau proposing as a preliminary schedule: six months for an outline, a year for a first draft, and a further three years for the final version. Buttafoco and the other Corsicans weren't to forget that Rousseau no longer enjoyed such good health as he once had, and that he was going through yet another 'stormy crisis', being attacked on all sides for his *Letters from the Mountain*.

The best thing, he then went on to say, would be for him to pay a visit to Corsica. But what a troublesome enterprise that would be! All the petty officials in the intervening districts would take pleasure in creating difficulties for the notorious Rousseau, public enemy number 1. Buttafoco tried to persuade him everything would be all right. In the meantime, Rousseau had been getting information from another source about conditions on the island, and was less keen about actually going there. However, things were becoming so hot for him at home (he was going to be hounded out of Môtiers, and later out of yet another refuge, the île de Saint-Pierre) that he began to wonder if he might not be able to go and actually *stay* in Corsica. Could the Corsicans provide him with 'a little house' in which he might spend the rest of his days in peace? Even if he didn't write out the complete constitutional plan, he'd at least try, as a sign of his gratitude, to do the history. But it would be better if he could come with no fixed commitment at all – he'd work better that way. Buttafoco replied that this would be possible, and that it would be enough for the Corsicans simply to have him on the island. But Rousseau should bring his own bedding, linen and kitchen utensils, because there wasn't much of that kind of commodity available in Corsica. At the idea of lugging pots and pans across Europe, Rousseau lost whatever inclination he'd had.

There were further reasons why Rousseau's initial enthusiasm about the drafting of a constitution had cooled. Some he expressed to his correspondent: he was, for example, more and more apprehensive that there would be too great a gulf between the ideas of the Corsicans and his own, which would mean a spate of disputes and quarrels, and he'd had a bellyful of those in his life. Then, he was less and less sure about the political context: he saw more and more signs that France was just biding its time to come in for the kill and make a takeover bid for this strategically situated island – in which case his labour would all be for nothing. Other reasons again Jean-Jacques didn't express in his correspondence, nor even in his theoretical texts, only in his autobiography, the *Confessions*. He says there that, fundamentally, whatever his interest in social theory, his nature tended to 'meditation in solitude' and that with this project he was going to be condemned to an 'active life' and be dragged back into public affairs that would both irritate and bore him. Add to that a little note (dated 'Paris 1758') appended to his study of the writings of the Abbé de Saint-Pierre. He says there that when you look at the nations of Europe, seeing that some are too big to be decently governed, while others are too small to be independent, when you consider all the accumulated prejudice in them, 'you have to be as simple-minded as the Abbé de Saint-Pierre to propose the slightest change in any government at all'. Even the Abbé de Saint-Pierre, incorrigible idealist as he was, looked on most human beings as children, and considered that if children are necessary for the continuation of the species and the population of states (he regularly fathered a bairn on his housekeeper), they were, in themselves, mostly not very interesting. To come back to Rousseau, if he was still ready to write social theory, he realized he got more real pleasure from his books on botany.

In fact, with regard to actual contact with Corsica, it was a young Scotsman, from Auchinleck, in Ayrshire, who was to take over from Rousseau. James Boswell was a much more superficial character than the Genevan, had nothing like the dimensions of the erratic Swiss, but he had sympathetic qualities and was not without talent. He also had a real sense of interesting personality and unusual, singular intelligence. Which is why he went to see Rousseau at Môtiers in December 1764, finally proposing to be Rousseau's 'ambassador' to Corsica. Rousseau, who, with his keen little eyes that could twinkle with humour, saw through him right away, said 'maybe you would rather be *King* of Corsica' (later on, at the time of the Anglo-Corsican kingdom, Boswell actually did put himself forward as the best possible choice for the post of Viceroy), but agreed to give him a letter of recommendation.

Boswell arrived in Corsica, at the port of Centuri, on Capo Corso, on 12 October 1765. Based at the mansion of Colonna d'Istria at Sollacaro, he went round the country, studied its history, had conversations with Pascal Paoli, and finally completed his first book, at Auchinleck, in 1768: *An Account of Corsica, the Journal of a Tour to that Island and Memories of Pascal Paoli.*

From that moment on, he was 'Corsica Boswell' – in much the same way as, some years later, T. E. Lawrence was to become 'Lawrence of Arabia'. Already on the island, Boswell was dressing up as a Corsican bandit, sporting two pistols Pascal Paoli had given him and, on his return to Britain, he turned up at a Shakespeare festival in Stratford-upon-Avon dolled up like some kind of Corsican Rob Roy. But it wasn't *all* superficial. He tried to persuade William Pitt to give the Corsicans a hand. He got dispatches printed in the *London Chronicle*, supposedly from 'Italian correspondents', but in fact all written by himself. He edited a collection of essays by various hands, *In Favour of the Brave Corsicans*, after launching a fund in Scotland that brought in £700. He sent cannon and cash to the island revolutionaries. What's obvious to a Scottish reader of his book is that a lot of this is transposition. Boswell was writing only twenty years after the Jacobite rebellion of 1745 and he had this on his mind. The Scottish reference runs right through the *Account*. It's there in the very epigraph, which is a phrase from what constitutes maybe the first recorded declaration of independence in Europe, the 1328 Declaration of Arbroath: *Non enim propter gloriam, divitias aut honores pugnamus, sed propter libertatem solummodo* (We fight not for glory, wealth or honour, only for freedom). Boswell says if you evoke the spirit of freedom, you think of Switzerland, Holland, Scotland – and Corsica. Later he speaks of mountains – those of Scotland, those of Corsica – as bastions of independence (to get at the Corsicans in their mountain fastnesses, the Genoese employed Swiss mercenaries, as the French did Pyreneans from the Béarn). He quotes this comment on the Romans by the Scottish chief Calgacus, as reported by Tacitus in the *Agricola*: *Ubi solitudinem faciunt, pacem appellant* (they create a wasteland and call it peace). He even draws a physical parallel between Corsicans and Scots, saying that they tend to be smallish in stature, but robust and vigorous – while admitting that there are exceptions on both sides. That said, Boswell was resigned to being a Britisher and was later to travel happily to other islands in the company of that most abominably English of Englishmen the earth has ever borne, Dr Samuel Johnson.

To come back to Rousseau, the 'philosopher of paradox', as Boswell calls him, although he'd given up the idea of any effective collaboration with Corsica, he still worked on and off at the project, noting an idea, developing a thought. For years, as he wandered over Europe, from Berlin to Edinburgh, he carried in his luggage, along with the manuscript of the *Confessions,* a folder tied with string marked *Affaires de Corse.*

Behind Rousseau's political thinking was society as he'd seen it among the mountain people (the *montagnons*) of the Jura. It was this he proposed as a model, with local adaptations, to the Corsicans. The adaptations took into account, for example, the size of Corsica – too big for a direct democracy, suitable rather for a mixed, that is, representative democracy. As to the economy, it would be agrarian or, as Rousseau says, 'rustic' – the same idea Jefferson had later for America: the only ultimate guarantee of independence. On that basis, despite 'the Genoese and the journalists', Corsica might flourish internally and at the same time exist in the world at large. With his own ten-page constitutional outline in front of him, Paoli might have agreed to these general principles. It was when the two of them got down to particular legislation that there would, without a doubt, have been significant divergences. To take only one example, for Rousseau, any man forty years old and still unmarried should be deprived of his civil rights (*'Excluds du droit de Cité'*). That would have excluded Pascal Paoli himself. When Boswell told him he should get married, to ensure an heir, Paoli replied that he didn't care to, he wanted to devote all his time to his work and, as to a family, what guarantee could he have that his children would think and act intelligently?

We can imagine Rousseau, settled on the island, and he and Paoli arguing the toss in Corte, with Jean-Jacques finally declaring: 'Ach, Pascal, to hell with it all, I'm away for a walk in the woods.'

★

Big bright moon and, in my head, a sense of the torrential river-system of Corsica:

the Aliso
the Bevinco
the Golo

the Ostriconi
the Fium Alto
the Alesani
the Bravone
the Tavignano
the Fiumorbo
the Travo
the Solenzara
the Stabiacco
the Ortolo
the Rizzanese
the Taravo
the Prunelli
the Gravone
the Liamone
the Sagone
the Porto
the Fango
the Ficarella...

Leaving Corte, I moved up the valley of the Restonica. I'd been told in Corte I'd find an inn up there. I did. What characterized this delectable enough albergo was that every room had a family name emblazoned on its door: Biancheri, Olmiccia, Ujlaki, Siatka, Fraceschetti... Poets of the island? Heroes of the Corsican revolution? No, football-players. It seems the owner of the hotel, an ex ball-champ himself, had found this way of giving his establishment distinction while perpetuating a noble tradition.

Not that the place wasn't patriotic. It was. In the dining-room, there was a bust of *Pascal Paoli – U Babbu di a Patria.*

After dinner, I went up to my room, and stayed out for a while on the little balcony, listening to the torrent rushing below.

At breakfast next morning, the waiter told me that *broccio* cake was better at this time of the year because the cheese-milk was fresh, the rest of the year they were made with powder. I had been warned.

The narrow valley of the Restonica was still in shadow, but an early light bathed the highest peaks, turning them into lumps of craggy gold. All around, great hulking pines and, scattered among them, little yellow chestnut-trees and fiery red beeches. The ferns were browngilt, and the last bees were buzzing busily in the grass. Up at the top of the glen was a grey boulder chaos and, scattered within it, several cabins. A notice informed the passer-by that here began the grazing grounds of the Commune de Corte, and supplied a list that might have been a line (or two) in a pastoral epic poem: *Bergeries d'Alzo, de Colleta, de Timozzo, de Rivisecco, de Spiscie, de Grotelle, de Cappellaccia, de Pozzi.*

I didn't see any shepherds or flocks – maybe they'd already all gone down into the plains for the Winter – only the blue van of the gendarmerie: *Secours en Montagne* (some tourists had got lost).

The shepherd's cabins looked very neat and trim and prosperous. Maybe the people living in them – from one or two, blue smoke was curling – weren't real shepherds at all, only weekend shepherds. Anyway, I didn't hear any *chiama e respondi* or any polyphonic *paghiella*, only, from the window of one of them, a little ditty whose refrain went like this: 'I do my cryin' in the rain'.

I raised my eyes to the hills, the great rugged mass of them. Then, back down in the woods, spent a long moment with a little mauve cyclamen.

★

The Greeks called the island Callista, 'the beautiful one', which, given all the lovely islands they had around them in the Aegean, was quite a compliment. They also named it Kyrna, which I take to mean 'the mountainous one'. Corsica is in fact the most mountainous of the islands in the Mediterranean. As to the name Corsica, where it comes from no one knows. There's a story that a squint-eyed woman named Corsa espied the island one day from the top of the leaning tower of Pisa, but you don't have to believe it.

Apart from old sourpuss Strabo, the meanest geographer in the books, who says Corsica is a rough country, hard to penetrate, inhabited by a people more brutish than animals (besides, they make bad slaves, preferring to commit suicide), the Greeks had all kinds of fine things to say about Corsica. Theophrastes in his *History of Plants* says it has marvellously tall trees. Diodorus of Sicily has this:

> The isle of Corsica is mountainous, full of fine forest, and is watered by great rivers. Its inhabitants live on milk, honey and meat, which the country liberally provides. They observe the rules of justice and humanity more scrupulously than other barbarians. Any one who finds honey in the mountains, in the hollows of trees, can be assured that no other islander will dispute his right to it. Flocks, once marked, can be left to graze with no one to watch over them. The same spirit of equity prevails among them in all aspects of their life.

If the Greeks found Corsica beautiful, it's because they had a sense of live chaos and open cosmos. The Romans, on the other hand (with the great exception of Lucretius), tended to be more citified and civilized, with a utilitarian or at most bucolic sense of nature. Juvenal talks about the good sea-food to be found there.

The Romans had two towns on Corsica – Mariana, founded by Marius, and Aleria, founded by Sylla: colonial outposts, strategic harbours for the Western Mediterranean fleet.

I'd come along the coast road, lined with ruddy vineyards and green olive groves, past marshy pools (*Il Stagno di Diana*), past also the 'penitentiary farm' of Casabianda. And there I was, standing on the main square of Aleria, looking at a ripped advertisement for a festival of Traditional Polyphonic Song. The Pizzeria Maracana was closed for the season, its grounds littered with red Autumn leaves. A café, offering an *assiette corse*, was open, but I didn't feel like going in. A wrecked and rusty Mitsubishi lay abandoned in a yard. The sun beat down. Total desolation.

I went up to the ruins of what was the old Roman town-centre: the forum, the Capitol, the baths, the shops... I knew, walking up the path, that, right under my feet, there were probably figures made of Phoenician glass, with big black eyes and shiny blue beards, fragments of red and black pottery from Greece, maybe a dully-gleaming Etruscan coin or two. But I couldn't get rid of that terrible, sun-beaten feeling of desolation.

It was to this place that the Roman writer, Seneca (Lucius Annaeus Seneca), born in Cordoba in 4 BC, was banished (*relegatio in insulam* was the legal term) in AD 41.

Seneca's father was a rhetorician, but for his son he had political ambitions, which is why he sent him up to Rome as soon as feasible. There, Seneca the younger got interested in philosophy, especially Stoic philosophy, but he toed the administrative line, becoming *quaestor*, then *senator*, making brilliant speeches, writing highly acclaimed texts, arousing thereby a lot of jealousy.

It was under Claudius, on a charge probably trumped up by Messalina, that he was exiled – to Corsica, where he was to remain eight years, eight long years.

Seneca wasn't one of those young men dreaming of adventure on an exotic shore that I evoked earlier. He had work in progress at the Centre of the World, and there he was in a no-place on the road to nowhere, surrounded by pukka sahib colonials and pompous military morons. He was, to say the least, a little downhearted.

He looked at the blue of the Tyrrhenian Sea and he did not find it beautiful. He looked at the mountains of Corsica and he found them unbearably ugly:

> *Barbara praeruptis inclusa est Corsica saxis*
> *Horrida desertis undique vasta locis*

He looked into his heart and saw... total desolation.

But the School of the Stoa says: stick it out, so he stuck it out and made the best of it.

He must have had a neat little villa there, and a shelf of books, maybe even a few jars of good Italian wine. Enough to make the situation at least bearable.

In the beginning, he tried to get the exile cancelled, or at least reduced in length. He even swallowed his pride and wrote a text that was more of a pathetic entreaty than a plea. All to no effect.

Well, damn them!

And, little by little, he was able to look up from his own life.

To begin with, bucking up his courage, he wrote poems imbued with a Stoic ethic, saying, for example, that 'the superior man' isn't characterized by wealth or display, but by his ability to put down fear and still the anxiety in his breast. He is not lured on by vain ambition, nor is he swayed by the fickle opinions of the vulgar crowd, but sees all this as beneath him.

He knows the joys of 'sweet quietness' and how to make deep use of all the time at his disposal:

> *Regem non faciunt opes,*
> *non vestis Tyriae color*
> ...

If in this frame of mind, Seneca can come at times to annihilate the world entirely (*hic aloquo mundus tempore nullus erit*) at others he takes a cool, quiet look at it and finds beauty – at night, for example, looking over the sea and up at the stars, and in the early dawn:

> *Iam rara micant sidera prono*
> *languida mundo. Nox victa vagos*
> *contrahit ignes luce renata...*

He begins then to ask himself questions concerning the relationship of man to the cosmos, and it's the *Naturales Quaestiones*, in which, among other matters, he talks about earthquakes, fishes and constellations.

And, from there on Corsica, his thought, moving along the coast of Andalusian Spain, and out into the Atlantic, becomes visionary, cosmographical. He evokes a 'great secret hidden in the ocean' that humanity will *one day* discover and says that centuries will come when the ocean will break all chains and confinements, when the great earth will lie open and new worlds will be found, for no Thule is ever the ultimate Thule:

> *venient annis saecula seris*
> *quibus Oceanus vincula rerum*
> *laxet et ingens pateat tellus*
> *Tethysque novos detegat orbes*
> *nec sit terris ultima Thule*

Lucius Annaeus Seneca was no doubt reconciled to the prospect that he would be buried in a brick tomb covered with tiles and with a coin on his lips to pay for his passage across Lethe in Charon's boat (that's how they did things in Aleria), when, in AD 49, he was called back to Rome to be the tutor of Nero.

That was probably the most abysmal period in Roman history, with Nero, that punky pop-star with power, getting madder and more murderous with every passing month. It might have been worse still but for Seneca, who, as a Stoic, still felt he had to do his social bit, even among the most unpromising circumstances. He stuck it out thirteen years. Then in AD 62, at the age of sixty-six, he requested permission to withdraw, offering to restore to the Emperor all the wealth he had amassed, an offer which Nero, eager to build a palace worthy of himself after the conflagration of Rome, ignominiously accepted.

The philosopher thereafter enjoyed a short period of leisure, study and meditation, till, in AD 65, he was accused of taking part in a conspiracy against the State and ordered to kill himself.

It is not at all impossible that, in Nero's rotten Rome, Seneca thought more than once, with regret and nostalgia, of his years of quiet exile at Aleria. If he had stayed there, who knows, he might have written a magnificent book on islands, *De insularum natura* or something like that, or a more meditative version of the kind of oceanic poem Avienus did four centuries later, with the *Ora maritima*.

Who knows...

★

'*Le Jour des Morts, il y a toujours tempête*' ('On the Day of the Dead, there's always a storm blowing').

I was seated at the glass front of a restaurant in the old quarter, the *terra vecchja*, of Bastia, and this was the proprietor talking. Rain was battering at the windows, thunder was crackling, lightning flashing. The twin towers of the church of St John the Baptist had blurred, also the red and green pillars at the entrance to the harbour. I had a plate of excellent fish and a bottle of palatable white wine from the Cape on the table before me.

I'd got into town that morning. I'd stood on the main square under the palm trees looking at the statue of Napoleon and the other monument *Aux deuils, aux triomphes, aux espoirs de la patrie* ('To the mournings, triumphs and hopes of our land'). I'd seen along the streets the high, seven-storied, Italian-type buildings with the decrepit fronts and washing hanging from many a window. I'd passed by the Quincaillerie Valéry (a hardware store), and the Agence Maritime Colonna d'Istria, as well as the Mobylines company: Bastia–Genoa–Leghorn. I'd read the Résistance Corse (1944) plaque to Jean Nicoli: *Condamné à être fusillé dans le dos, décapité* ('shot in the back and beheaded'). I'd made out on a wall the old advert of the Maison Alessandrini: *Pâté de merles – fabrication corse – aux parfums du maquis* ('blackbird paté – made on the island – all the fragrance of the backcountry'). In the harbour, I'd seen the *Kalliste* and the *Odyssée* and the *Cipango* swinging at anchor. I'd noted the by now familiar graffiti: *Corsica Nazione – Autonumia*. I'd drunk coffee in bars named Le Pied Marin or Ciao Bella. I'd climbed up among the palm trees and the laurels of the Jardin Romieu to the Citadel, where it was written in stone that such and such a governor had purged this island 'rife with criminality' – *insula rapinis et latrocinis plena*.

It was just after I'd come out of the Citadel that the storm started. The sky took on a deep violet blue, and a wind sprang up from nowhere, howling, raising dust and leaves in great suffocating clouds. There was the noise of shutters clattering and of café terrace chairs and tables being hurriedly stacked away. The sea had white horses by the thousand. Noon tolled from the Citadel bell.

It was then I had made for the restaurant.

As I lingered over the wine, I read a musty, yellowed number of the *Bulletin of the Historical Society of Corsica* I'd picked up in an old curiosity shop in the backstreets of Bastia. There it was, lying beside a phonograph with Italian records, a school map of the New World and a packet of Marseilles Tarot cards. What had attracted me as I flipped through its pages was an article on a literary society that had existed in Bastia in the nineteenth century, the Accademia dei Vagabondi. The Academy was so called apparently because its members had all travelled abroad, mostly to Italy, where they'd studied at Pisa, Genoa, Padua or Bologna. The literature quoted didn't interest me that much, but there may well have been other work this particular article hadn't thought fit to consider. Anyway, it was the name itself, Accademia dei Vagabondi, that intrigued me, and gave me space for thought.

An hour later, the storm was abating, pigeons were flying again around the towers of St John the Baptist, gulls were moving out to sea again.

I went back out into town.

The harbour was bathed in a blue and golden light. On clear days you can see from Bastia the political island of Elba and the romantic island of Monte Cristo. But that evening on the horizon there was only a dark, smouldering blueness.

★

On the morning of 3 November, I left Bastia with the intention of moving round Corsica's northern cape, the Capo Corso.

The sea was bright blue, the horizon rosy pink. All along the coast road, villas with gardens full of luscious high-colour bougainvilleas, lantana, hibiscus and the flickering pale grey-green-silver of olive leaves.

Pietranera, Erbalunga.

At Erbalunga, the old mansions of wine-merchants and the ruins of a Genoese tower.

But it was mainly a village called U Campu I had in mind.

U Campu lies three kilometres west of Santa-Severa on the road to Luri.

Why was I so keen to get to U Campu? Well, this is where Dominique Cervoni was born – the Corsican seaman Joseph Conrad liked so much and esteemed so highly, whom he had first met in 1876 when Cervoni was second mate on the *Saint-Antoine* out from Marseilles and who was to be the basis of some of Conrad's characters, such as Jean Peyrol in *The Rover*, Tom Lingard in *The Rescue*, Attilio in *Suspense*, and Nostromo in the novel of that name.

When I finally got to U Campu, a little village wrapped in silence and the smell of wood-smoke, it was to see that there was nothing remarkable about the Cervoni house itself. But it bore this plaque to the seaman's memory:

> Dans cette maison est né
> le 28 août 1834
> Dominique André Cervoni
> navigateur et grand aventurier
> il y mourut le 27 juillet 1890

For Conrad, Cervoni was 'one of us'. By that, he didn't simply mean one who belongs to the general fraternity of the sea, but one who seems somehow a stranger (an *isolato*) amid his fellow-men and who may transcend their codes, even those he most respects, in the name of something else, accepting as judge of his secret ways and acts only the empty sky and the implacable ocean.

Having saluted Cervoni, I moved on.

In Macinaggio, at the shipchandler's, there was talk about pensions, in particular Catégorie 3. One man had it, and thought his friend should be entitled to it. 'Yes', replied the other, 'but I'm in the fishing-trade, we don't work all year round.'

Vineyards: Nicrosi, Goielli.

On the tip of the Cape, at Barcaggio, a little harbour and in it two or three barques registered in Bastia. Just offshore, a small green rock island with a dazzling white lighthouse.

More yellow-red cliffs and headlands.

Commune de Centuri.

Green schist roofs. The tinkling of goat bells. The roar of the sea.

More vineyards: Marfisi, Patrimonio.

And then the Gulf of San Fiurenza.

Sitting in a café on the waterfront at St-Florent, I watched the sun go down over the Désert des Agriates, and the sky turning rose to violet.

It was there I got into conversation with Joseph Bastianelli, or rather that I listened to his dromomaniacal monologue.

Joseph started off by telling me that he was just back from six weeks in Paris, where he'd been looking for a job. He'd spent all his savings up there. But no luck. So he'd come back to St-Florent:

'I was born on the 19th of July. There may be no connection. But I heard somebody in Russia committed suicide on July 19th. I was born in Marseilles and I'm completely off my head. At Marseilles they would always be telling me: anything's possible, you just have to pay the price of horror. I was always ready to pay the price, in cash – but not the price of horror. Paris is my capital, France is my country. We fought for that. We were in all the wars. I'm not for autonomy. It's a principality I'd like. In Paris, I spent eighteen hours a day making pizzas. They crushed the grey matter of my brain. My mind isn't totalitarian, but I can see everything, especially when I close my eyes. I see things the government folk see three years later. I suffered a defeat, it's my Waterloo. I lost on sentimental grounds. I fell into the gulf, even the fish don't want me. I have no qualifications. The history teacher told me about the Soissons vase. He said they broke it. I wanted more details. How many pieces? He threw me out of the class. That's why I never completed my education. Anyway, nobody bothers about education any more. Sport's the thing now. I write a fine hand. At least when I'm inspired. It lasts two or three minutes, then it all breaks up and me with it. Some leave with a hundred wrongs and arrive with a hundred rights. I left with a hundred rights, and I arrive with a hundred wrongs. I shot a well-balanced arrow, but I didn't hit the mark...'

He kept silent for a while, then added:

'I've talked enough. *Bonne route*, friend.'

I could no longer see Joseph's face, his voice (another of those 'inner voices' of Corsica) was coming out of the darkness.

'*Bonne route* to you too, friend', I said.

★

It was more and more definitely Autumn.

I was sitting at the terrace of a café on the Place Paoli at Isola Rossa. There was a great rustling at the tops of the plane-trees and the palms, and hordes of dry leaves were blowing across the ground.

'*Le temps, il change – ça fraîchit*' ('the weather's changing'), said a man at the next table.

I'd just crossed the Désert des Agriates, which isn't a 'desert' in the modern sense of the word, but in the old sense: a savage expanse, a wilderness. It's a wilderness thick with crimson-fruited arbutus and darkgreen cactus, scattered with hummocky rock, a wild wind blowing across it, empty blue sky above it, and the *whee-oo-whee* of hawks, the shriek of jays, the cawing of grey-black crows. Here and there, in a little clearing, a clutch of bee-hives. Now and then, a little herd of goats. A battered old building, maybe a forlorn attempt to create a wayside restaurant: L'Oasis. An abandoned rusty old van: *Déménagements Corse-Continent*. A pair of goat horns affixed to a tree, painted red.

Images such as these were going through my mind as I sat drinking a coffee at Isola Rossa, before making for Calvi.

There had been the dark centre, the windswept emptiness

of the Cape, the wilderness area of the Agriates, now Corsica was a garden – a garden between sea and mountain: la Balagne. I passed through villages – the houses pale rose, washed ochre, mustard yellow: Belgodere, Occhiatana, Speloncato, Muro, Avapessa, Cateri, Sant'Antonino.

In the church of Sant' Antonino, I saw a skeleton with wings, something I'd never seen before, not in any church from Dublin to Byzantium. In a lane, I made the acquaintance of a little donkey, brown and grey, with sturdy legs, carrying two shining milk-cans, who looked at me with rheumy eyes full of the measureless pity of time. On the square, it was a little human scene: a butcher's van stopped for business, the butcher, a young man, slicing meat, an old woman, chaffing with him, saying: *'S'il y avait une belle fille à ma place, vous vous couperiez le doigt'* ('If there was a young girl standing here instead of me, you'd cut your finger).'

When I got into Calvi that afternoon, the place was packed with Foreign Legion men wearing white képis, wandering around aimlessly in groups, talking to one another in half-a-dozen languages and rummaging in the Maison de la Presse for Sex and Sport magazines.

I decided I'd try to get a better idea of the town in the morning and went to look for a hotel. What I found was a Roman villa – or at least the nearest thing to a Roman villa Corsica had seen since ancient Aleria. As evening came down and the mountains took on a magenta tinge, I stood at my window looking down at the classical garden and over at the sea and the massive citadel. Later, cold blue moonlight flooded the scene.

When I woke, the sun was shedding white light over the mountains. *Very* white light. It took me a moment to realize it was because snow had fallen. In the immediate surroundings, it was still Autumn, with a drift of blue smoke over the hills, and the twittering of small birds in the garden. But up there, on the Monte Cinto, on the Monte Grosso, on the Monte Longu, on the Punta Radiche, it was already the silent gleam of Winter.

Around ten, I went down to the harbour, took a seat at a café terrace under the citadel, and admired the spectacle: all the sea-panorama over to Punta Spano, and close to hand the palms that line the waterfront, and the cacti and Barbary figs clustered at the base of the citadel rock. The *Colombo* sight-seer (Calvi prides itself as being 'the city of Christopher Columbus' – many members of his crew had Corsican names such as Brando) had ceased its activities for the season. An old man was mending a blue net.

The sea was rough, and in colour a deep violet.

That morning, Calvi felt less like a stage-set for some film that would start in a barracks and end up at the crazy sun-pulsing centre of the Sahara, and more like a runway for a supersonic flight of the mind to the American side of the Atlantic.

I ate a plateful of *beignets de murène* there on the waterfront at mid-day, then got out on my way.

I took my time, on a road that at times followed inland valleys, at others opened out again on to a seacoast rimmed with red-ochre rock.

When I got to Porto, with its cluster of rosy-coloured houses, it was like a deserted village, a ghost town. Le Romantique was closed, L'Hôtel Moderne was closed, Le Robinson was closed. Everywhere was the sign: 'End of season'. I liked that atmosphere (end of a century, end of history?), even if it meant that it was difficult to find a place to stay. Anyway, I didn't try too hard. I had my mind set on the village of Piana farther still down the coast. There I found a congenial room.

In the early morning, I climbed up the rock behind my lodgings, and looked out over the colours and shapes of all that superb volcano-plutonic complex I had before my eyes. How many contradictory forces have come together to create such an extraordinary mass of matter! It was as if floods of energy from the sun had taken on expressive shape.

That moment on the rock was my ultimate Corsican meditation.

As I took my breakfast on the terrace of my room, I noticed a swallow's nest up in a corner of the roof.

The swallows had gone.

The Big Andalusian Trip

The old Málaga Palacio is situated at the heart of the city, just in front of the cathedral, at the corner of Molina Lario street and the Cortina del Muelle. The room I occupy, on the eleventh floor, has two windows, one looking out over the harbour, the other up to the ruins of the Moorish fortress and the Castillo Gibralfaro. It's Autumn, almost the end of October, but the sun is still strong, so strong that, in order to keep some kind of coolness in the room, I've closed the curtains. Those curtains are satiny green, so that it's in an emerald kind of atmosphere that I'm beginning this account of my transcendental travels in Andalusia.

★

I got into Malaga a week ago.

For the first few days, I just wandered about the town, getting the general feel of it. I climbed up the cactus-lined path of fire leading to the Alcazaba which, before it was a Moorish fortress, was maybe a Roman *castrum* and, before that, a Phoenician observation point. From up there, you get a panoramic view of the city: the tenements of the Malagueta that look down into the Plaza de Toros, the harbour with its twin towers of Goliath Cement, and away over to the River Guadalmedina.

I sat at the terrace of the café El Jardin, just behind the Cathedral – all velvet and rosy inside, with stucco portraits of local poets on the walls, and, outside, a little garden of palm trees and mandarine trees, with a fountain playing. It was in there I heard a voluble Andalusian explaining to an earnest American: 'There is Andalusia, and there is the rest of Spain – peasants. In Andalusia, you must also make distinctions. Eastern Andalusia is all graceful, gentle, erotic ("your teeth are like grains of rice in milk"). In western Andalusia all is knives, blood and bulls.' I frequented too another similar establishment, La Buena Sombra, decorated with the drawings of José Parejo who, as a memorial plaque indicates, 'ennobled with his lively caricatures the little art-world, the *mundillo del arte*, of Malaga.' Then, in the Calle Moreno Monroy, there was El Chinitas, a more rustic place, with banquet-halls on the second and third floors containing each one a huge round or square table. The bottom floor was decorated with hams hanging from the ceiling and, on the walls, lurid redblackyellow bullfight posters. In El Chinitas, Federico García Lorca situated a bullfight ballad (*Dijo Paquiro a su hermano...*), the first stanza of which, Englished, would go something like this:

> *Said Paquiro to his brother*
> *Of us two I'm the stronger*
> *Right, said the brother, we'll try*
> *I say at six that bull will die...*

I've been told it's apocryphal, and was probably written in El Chinitas, after a couple of bottles of ruby-red rioja, by somebody fed up with all the Lorca-lyrical ballad business. Anyway, there it is, translated by myself on the spot after a solitary bottle of dark Bull's Blood.

The Arabs called Malaga an 'earthly paradise'. It's hard to subscribe to that today. When I first settled into my room, what I was most aware of was noise. There were palm trees interspersed with pines down there on the Paseo del Parque, but the din of traffic, especially innumerable buzz-bikes, and the strident whines of police-cars and ambulances, made it seem like a machine-mad jungle rather than anything remotely resembling a paradise. The same goes for the rest of the city. I met a Madrileño who'd been living for three years in Malaga and felt exhausted every time he came out of a café or a restaurant, because of the sheer din: 'Everybody talks, nobody listens.'

That said, there are flowers and fruit-trees everywhere: jasmin, oranges, lemons... So that even across the dust and noise you do get an occasional whiff or glimpse of a heavenly garden. The light too is golden, golden and warm.

It was when walking one afternoon in the area between the Customs House and the Facultad de Filosofia y Letras that I met Salomon. There he was, in stone, looking on I thought somewhat sadly as two Malaga workmen played football (*futbol*) with a lemon.

As an intellectually minded Jew born in Malaga (*ha-malaquí*, 'the man from Malaga', was how he liked to style himself), raised in eleventh-century Andalusia, Salomon Ibn Gabirol was a Hebrew poet and an Arab philosopher, knowing by heart the Old Testament and carrying in his head the body of Greek philosophy (Plato, Aristotle, Plotinus) as translated by the Arabs.

In Andalusia at that time they were deeply aware of all that was going on in the whole Mediterranean world – as the saying went, if a crow squawked in Iraq, they heard it. Life would have been pleasant, extremely so, for Salomon, in his 'earthly paradise', if he hadn't suffered from a horrible disease that brought out boils full of pus and blood on his skin and killed him off (he saw it coming) at an early age. But since from his teens he'd devoted himself entirely to poetry and philosophy, he was able to surmount his misfortune and accomplish a great deal of marvellous work. His principal book, *The Source of Life*, written in Arabic, gathered together all the floating philosophical elements in the Arabo-Andalusian world. In Arabic too he wrote *The Correction of Character*, a treatise on ethics based on the theory of the four humours derived from Aristotle and propagated by a Jew of North Africa, Isaac Israeli. Then there was *A Catch of Pearls*, consisting of aphorisms and fragments of verse. And lastly, written this time in Hebrew, *The Royal Wreath*, a book of poetic cosmology. His poetry was basically biblical-synagogal, but he incorporated into it also Arab elements: the ancient poetry of the desert, as well as the more easygoing pleasant verse of Baghdad. In one of his poems, he has this: 'I have written of Autumn with the colour of its rains.' It was all this made me think Salomon would be an ideal travel-companion for a while in Andalusia.

'Salomon', I said to him one evening beside his statue, 'how would you like to come with me on a little trip around the country?'

'I would love it immensely', he said, jumping down from his pedestal, 'I've been getting ankylosed up here.'

Once down on the street, he added: 'Call me Schlomo.'

★

A golden shower of rain was falling over Malaga as, on the morning of 18 October, we left, Schlomo and I, for Cordoba.

We were in a little dark blue Opel Corsa and were moving out along the Arroyo Los Angeles when we heard a burst of Arab music coming from behind closed shutters:

'*Shir ha shirim hasher...*', murmured Schlomo.

'What's that?' I said.

'Just a song I know.'

We were by now on route N331 – it was announcing Cordoba via Antequera. 'Schlomo', I said, 'how does it feel to be a Jewish peripatetic neo-platonist?'

'Superb', he said, laughing. Then, after a pause:

'What does it feel like to be an encyclopedic mahayana Scotist?'

'Great', I said.

I had the feeling that this was going to be indeed a great trip, a real ecstasy journey, an ecstasy journey through the *ciudades* and across the *sierras*, going on in several dimensions at once, the way I like it.

It was hill country first of all, rolling hill country, and the hills came in all colours, desert colours: palegreen, peppery, mustardy. When the lower earth showed through, it was red, and there were outcroppings of papery, wasp-nest rock. Here and there, olive trees, pines, cacti. Back of the hills, great grey craggy masses. Dotted over the landscape, gleaming white *haciendas*, *fincas*, *cortijos* – big farms, little farms: clean-lined, cubic.

When we arrived in Cordoba, wind was blowing the dust about and giving a lazy sway to the palm trees. 'Schlomo', I said, 'I know you were born in Malaga, but your father was from Cordoba, is that not so?' 'That is precisely so', he answered. 'In Arabic, I was called Abou-Ayyoub Soleiman, son of Ya'hya ibn-Djebiroul al-Kortobi. I am glad to be in Cordoba again, the city of my ancestors.'

We made straight for the Jewish quarter, the Judería, had a bite to eat at Pepe's tavern there, then went out to make closer acquaintance with the town.

We'd hardly been walking a couple of minutes in its blazing white labyrinth when we came up against the Old Synagogue, and in we went. That might have been a good, meditative moment, but it wasn't, because the place was packed with a tourist group from Israel and their guide was booming information at them as if he owned the place, God's right-hand man.

Schlomo watched, mesmerised and bemused, as one obstinate-looking tourist stepped over a rope that protected its niche and began methodically picking red wax from a seven-pronged candlestick and stuffing it into a bag, while his wife pleaded with him all the time to come the hell out of there. I looked at Schlomo, he looked at me with downturned lips, hunching his shoulders, raising open palms, and we went out again into the common street.

It was then we came across the statues of Maïmonides, whom Schlomo called Moshe ben Maïmoun, and of Averroës, who for him was Aboul-Walid Mo'hamed ibn-A'hmed ibn-Roschd. Schlomo was delighted and wanted to introduce them to me in detail. He could hardly believe that as a Hyperborean Caledonian from beyond the frontiers of philosophy I should know much about them at all. I had to tell him that, although I had never actually come across Maïmonides and Averroës during my local years of formation, I had made close acquaintance with followers of their tradition here and there later on. In the Ardèche, when I lived in that area, there was Joseph ibn-Kaspi of Largentière, who wrote a summary of Aristotle's *Organon* as well as a commentary on Maïmonides' *Guide for the Lost*. And in the Pyrenees, there had been Abraham ibn-Bibago of Huesca, who wrote a commentary on Aristotle.

But Schlomo did undoubtedly know more about it all than I did, so I was glad to listen to him.

'Ah, the School of Cordoba', he said, 'the formidable School of Cordoba!' That was when the Jews, intellectually emancipated from the religious authority of the Babylonian Academy of Sora, were picking up on Greek philosophy, mainly Aristotle, brought in by the Arabs. They gathered in texts by the handful, translating them into Hebrew. That was what Maïmonides did, doing a reading of the Bible and trying to get some kind of order into the confused mass of Talmudic texts. It was the rabbis too who saved Averroës. When the orthodox Muslims accused him of heresy, the Cordoban Jews studied and translated his work. Averroës worked not only at the Koran, but at the philosophy of Aristotle, and at all kinds of sciences, and he also practised poetry. It was said, went on Schlomo, that Maïmonides used up ten thousand sheets of paper, writing treatise after treatise, pushing Aristotle maybe even farther than Aristotle wanted to go. Aristotle had written a book about the soul, but it didn't satisfy Averroës, who wrote a beautiful little text: 'A treatise on the hylic intellect and the possibility of conjunction', that was Schlomo's favourite. The hylic intellect, that's ours, and the 'conjunction' was the possibility of getting that personal intellect in contact with the Universal Intellect. There was a phrase in that book that delighted Schlomo: 'Me you can't see, but look at the mountain.' Oh, the Christians were always talking about *passion* – passion for this, passion for that – but what counted was *conjunction* and *ecstasy*. That's what he himself had worked at: first matter and form; then, the creative world, the faculty of abstractive, poetic power; finally the primal substance... 'Me you can't see, but look at the mountain.'

Leaving Schlomo in contemplative ecstasy at the core of the Judería, I continued my itinerant investigations.

Tiled patios, with fountains full of flowers, the scent of jasmine...

I went into a little paper museum that laid out the paper road from China via Baghdad to Cordoba and displayed manuscripts in Hebrew and Arab script. One in particular fascinated me: written in black and red Hebrew script, with an underlining of earthy brown on the black. One hears here and there that the Paper Age is over. Well, anyone who says that books have had their day is either a nitwit, a demagogue, or a computer salesman. The book is still the place for maximal concentration and mindblowing beauty.

After the paper-and-book museum, I went into the bullfight museum, seeing the portraits and reading the lives of matadors such as Lagartijo, Machaquito, Bocanegra and Manolete. I even saw Manolete's bloodstained shirt, alongside the hide of the bull Islero that got him on the afternoon of 28 August 1947 in the arena at Linares. It takes courage to be a bullfighter, no doubt about that, and, living with death, those bullfighters have a dignity and quietness that is the opposite of noisy vulgarity. But courage can be shown in all kinds of contexts, and the blood-and-sand arena is maybe not the most interesting. I found myself looking more and more at the magnificent bulls, those so-called *toros de muerte*, who would certainly had rather been left to roam about the hills, and would have provided the human mind with an image of greater expansion that way. Their great heads are there on the wall: Indiano, Hortelano, Carbonero, Costillares...

I had been vaguely looking for traces of Seneca, born here in Cordoba, the man who wrote that *one day* the secrets of the great ocean would be revealed. And I found him, just outside the walls of the Judería. At least I think it was him, or maybe his father, the rhetorician – a bush hid the inscription on the stone.

I ended up late that afternoon in the Mosque, the *mezquita*, walking through the arabesque grove of slender pillars and seeing, over there in the background, the head of the poet Don Luis de Gongora grinning through the gothic gloom, whistling a little tune, singing to himself and to sheer Nothingness:

> *Da bienes fortuna*
> *que no estan escritos:*
> *cuando pitos, flantas*
> *cuando flantas, pitos*

'Fortune bestows gifts, not according to the book. When it's flutes you want, you get whistles. And when it's whistles you're expecting, you get flutes.'

Schlomo had gravitated there too, I saw him over in a dark corner, like a shadow. We sat for a while, before going up to the *parador* on the Avenida de la Arruzafa to spend the night.

★

Next morning, around seven, from my room at the *parador* I could see Cordoba spread out below in twinkling lights, with a line of broodingly dark hills on the horizon. After breakfast, which we took under a big painting of hunters and dogs on the Sierra Morena, we went down to the Alcazar, the old palace.

Of the rooms and halls, the one that interested me most was the Salon del Océano, with its whitewashed walls, its two mammoth chairs, its mosaic presenting the shaggy head of Neptune surrounded by fish, and its table with, inset, a map showing Africa, Asia – and the Mare Oceanum.

We then went up into the gardens – dusty and unkempt, but still despairingly beautiful.

A mosaic of black and white pebbles along the walks.

Lemons and oranges thickly clustered on little darkgreen trees.

A pool, in it clouds of gold and silver fish.

On a plaque set in a wall, this Spanished line of Martial: '*En tierras tartesas hay una casa celeberrima*' ('In Tartessan lands there is a famous house')...

It was Sunday morning, and the bells of Cordoba were ringing over town and countryside. A light wind was bending the reeds in the Guadalquivir River and a band of rooks was flying over the grey-green slowflowing waters.

★

Now we were out on the *Autovía de Andalucía*, making for Seville.

Spain is a rocky peninsula, from the Cordillera Cantabrica in the north to the Sistemas Beticos in the south, from the Pyrenees to the Sierra Morena.

But it's just as much a land of plains, and that morning, warm, hazy, bluegreyish, we were moving across a great rolling plain: Sevilla, 119 km.

Brown, khaki, burntyellow land, blazing white haciendas. Olive plantations. And cotton fields, with bolls of pale cotton blown on the wind and shreds of it scattered all along the road...

Arroyo Garabata.

La Luisiana.

Cañada Robal.

Carmona.

Carmona seemed to have religion written all over it. It was there in the names of streets and squares: Calle Sacramento, Plaza de Cristo Rey. It was inscribed into the walls: '*Ave Maria*', '*Ducam eam in solitudinem et loquar ad cor eius.*' The whitewashed lanes were full of the fluttering of pigeons' wings. Hemp shades, archaically rough, hung out over the windows. When a very beautiful, very graceful young girl came out of one of the patios, Schlomo stopped in his tracks. As we moved on, I heard him murmuring. 'What's that?', I said. 'Throughout my life I had no companion other than my thought, I sought her everywhere, enamoured of her beauty.' It sounded familiar. I wasn't sure if it was from my Solomon, or the other Solomon, or from Plato. Anyway, it was a very Solomonish and also very Platonic thing to say. A little farther on, obviously thinking all this over, Schlomo said: 'You know, I think there was a lot of sublimated sensuality in my Platonism.' And then he added again: 'Maybe there was a lot of sublimated sensuality in Plato's Platonism.'

A few miles farther on, and we were in the suburbs of Seville.

A Coca-Cola plant.

A Pepsi factory.

Then we were moving into Seville on the Avenue Kansas City.

'Oh, Christ', I thought. 'Will Spain also sell out?'

On the Paseo de Cristobal Colon, that big thoroughfare that runs parallel to the Guadalquivir, a lot of noise, South American brand, was coming from the Festival de las Naciones.

A big poster bore this message:

SEVILLA

PUERTO DE POETAS

1927–1997

I wondered what that could mean, probably nothing worth bothering about.

★

We found ourselves a hotel up in the Cathedral quarter: the Hotel Doña Esmeralda.

Brown lounge, with ten smokey dark paintings on the smokey walls.

We were led along a passageway lit by red lamps.

Had a look at the rooms, and decided, both of us, we wanted something else.

We were then led along a passageway, a floor farther up, this time lit by blue lamps.

Same scenario.

We then went another floor up and were led along a passageway lit with white lamps.

Okay.

The room I had, and I suppose Schlomo's was the same, was still full of thick red and dripping gilt – like so much of what passes for art in Spain, and in Latin America: rococo rhetoric, baroque blabber. But it had a beautiful view over the Cathedral, and the old Moorish tower, and the city.

Schlomo said he had a lot to think about and preferred just to stay in his room. I wanted to go out on the town, absorb as much as possible, you never know what can turn up: flutes or whistles, whistles or flutes.

'*Quiere hacer un paseo?*'

That was the driver of one of those horse-drawn cabriolets stationed on the Cathedral Square, the horses very still and patient, with flies crawling around their eyes.

Thanks, I said, but set out determinedly on foot.

Turning left at the Cathedral, I skirted the old Jewish Quarter, making into the Barrio Santa Cruz.

I passed by the Academia Sevillana de Buenas Lettras (founded 1751). Then the house of José Blanco White, born in the quarter in 1775 and who spent '*una vida dedicada a combatir la intolerancia*'. Then by the Fondación de Arte Flamenco, as well as another place offering tuition in *Sevillanas, Palillos, Rumba*, and a guitar shop: *Guitarras de Artesania*. On the Plaza S. Leandro, there was an ancient tree (a laurel of India), a fountain, and pigeons. On the Plaza Jesus de la Pasión, the smell of roasting chestnuts. After that, it was the Plaza de la Alfalfa and the Plaza de Salvador, nearby which is the site of the prison where Cervantes '*el principe de los ingenias españoles*' is supposed to have begun *Don Quixote*. There was a guy there in the middle of the road, on his knees, arms outstretched, with a notice beside him: '*Soy el padre de cinco hijos*', exactly like something out of one of Cervantes' exemplary stories.

By this time, night had fallen and I was feeling hungry. I had been told in Malaga about a restaurant, the San Laureano, but I hadn't a clue how to get there, so I hailed a taxi.

It was a young guy, with a shaven skull, at the wheel:

'American?'

'Yeah', I said, putting it on.

'Where from?'

'Chicago.'

'Where go?'

'San Laureano – the restaurant.'

'*Para comer?*' (to eat?)

'No, to play baseball.'

'*Gaspacho?*'

'Who knows?'

'First time Sevilla?'

'No.'

'A city tour?'

'Nope.'

We pass by a little street: 'There lives my *querida*', he says, 'my darling. We go there?'

'Look, dude, quit the hustling and just take me to the San Laureano restaurant, OK?'

Before he stops, I get the impression that he knocks the meter to jump it up. I'd seen it was at 575, now suddenly it was at 1,073. But I wasn't sure, I'd been looking out the window, and, who knows, maybe Sevillian meters do take wild leaps like that. I was willing to give him the benefit of the doubt.

'1,073 pesetas', he says.

I hand over a 5,000 pesetas note.

He gives me back 2,900.

'What about the other 1,000?', I say.

He hands it over without a word.

In the restaurant, I order myself an austere but delicious meal, with a strong-bodied bottle of Marqués de Arienzo.

At the table next to me there's a mixed bunch of Spaniards and Americans. They're doctors, from some Congress – there seem to be congresses of all kinds all over this city. One little American woman is the life of the party, she keeps bubbling with laughter. Her husband is already blotto and solemnly somnolent, but he wakes up to declare with reckless romanticism to his Spanish neighbour: 'I adore you.' The Spanish woman, who is smoking like a volcano, thinks maybe *she* should be a life of the party too, so she tells about some party she was at the other night where a doctor, from Dallas, Texas, put his hand on her butt saying: 'This is a hell of a party, honey.' She said: 'We don't do that kind of thing in Spain.' He said: 'Well, we do it in Texas.' At this, the little American woman positively rocks with laughter. Another American is declaring: 'I have a cousin in New York who knows good wines. You know, ten thousand pesetas the bottle kind of stuff. Me, I like to drink cool, so I always put ice in it. He goes berserk.' The little American woman rocks again. She is really doing her bit. The Spanish men seem to be just grinning and bearing it (there are no doubt big-numbered bucks in the wing as compensation).

Next morning, it was raining. Black tarpaulins had been drawn over the carriages clustered round the Cathedral. The horses had fewer flies round their eyes and nostrils.

Schlomo and I decided to visit that Mecca of original Americanism, the Archivo General de Indias, which had been my principal motivation in coming to Seville at all. The archives, the *papeles de Indias* have been stored for two centuries now in what used to be the Merchants' Hall of Seville, the Casa Lonja. It was José de Gálvez, in the early 1770s, having seen the desperate disorder in the royal library at Simancas, who'd first expressed the need for a New World archive, suggesting that it should gather in all the relevant documents (letters, reports, logbooks, maps, books) from all the various institutions concerned: the Casa de Contratación, the Consejo Real y Supremo de Indias, the Consulado de Cargadores... This collection and organization of the documents became all the more urgent when William Robertson's *History of America*, out from Edinburgh in 1777, attacked unequivocally Spanish practice in the New World. A Spanish answer was imperative. The task fell on Juan Bautista Muñoz, *cosmógrafo major de Indias*, and everyone agreed that he should have all the documentation concerning the *territorios de Ultramar* at his disposal, in as rational an order as possible.

I haven't read Muñoz's *Historia del Nuevo Mundo*, but *I have* read *The History of America* by William Robertson, DD, 'principal of the University of Edinburgh, historiographer to his Majesty for Scotland' – three fat little volumes of it, bound in brown and red, bought in Paris, have been on the shelves of my own 'Atlantic library' for years. It's true that Robertson's portrayal of Spain is hard: a nation of 'tedious formalism', 'slow and dilatory in forming all its resolutions', and that his indictment of Spanish New World policy is harsh. His opinion of its laws at the time of Columbus, Ferdinand and Isabella, especially Ferdinand, is less than flattering, and his description of Spanish ways in both discovery and settlement is one of lack of foresight, greedy avarice, criminal licentiousness, narrow-minded ambition, mean jealousy, ignominious cruelty and obstinate stupidity. Who in fact could deny it? It's undeniably true that, over there in the 'New' World, there was Aguirre, the crazy Basque, and Francisco de Carvajal, the *Demonio de los Andes*, it's true that there were hordes of illiterate adventurers marked by ignorance, incapacity and prejudice swarming over the new lands. But maybe Robertson overdoes it a bit. And his moral-political criticism leaves out all the investigations, all the cosmographical and cartographical labour, all the navigational poetics. He simply has no sense of this. In other words, his sense of things is only *common*, in a context that was exceptionally *un*common.

For my part, moving through those marvellous halls with the dark cedar wood walls and the marble floors, looking at the thick yellow archives, shelf on shelf, of the *Sección Contracación* (the papers of the Casa de Contratación, also called the Casa del Océano, which not only organized expeditions and controlled, or tried to control, emigration, but also ran a school of pilotage and map-making), I can only feel unreserved exaltation.

All around me are eighty million pages of documentation covering all the territories from Tierra del Fuego to Texas.

I practically run amok.

Here's Juan de Gardenas, *Problemas y secretos maravillosos de las Indias*. The marvellous secrets! Here's Fernández de Enciso, *Suma de geografía que trata de todas las partidas y provincias del mundo, en especial de las Indias*. Here's Antonio Vásquez de Espinosa, *Compendio y descripción de las Indias Occidentales*. Here's Juan López de Velasco, *Geografía y Descripción Universal de las Indias*. Here's Alonso de Santa Cruz, *Islario general de todas las islas del mundo*. All the islands in the world! Here's Juan Pedro de Medina, *Arte de navegar*. Here's Martin Cortés, *Breve compendio de la esfera et de la arte de navegar*, the first mention of the magnetic pole. Here's Andreas Morales's treatise on Atlantic currents. Here's a *Mapa Corografica de la Nueva Andalucía* (that is, Venezuela) by Luis de Surville. Here's a *Mapa de las costas del golfo de México y de la América Septentrional hasta Terranova hecho por el piloto Martin de Echegaray en Sevilla el 20 de abril de 1686*. Here's an *Idea topográfica de los altos del Mississipi y del Missouri*. A topographical idea! Here's a *Gramática en la lengua general del Nuevo Regno*. A grammar of general language!

Enough to drive an intellectual nomad crazy.

Schlomo is amused by my excitement, but I don't think he really understands. For him, fundamentally, there's only *one* book – the thing in his eyes is to learn how to read it right, which can mean, among other instrumentations, wearing spectacles made by Plato. But his mind is in that book, not in the world, not on the earth and on the sea. He's a Platonist poet. I'm a nomadic geopoetician. We nonetheless have a lot in common.

That night, in my room at the Doña Esmeralda, I was reading a book I'd picked up during my Sevillian rambles in a wonderful bookshop, the kind of bookshop I delight in, packed full of philosophy, itinerancy, cosmography: Juan de Escalante de Mendoza's *Itinerario de Navegación de las mares y tierras occidentales*. The manuscript is dated 1575. But Mendoza never got a licence to print it, the authorities allegedly fearing that, if that book got about, with all it revealed, it would upset the geopolitical *status quo,* so it stayed in manuscript for four hundred years.

Fired with the idea of the New World, full of an ocean-sense that was to expand with the extension of his knowledge, Mendoza, who calls himself *'marinero de ciencia y experiencia'* (he has the gift of the compact formula, as well as that of the space-opening phrase), came to Sevilla as a young man, to the house of his uncle, Captain Alvaro de Colombres. He sailed first with Colombres, then on his own account. And he was to die, on the American continent, at Nombre de Dios. All the time with a book on his mind.

This man was not only a seaman, he was a writer, and of no common sort. He says his first studies were in Latin: Virgil, Pliny – and I'd bet a million pesetas that he also read Seneca. He read these authors with *'vigilencia y diligencia'* (again, the formulation). All his life, he says, was devoted to 'attention, study, speculation' (I remember another cosmographer I read whose motto was: 'Go, study, consider'). And when it came to *materias marítimas*, that meant a particularized, specialized study: *'muy particular y específico estudio y especulación'*. He read all the available documents: *'todos los memoriales y relaciones particulares'* before, on the basis of his own experience, plunging into his own manuscript, tracing out his own text, making out his own mental map. And he does it with that sense of space and expansion I mentioned earlier, coming up again and again with phrases such as these: *'tan larga navegación'* (such far-ranging navigation); *'tan grandes y espaciosos mares'* (such wide and spacious seas); *'aquella grande inmensidad de tierras y regiones e islas occidentales'* (that great immensity of lands and regions and islands in the west); *'por golfos largos y por mar muy alta'* (through broad gulfs on mighty seas). Ah, a man after my own heart, after my own mind! You can take all your rococo poetry, all your baroque novels and leave me, poetico-cosmographically, with that one phrase: *'por golfos largos y por mar muy alta'*.

We begin on the banks of the Guadalquivir, here in Sevilla:

'Para dónde va ese barco?' cries the traveller-writer, the poet-cosmographer, and the answer comes back:

'Para Sanlúcar!'

When the incipient writer starts putting his questions, the first interlocutor, no doubt a common sailor, says the man to give the answers is the pilot: *'ese hombre viejo vestido de azul'* ('that old man dressed in blue').

The book then consists in a long informative and inspiring dialogue between writer and pilot.

'What's the best wind for going down the river?' is the initial question. The *'nor-nordeste'* is the answer. 'How come there are so many accidents on the Guadalquivir?' Because there are dangerous and difficult areas: the piles of an old bridge, the shallow waters where the river divides, and there's another shallow part called El Naranjal. Then, some pilots are better than others – some get drunk and don't know what they're doing. Add to that the passenger boats: they take on too many people and try to go too fast, not respecting the ordinancies. That's why there are so many collisions and capsizings between Sevilla and the coast.'

'How far is it from here to Sanlúcar?'

'Sixteen leagues – *16 leguas de camino*.'

★

We were out on the *Autovía*, going down to the Lower Guadalquivir, Baja Andalucía, along by Bellavista, Dos Hermanos and Los Palacios.

A tropical wave had hit Spain and the rain was pouring down torrentially. Through a grey curtain we got glimpses of the river, pine trees and cotton fields.

Farther down, we passed by a territory called Cerro del Fantasma.

And then, at Las Cabezas de San Juan, we branched off on to the yellow road going down by Lebrija and Trebujena to Sanlúcar.

There the rain slackened off a bit.

To the left, cotton fields with bedraggled bolls and the occasional vineyard. To the right, a wasteland, in which at one point I saw a man on a donkey herding a double flock of cattle and sheep, the cattle gathered in a black and white cluster, the sheep drawn out in a long grey straggling line.

A huge notice blared out: *El futuro està aquí!*

Further on, another huge billboard announced UN RÍO CON OPPORTUNIDADES ('a river of opportunity').

Flatlands, here and there slightly rolling. Every now and then, a dump. The impression of travelling miles and miles through a dead end.

Seven more kilometres to go.

Sanlúcar de Barrameda.

★

I don't know what I expected to see at Sanlúcar. Maybe I didn't want to expect anything (you know, flutes and whistles).

But there it was: strangely empty, strangely silent.

Maybe it was just the time of day.

I noted a monument to Labouring Youth, several manzanilla co-operatives, a *Fabrica de Dulces*, and that was that.

Suddenly five buzz-bikes buzzed out of nowhere, stopped, at a red light, fuming and farting and whining, then buzzed off into another nowhere. Like mad insects on a hopeless migration.

We stood on the harbour front, Schlomo and I, looking out over the brown waters.

That's when I started to do a little imagining and conjure up a scene.

This whole Atlantic coast of Andalusia was once frontier territory, not only in the sense of the Christianity–Islam conflict, or the Spain–Portugal rivalry, but because once out there beyond the bar, the way was open to unknown seas and uncharted archipelagoes, with all kinds of opportunities for discovery, adventure, the amassing of wealth, the spreading of the Santa Fé or just getting away from everything habitual – all kinds of motivations were in the air, often mixed.

Here at Sanlúcar was the Capitanía General del Mar Océano.

Columbus himself didn't sail from here. But he was around, as at Puerto de Santa Maria, asking questions, looking for small, sturdy boats easy to handle and good for exploration, before leaving from Palos. So, Sanlúcar wasn't Columbus's port, but it was Magellan's, it was Champlain's. Pedro de Menoza's expedition got ready here before making for Río de la Plata. Hernández Serpa sailed from here to Guyana.

The streets and taverns would be full of a hubbub of voices in many languages: Spanish, Basque, Italian, French, Breton..., with exotic names and unfamiliar words cropping up again and again in the conversation: La Habana, México, Perú, la Zona de Darien, La Bahía de Santa Marta, Las Antillas, Santo Domingo... What was the best way to get over that damned bar? So many boats had wrecked there, on the way out or the way in: the *Santa Barbara, El Fenix, Nuestra Señora de la Luz...* How far to the Canaries, how far to Dominica? You must get through the Bahamas before August. There are Indians and Indians: the Caribs are cannibal, not the Arawaks. Is there any cure for the *fiebre amarilla*, the yellow fever? And stories would be told. About that *muchacho* from Malaga, shipwrecked on an island, who ate his own arms. Or about that Juan Ortiz, captured by Indians in Florida, who lived with them for years, and when he finally escaped and met up again with Spaniards, in order to identify himself, could only get out one word, badly pronounced: 'Xbilla, Xbilla' (Sevilla, Sevilla). Maybe one, away in a corner, while listening to all the stories, is following in his mind an obscure path, ranging along coasts amid a labyrinth of islands, with eyes open for currents, the flight of birds, the movement of seaweed...

After a couple of hours of just staring out to sea, we went a bit farther up the coast to Bonanza.

Stood there on the pier, looking out over the now sandy-coloured waters under a paleblue sky, and along the coast to the north where piles of salt rose like gleaming little mountains.

Bonanza is the fishing port, run by the Asociación de Pescadores Nostra Señora del Carmen. We went into the

Cantina del Pescador, where we ordered two *finos*.

Schlomo was saying that, in his time, it wasn't any New World they were interested in, but the newness of the world, how it arose from primal substance, and the attempt to get as close to that as possible. I said I liked the idea, and that what interested me in the New World thing wasn't project and purpose, far less the constructions, but the actual movement, the stretching out into unfrequented space...

We left the theme floating in the atmosphere.

As we came out of the cantina two egrets were crossing the water towards the Punta de Mulandar.

★

In the Fisherman's Tavern at Bonanza I'd unfolded a big map of Andalusia so that Schlomo and I could decide where we'd go next. We finally picked on Arcos de la Frontera.

That meant a series of little yellow roads and little red roads. Palebrown earth. Paleblue sky. Villages lying like handfuls of sugar cubes on the hillsides.

Arcos turned out to be a very fine little town, white as white could be, with steep streets running up to the citadel height that gave it its name.

Up on the embattlemented heights of the citadel, there's a memorial to Diego Ximenez Ayllon (1530–1590) who was not only '*capitan de los tercios de Flandres*', not only '*primer poeta gaditano en lengua castellana*', but also '*regidor de esta ciudad*'.

It's the old regidor's or corregidor's house that has become the *parador*.

I took to it straight away. So did Schlomo. In the hallway there was an old print of the Academia Platonica, so he felt totally at home.

My room, whitewashed, with darkred furnishings, looked down over the cliff face inhabited by glossy black choughs, brown-winged kestrels and little blue pigeons, and out on to a wide space of plain and hill covered with vines and olive trees, and frosty-looking fields of cotton in the distance.

It was astoundingly beautiful.

When I kept the window closed, I could hear the wind tearing at it. When I opened it and stood on the little balcony, I could hear the cries of the kestrels.

The sun, in its setting, shed a misty russety red over the landscape.

Because maybe he was suffering from his boils, Schlomo had decided to stay in his room and have a meal brought up to him.

For my own part, I went down to the dining-room, ordering a dish of hake, 'in the style of Sanlúcar', that is, stuffed with gambas and grapes, along with an exceptionally epicurean bottle of 1986 Marqués de Cáceres.

Back up in my room, listening to the wind, thinking of the hawks, I wrote a long, rambling, geopoetical poem, 'Autumn in Andalusia'.

When I came down next morning, Schlomo was standing at a table in the foyer reading an article in *El Mundo* about the effects of global warming: by the year 2050, there would be no Nile delta and the Sahara would be advancing into Spain.

He looked horrified.

We left Arcos by the snow-road, El Camino de las Nieves.

★

Our departure from Arcos took place under rain, but pretty soon the sun was streaming incandescently through the cloud.

We were up on the sierra of Grazalema: grey wisps of cloud clinging to grey, calcareous rock; groves of darkgreen oak.

Grazalema itself proved to be a quiet little mountain township, all white, with the Rio Guadalete running through it.

We sat on a bench in front of the Iglesia de la Aurora, watching and listening to the doves, with blue woodsmoke drifting across the roofs, in our nostrils the smell of smoke, wool and honey.

We then moved up to Zahara, across the Sierra Margarita, seeing a couple of inquisitive eagles and a roving band of vultures.

★

'Who's that?', said Schlomo.

We were sitting in the lounge of the old Reina Victoria hotel in Ronda, where I'd ordered us a couple of *finos* and a bowl of almonds.

'Who, where?', I said.

Schlomo indicated discreetly with his chin a dark corner of the room.

At first I saw nothing. Then something materialised. A man with a wispy beard, a drooping moustache and big wide-open eyes, his whole manner at once frail, stiff and vague.

'What's he saying?', asked Schlomo.

The man in fact was murmuring to himself in German, with an Austrian accent: 'Prague, Munich, Russia... Monasteries, pilgrimages... Paris... Now this place built over an abyss, and the silent sierra... Alone, like a mineral.'

I recognized Rainer Maria Rilke, who was living at the Reina Victoria at Ronda in the Autumn of 1912, and told Schlomo so, saying how much I admired his poetry, especially the *Duino Elegies*. But I did not care to disturb him and pretty soon he disappeared, leaving only the perfume of a rose.

The Reina Victoria is a white building with green shutters, somewhat like a Swiss chalet, on the edge of Ronda, looking out over the burnt expanse of the Sierra: a great abstract space, with the tinkling of sheep and goat bells in the near distance, and, in the far, the silent flight of sierra birds. The hotel was started up in 1906, linked to the construction by the British of a railway line, and frequented at the beginning mostly by Queen Victoria stalwarts from Gibraltar.

I went to sleep with the tinkling of bells out in the sierra, and I woke early, to the sound of a lone dog barking away out there in the first light, seeing the red of the rock turn into grey and the grey into blue.

After breakfast, we started strolling round Ronda.

Ronda is a famous little town in Spain because it attracts candidates for suicide: that chasm over which the *ciudad* is built is really too tempting. It's also famous for Pedro Romero, the man who started the fighting of bulls on foot instead of on horseback and on whose statue raised in front of the Plaza de Toros in Ronda can be read this phrase: '*Mas cogidas da el miedo que los toros*' ('fear gives more blows than the bull').

I lost Schlomo at the chasm, and, hoping he wouldn't be committing suicide on me (that news about the future of the world had shaken him), went on over the fatal bridge on my own.

Just beyond the bridge, I went into an antique shop. The owner, who'd been standing at the entrance, came in behind me: a thin, stringy fellow of about thirty, with a bushel of black hair and big, brown luminous eyes. I was looking around at the accumulated jumble when he started talking to me, through clenched teeth – about Napoleon. He went on and on, never unclenching his teeth, the only word I could make out being 'Napoleon'.

'Sorry', I said at length, 'but I don't understand.'

'You understand well enough.'

'No, really, I don't.'

'Oh yes, you do, but you do not want to.'

I shrugged my shoulders, with an open gesture of my hands.

'*Soy un hombre libre*', he said ('I'm a free man').

'Sure', I said, not wanting to argue with him, and got out before he started screaming.

I ended up in the Museum of Banditry. There used to be a lot of bandits in this area: the Guardia Civil was created to put them down, which is why some of them left for Mexico and got into films. It was here, in the Serrañia de Ronda, that the last real Andalusian bandit, Juan José Mingolla Gallardo, known familiarly as Pasos Largos, was shot, on 18 March 1934. And here's the story of José Ulloa, known as El Tragabuches. José was a member of the bullfighting school here in Ronda. One day he left for Malaga, to do a gig in the bullring there. On the way, he fell off his horse, and was in a coma for a while. But he made it back to Ronda, with an idea of vengeance in his mind. He'd long suspected that his wife was having a little tilt with this character called El Listollo, so he bursts into the house, finds El Listillo tucked away inside an earthen jar, sticks his knife in him a couple of times, and then throws his wife out the window. After which, he runs off to join the gang known as 'The Seven Lads of Ecija' (*La cuadrilla de los siete Niños de Ecija*).

That was Ronda in the good–bad old days.

I found Schlomo again at the state hotel, the parador, sitting at a corner window looking down into the abyss, like an angel in Paradise.

That night in the Victoria, Schlomo and I had a couple of American businessmen behind us at dinner. They'd been prospecting Andalusia and making some deals. There was much talk about 'the product guy'. After listening in for a while,

Schlomo commented ruefully: 'Columbus should never have discovered that America.'

★

I'd thought maybe we might call it a day there and go back to Malaga. But Schlomo wanted to go and pay a visit to Moses ben Ezra in Granada. So Granada it was going to be, but we'd take the long way round, by the coast, which I was curious to see in detail.

That meant, in the first place, a journey down through the Serranía de Ronda, the Sierra de las Nieves, and the Sierra Bermeja.

Red and grey country: grey rock, red earth, dotted with fir. At times, from the heights, glimpses of the Mediterranean: a grey mirror, slightly bluer down by Gibraltar.

Then it was the coast, at San Pedro de Alcantara.

To leave the hills and to go down to the coast at that point is, as I learned, to leave austerity for vulgarity.

Club Playboy: Picasso Bar – Escort Sauna – Live Show.

Costa del Sol: Costa del Golf.

Disco-Pub Micmac.

Marbella.

Fuengirola.

Torremolinos.

The highway – the *Autovia del Mediterraneo* – runs between little Disneylands of pastry architecture, and a dirty, dismal, tired-out beach.

Even the sea looks exhausted, extenuated: palerose, pale-green – as if it had been turned into a tepid fruit squash.

Here and there, amid all the architectural pastry, the remains, for how long, of authentic little fishing villages.

Tierra de luz, paz y speranza, they call it – I mean, the publicists call it.

Shit.

Shit.

And more shit.

'*Hevel, havelim, hakol*', said Schlomo.

'What's that?', I said.

'Hollow as hell is all this – vanity of vanities.'

'You can say that again', I said.

He did.

After Malaga, the country seemed to get a bit rougher, less built up.

We became aware again of headlands.

Just after Salobreña we moved back up into the hill country.

Up along the River Guadalfeo, via Velez de Benaudalla, Puerto del Suspiro del Moro, to Granada.

And then, there, red on the horizon, the walls of the Alhambra.

'*Alqala hamrâ*' ('the red fortress', in Arabic), murmured Schlomo.

★

Two in the afternoon on the Bib-Rambla in Granada. The iron shutters of the shops were being pulled down with a screech and a rattle. A little brat was chasing the pigeons on the square, other kids were roller-skating or tricycling. The flower booths were resplendent with golden chrysanthemums. Autumn leaves were falling, and there was already a slight chill in the air, with a cold wind blowing down from the Sierra Nevada wrapped in cloud.

We'd been walking through the city centre, past the Souk Alcacería full of tinselly trash, past the Ecclesia Imperial de San Mateas, over by the Placeta de los Peregrinos.

Back to the Bib-Rambla.

On the Bib there's a fountain held up by four old bearded guys, monstrously deformed. At first glance, you think one is smoking a cigar-butt. It turns out to be a water-spout, and no water running.

I'd wondered if there might be rooms available for Schlomo and myself on the Placeta de los Peregrinos, which would have been nice for symbolical reasons, but the symbol would have had to have triple-glass windows and be lined with cork, because Granada also has its horde of Vespas and waspy little Vespinos.

We took rooms on the hill, in the Alhambra Palace, an exotic edifice left over from some World Exhibition.

The idea had been to visit Moses ben Ezra. But Schlomo had no idea where Moses had lived. He was totally confused in the modern Granada. Walking in the streets, I could see him visibly panicking. That night at dinner, he was gloomy.

Next morning, in order to at least get some initial bearings, we went to visit the Alhambra, the old Alhambra.

You could hardly move there, what with the hordes of serious Germans and camera-clicking Japanese, with families of voluble Americans in between.

Drab ruins, dusty gardens.

Torre de las Infantas.

Schlomo kept saying the architecture of the place had esoteric significance, but he could no longer read the lines.

In the Church of Santa Maria de la Alhambra, I tried to get him involved in a conversation with San Francisco and his acolytes, San Pancracio and San Expedito. In the Alhambra museum, I tried to get him interested in two Koranic books probably from a Koran in sixty volumes composed in a scriptorium of Sevilla or Marrakech and later dispersed. But he was having none of it. He was in the throes of an abysmal depression.

I thought a walk in the Albayzin district, the Moorish Quarter after the Christian *reconquista*, on the other side of the Darra River, beyond El Paseo de los Tristes ('the pass of the Sadnesses'), might do him good.

On the Plaza Nueva, under the trees, there was a gathering of all kinds of tramps and vagabonds accompanied by their dogs, with drums and flutes playing here and there. We passed by the bars: the Pasodoble, the Vatican, the Valparaiso. The only time Schlomo looked interested was before the rusty iron gates of an old ruined house with a wildered garden called the Carmen del Negro, but he couldn't remember why.

No sign anywhere of Moses ben Ezra and nobody had ever heard of him.

Schlomo was so desperate he decided to retire early to his bed that night and try to forget the whole thing.

Leaving him in his room, I went down into the city.

Night was coming on.

I padded down one stairway after another, past one *carmen* (quiet little walled-in residence) after another, going down into the low town.

There was Little Dog Street – Callejon del Perro.

Cats were prowling in the gathering dark around the backstreet ruins.

I kept going down.

Till I came to a river and a bridge, where Africans were selling belts, umbrellas and ties.

Then I found the main central thoroughfare.

It was there I came across the *Feria del Libro*, a great book fair, *'para la promoción de la lectura'* (you could get sixteen plaquettes of *poesia contemporanea* for 1,000 pesetas), with bookshops represented from all over Spain, but mainly from Andalusia.

I went from stand to stand.

And finally found him, Moses ben Ezra.

There he was, on the display table of a new publishing house, Bibliotheca Andaluciana, a bilingual edition of his philosophical-poetical treatise: *'Arougath ha-bosem* ('The bed of aromatics').

I bought it.

Took it back up to the hotel, and left it at Schlomo's door.

I hoped it would perfume his sleep and thereafter brighten his day.

★

It was a bright blue morning, a blue illuminate and rose-dewy morning.

Behind Granada lay the dark mass of the Sierra Nevada, with snow patches here and there.

We decided to go up into it.

Schlomo was feeling a lot better, thanks to ben Ezra's aromatics.

Autumn-bitten leaves along the road. Cloud moving slowly along the crests. White webs on the tips of pinetree branches. Magpies.

The Camino del Veleta, said to be the highest road in Europe.

At the top, a battered meteorological observatory and a statue of the Virgin.

Grey peaks, dark stone.

'Al-Nadja', said Schlomo.

'What's that?', I said.

'Deliverance – a term used by Avicenna.'

There was a strong wind blowing.

'Nephesch, roua'h, nescha mâ', said Schlomo.

'What's that?', I said again.

'The three Hebrew words for soul', he said.

142

'I see what you mean', I said.

'The world at creation', he said, 'hahh, hahh, hahh – the cosmic wind!'

We stood up there for a while, Schlomo looking ecstatic, me pretty ecstatic myself, but looking over the terrain: signs of glacier flows.

Well, we couldn't stay up there forever, so we left to have a look at some of the Sierra Nevada villages.

At Lanjarón, a place of Arab origin, in the southern fold of the sierra, fifty kilometres from Granada, we went into this *tienda gastronomica* called El Arca de Noe for a bite to eat: cheese and ham served on a wooden platter, with a glass of darkred wine.

Then went on to Capaleira.

In Capaleira of the white lanes, in Capaleira of the cool heights, where you look down over the cloud in the valley, there is a lane called Calle Silencio.

'The tenth sphere', said Schlomo as we walked along it, 'is the sphere of intellect. There the mind is elevated beyond all elevation, looking out over the thirty-two marvellous paths of wisdom. In philosophy, one can go from labyrinth to labyrinth. But *there* is the source of light and life.'

'Agreed. Glad you came, Schlomo?'

'Very glad', he said. 'For this!', and he stretched out his arms.

'Flutes and whistles, eh?'

'Whistles and flutes.'

After spending the night there in Capaleira, we made back to Malaga.

★

Back at the starting point of this Andalusian journey, I waited while Schlomo climbed back on to his pedestal.

'See you again some time', I said.

'Any time you like', said he.

I walked away from him, giving him a final wave of the hand.

'*Adiós!*'

'*Hasta luego!*'

I think we will indeed meet up again one of these days, on foot or in the mind, in that lovely country, that limit-country, Andalusia, and walk along the lane called Calle Silencio.

Rainy Margins and Misty Horizons

To come into Portugal from Spain, especially the areas of Castille, Leon or La Mancha, is to leave those red and yellow deserts, those endless stretches of grey-green olive plantations, for something like natural, variegated growth. You leave a sun-burned monotony that can rise into a transcendental meditation for a soft, dark, baroque confusion.

It's there in the language too. Portuguese is a kind of fishy Spanish: it glides and elides in a liquid obscurity, seeming almost invertebrate compared with the sonorous angularity of Castilian. Pronounce the Spanish words *Español* or *Castillano*, and then *Portugues* ('*Portoogaish*'). See what I mean?

★

I came into Portugal, Europe's misty-oceanic margin, that late September, via Viseu, which is in the heart of the Beira Alta, way up miles north of Lisbon and other Lusitanian parts that used to be frequented by all the exiled princes of Mitteleuropa, among German spies, card-sharpers from Mexico, belly-dancers from Brazil, and chancers from everywhere.

The hotel I checked in at in Viseu, the Grâo Vasco, told me I'd got the last room available, they were full, full to capacity. Full at the end of September in the Beira Alta? said I, beginning to fear that my hopes of quiet days in the Autumn of Portugal were going to be blasted. Ah yes, indeed, they'd been chosen as a stopover place by the Transportugal Motorbike Rally that would be arriving that night around eight.

'Great', I thought, 'that's all I need.'

In Viseu there's a street called 'Straight' (Rua Direita) that is all bends. I walked along it, making side excursions into adjacent streets, mostly cobbled, often mossy, such as the Rua Senhora da Piedade (two blind beggars there singing *fado*), the Rua Senhora da Boa Morte and the Largo S. Teotônio (big banderoles of the Portuguese Communist Party proclaiming 'No to a New Conservatism!'), glancing in at one little shop after another: the cobbler's shop, 'O Sapateiro', advertising *Rapidez e Eficiência*; the embroidery and lacework shop; the shop selling pewter; the little bric-à-brac place full of heirlooms and vestiges of the twenties and thirties; the wine shop offering mature red wine (*tinto maduro*), mature white wine (*blanco maduro*) and green wine (*tinto verde*). A thin drizzle of rain was falling, and people were going about under umbrellas. I knew I wasn't seeing Viseu at its gayest and most smiling, but it appealed to me: a compact, lively little place. And the young girls didn't seem to be worried too much about the ominous information chiselled into the stone of the street called Straight, according to which 'Mary conceived without original sin' (*Maria concebîda sem peccado original*).

I found myself finally in front of a grey granite building on Cathedral Square. This was the art museum known as the Grâo Vasco, the same name as my hotel. I'd thought, vaguely, that the 'great Vasco' in question was Vasco da Gama, but he turned out to be Vasco Fernandez, a painter who'd been one of the leading lights in the, I learned, famous Viseu Painting School of the sixteenth century. Most of this was ghoulishly religious stuff (Santa Luzia, with her eyes on a plate, for example), but the old landscape-school of Viseu seemed to have been continued into modern times, and I stopped for a while before A. C. da Silva-Porto's *Railway Station at Night* (*Estaçaô do Caminho de Ferro a Noite*), and J. J. Sousa Pinto's *Na Bretanha*, showing a church, a lighthouse and a pensive child on a cliff.

After that I went into the cathedral, passing just inside the door a Christ on the Cross, *with real hair* (that must really put a shiver down the backs of the faithful), and an advertisement for the Seventeenth National Congress of the Students of Theology, the theme of which was to be *O ressurgir do religioso no final do milêno* ('the return of religion at the millennium's end'). There were about ten people on the benches: nine old women and a very old man, waiting for the six o'clock mass. And three young boyos were stalking along the aisles. One was a halfwit, dressed in baggy pullover and pants, perpetually chuckling. The other two wore three-quarter length jackets, one with jeans turned up largely at the bottom, peasant-wise, the other in smarter, thinner black serge trousers, obviously the Number 1.

Just as I came out of the Cathedral, a car with a young woman at the wheel was driving up. The parking-man (self-appointed), a scruffy rundown old fellow, made to guide her to a place. But Number 1 of the trio I'd seen in the Cathedral and

who were now on the square themselves, decided to take over.
It was he who, intervening between the older man and the car,
assumed the task of guiding the young woman in to a safe
berth. The older man had expressed his righteous indignation,
to which Number 1 had paid no attention. It was only when
the car was parked that he very deliberately took off his three-
quarter length coat, folded it, handed it to the halfwit, who was
trembling with delight, and went up to the older man, poking
him on the chest with his finger and spoiling for a fight. But the
old man simply backed off, mumbling, leaving Number 1 to
recover his coat from the howling halfwit and the smiling
henchman. The trio then ambled off into the city, like something out of a B-series Hollywood movie with Portuguese sub-
titles.

Since the rain was falling harder, I decided to buy myself an
umbrella, under which I kept wandering round the streets till
nightfall: Rua Escura, Rua de S. Lazaro, Largo Mouzinho de
Albuquerque.

That evening, in the dining-room of the Great Vasco, lit
dimly by artificial candles, and where the waiters looked as if
they'd be happier howking manure, I ordered a plate of cod-
hash (salt cod, egg, potatoes, onion – mixed) with a bottle of the
local red wine. The wine was good. As to the cod-hash dish,
well, it was part of the patrimony. Nobody, at least in Europe,
eats more fish than the Portuguese, and, in the old days, cod
was next door to God. At that time, it probably came straight
from the Grand Banks of Newfoundland. Now it comes down
from Norway in frigo-trucks and it's getting rarer every year.

The Rally folk may have arrived in Viseu around eight, but
they must have dined elsewhere. I heard them whining, crank-
ing and tramping in to the hotel around midnight. And at
breakfast, I saw them. They wore zip-suits with multi-coloured
plastic guards at elbow and knee. There was one wench with
them, a real tough chick. I watched her fill a plate with canned
peaches, then pour on them pink-coloured yoghourt. What she
did with it after that I don't know, because I looked away. I
was glad to hear that they were heading north to the Tras os
Montes, while I was going in the opposite direction, down
towards Coimbra.

If it had been raining in Viseu, it was deluging in Coimbra, the Mondego River was just a thicker version of what was going on in every street. But I had my umbrella, remember, and was ready to go.

As every transcendental traveller knows, the most interesting places in any town are the library, the station and the cemetery. If you don't know that, you may as well stay at home and watch television. Now, Coimbra has, reputedly, one of the finest libraries in Europe. It was got together by one of the Joâos, I forget his number, and it is housed on that hill overlooking the Mondego River. I was determined to see it. So I upped with my umbrella and ventured forth into the lanes and alleys.

Starting out from the Largo do Portagem, I went up the Rua Ferreira Borges, went under the arch of the Old Medina (sounds of *fado* from a cassette-player, and the smell of old books), then up a labyrinth of flaky, scaly, cancerous little streets (one of them called Quebra-Costas, 'Breakrib Alley'), till I emerged at the top of the hill.

Once up there, I accosted a fellow umbrella-carrier and asked him where the old university was, the one with the big library (I didn't want him to direct me to some new place full of computers that teaches hotel management). He gave me directions and I was already following them, having said my *obrigado*, when he called out to me:

'Enjoy Coimbra!'

I pumped up my umbrella twice in reply and sloshed on through the flood.

I was really determined to get to that library.

Get to it I did. To find about thirty people under umbrellas queueing on its stairs. Hell, I thought, but resignedly took my place. After about ten minutes, two or three people dribbled out, and two or three in the queue dribbled in. Christ Almighty, I thought, if this is the rhythm, I should be able to get a glimpse in sometime around 2010. But I was still determined.

Two or three more dribbling out, two or three more dribbling in. At last my turn came. There I was actually on the threshold when a woman just to my left said in a prim sharp voice:

'Do you belong to the group?'

'I beg your pardon?'

'Are you one of the group?'

'The group? What group?'

'My group.'

'No, I'm not one of your group, whatever it is.'

'Then please stand aside to let my group in.'

'Look', I said, 'I've been waiting patiently half-an-hour to get in to see this library...'

'But you're not one of the group', she said.

I could see I wasn't going to get anywhere with this bitch, especially as she'd been reinforced by a burly fellow with a badge. And pressure was growing behind me. If some of her group had been waiting there on the stairs under umbrellas along with lone individuals like myself, others had obviously been waiting elsewhere, in some dry place, and having now been given the sign, were swarming up like ants to a bit of pizza.

'Please stand aside', said the bitch again. And the man with the badge made a fat fascist authoritarian gesture with his arm.

Rage rose in my Scoto-Celtic belly.

'Damn you', I said to the woman. 'Damn tour operators, and all tour groups. Damn the University of Coimbra for allowing this kind of thing to happen', and made off into the rain under my black anarchistic, individualistic, no doubt politically damnable umbrella. 'Damn you too', I cried in passing to the statue of the man, João the Somethingth, who had wellmeaningly founded the place with its noble inscription: *Lusiadae, vobis hanc sapientia condiduit arcem* ('Lusitanians, wisdom raised for you this citadel')...

Then I started laughing. At the situation, at myself, at everything.

And laughed my way back down the hill.

★

My place of residence in Coimbra was the Astória hotel, on the Avenue Emidio Navarro, which runs along the river. I'd seen the Astória described in some guide-book as the one-time rendezvous of poets, artists and *fado*-singers, a jewel of Portugal. Well, it may have been a jewel around 1927, but by now it was a dump – a drab, gloomy, dismal dump. The first room I was shown had 'Suicide for certain' written above its door. The second wasn't much better, its motto might have been 'Abandon all hope'. I finally settled for room 109, which, once you abstracted from the omnipresent dinginess of the materials and the atmosphere, had a kind of attraction. A lot of buildings in Coimbra are built edge on to a square, and advance like the prow of a ship. The Astória was like that, and my room was right there at the prow, with three windows, and views that took in the Street of the Cats (Rua dos Gatos), the pink façade of the Banco do Portugal, the Largo do Portagem (Tollhouse Square) and the Mondego River. It was a bit noisy, because trams, buses, cars and motor-snorters were in perpetual motion just a few feet below, but the topology suited me.

At seven-thirty, the yellow street lamps came on against a darkblue leaden sky.

At eight, I made my way along the bright green emerald hall-way, down the musty darkbrown staircase, into the dining-room.

Rosycoloured pillars. Goldfish in a case swimming in *saudade* (that 'undefinable', as they say, Portuguese sensation of existence). A tray of cheeses slowly turning into art déco and a couple of flies showing their appreciation. On a mezzanine, a forlorn piano (flanked by four chairs for players of those Portuguese onion-shaped guitars) from which, perhaps, in the old days, fervently mellifluous *fado* was sung.

I ordered a dish of mullet.

The waiter was a moony kind of fellow with a droopy moustache. I'd talked with him earlier. It was a weird experience. I'd ask a question, nothing metaphysical (like 'What is God?'), nothing even existential (like 'How are things, man?'). Just a plain chronological: 'When's dinner?' Time passed. The question seemed to have gone along a long mental labyrinth and got lost in the cosmos. I'd given up all expectation of an answer when out it came: 'Thirty-seven'.

When the mullet turned up, they were as tough as Michelin tyres.

I called over the waiter and, in a quiet way, said: 'This fish, my friend, is overcooked.'

After I'd made my statement, a month passed. The goldfish felt *taedium vitae* weighing on them heavier and heavier, the flies got blasé about art and buzzed off into a bleak night of nihilism, I myself began to feel I had pronounced humanity's last word, when the answer came:

'Ah, yes, it is always like so in Portugal.'

There's *fado* for you, from the Latin *fatum*, meaning destiny.

Destiny, disaster and doom, not forgetting dire despair.

I poked stoically at the maltreated mullet for a while, drank a coffee at which the flies showed a reawakened interest in life, and went back up to my room.

The traffic was still busy and noisy.

Navarro's Bar down below was offering Pizzas and Coca-Cola.

The rain was falling heavy again.

Mondego Blues.

Exploring the mini-bar, I discovered two whisky miniatures, one red, one black. Not much, but it would do.

And moved into a cinematic kind of meditation.

Images, local images to start with: the Barbaria Universal (the Universal Barber Shop) in the Rua Ferreira Borges, with its antiquated chairs and its big ornate mirrors; the Cervezeria (beer-shop) in the old town, lined with blue tiles depicting boats plying on the Mondego River...

I sat there, sipping the whisky now and then, till dawn broke and the sky was white.

★

Later that morning, I left for Bussaco, which I'd read about in a book picked up in Coimbra.

To go from Coimbra to Bussaco is to go back up north a bit. But I didn't mind that. It's the kind of thing (zig-zagging, to and fro-ing, back and forward-ing) I do all the time. And this place seemed worth it.

Bussaco is a forest, a monastery, and an architectural folly that was meant first as a royal retreat and later became a luxury hotel.

It still is a luxury or, shall we say, semi-luxury hotel, but in it you'll meet up with groups of businessmen from Yorkshire (there is a baleful English influence on Portugal), bevies of convivial Americans ('where have you guys all bin?') hordes of giggling Japanese snap-shotting one another, and the publicity tells you that Agatha Christie (or worse) lived here. Enough to put you off, but they're all at it, they've all gone down that crowded road.

When I arrived at the Bussaco Palace, it was still only ten-thirty in the morning, so that the room allotted me (I'd phoned from Coimbra), was, understandably enough, not yet ready. I went to the lounge, a huge place that could contain two foxhunting parties, with their horses, and ordered a coffee. I was sitting there quietly, idly gazing at the Midsummer Night's Dream frieze that went round the room, when the Yorkshire group came in, soon followed by the Texan group. It was then I decided to go for a general look at the premises.

The hallway was lined with coloured tiles depicting, on one side, the Battle of Bussaco, 27 September 1810, in which Wellington defeated Masséna, which didn't interest me a lot (but that's where England got its final boot and foot in Portugal), and, on the other, Portuguese navigations to Africa, Asia and America, some scenes of which (great winging gulls over a coastline) were really beautiful. Thereafter, the monumental staircase leading up from the entrance hall carried portraits of Henry the Navigator (with his motto: *Talant de bien fere*), Vasco da Gama, Pedroalvares Cabral, Alfonse de Albuquerque, Joao de Castro and Francisco de Almeida – captains, explorers, governors: a pageant of all the ancient pride of Portugal. On the landings, chairs, couches and chest in dark exotic wood: Afro-Portuguese, Indo-Portuguese, Sino-Portuguese.

As to the outside, if you can put together in your mind's eye a gothic cathedral, a Hindu temple, a sea fortress, a coral reef and a bride's cake, you have, approximately, the Bussaco Palace. It's architecture gone riot, and since it's built of limestone, easily workable, it's decorated with a medley of grotesque gargoyles, lacey pinnacles, kitschy cornices, along with festoons of ropes, chains, leaves, liverworts and seaweed.

Around noon, a bellboy came to tell me my room was ready. It was a big room, with a view over the forest, then a haze of bluegreen hills, and, to the right of the window, a great pine tree from Australia, an araucaria, that, as a little plaque informed me, the aboriginals call the *bunya-bunya*.

In the afternoon, I went for a walk in the woods.

★

The Bussaco woods, consisting of about 260 acres, situated on the north-west slope of the Sierra de Luso, are among the most magnificent woods I know. In addition to local oak, yew and holly, you'll find in them parana pines from Brazil, cedars from the Himalayas, sequoias from Oregon, red ash from Pennsylvania, Atlas cedars from Morocco, eucalyptus from Tasmania, giant ferns from the West Indies, as well as all kinds of mosses and lichens. The area constituted a 'sacred wood' (that's what Bussaco means: *bosque sacro*) from early on, maybe Celto-Iberian times, and when the Barefoot Carmelites set up in it their 'desert house' in the early seventeenth century, they cherished it, nourished it and protected it. They built a 3-metre high wall, 5,750 metres long, around it, and got the Pope to issue a bull threatening with major excommunication anybody who cut or damaged a tree, which is the most intelligent bull I've ever heard of. When the Carmelites faded away from these parts in the mid-nineteenth century, the Forestry Commission took over, and, *mirabile dictu*, continued the good work.

I spent four hours wandering through the wood's quiet misty atmosphere, amid the sounds everywhere of platchering water, for there are fountains here galore. There's also a little lake, with a small bridge leading to a diminutive rocky island on which a lone willow grows. The waters of the little lake, at least on that day, were earth-coloured, and it was difficult at times to distinguish the goldfish who swam in it from the red leaves of Autumn that floated on it.

It was in 1628 that the Bishop of Coimbra ceded the forest to the Carmelites. Those Barefoot Carmelites were among those who were out to reform the Catholic Church from within (though they went about it more quietly than 'God's dogs', the Dominicans), and when they set up the Monastery of the Holy Cross of the Desert of Bussaco, it was on the basis of solitude, austerity and silence, according to the lesson of St Theresa of Avila and San Juan de la Cruz. They built the monastery out of local schist and quartz, decorating the front with white chuckies, bits of black basalt and pieces of red ironstone, and lining the inside, both for warmth and decoration, with cork. They also built little hermitages here and there in the woods. There were never many of these monks, never more than twenty-four at any one time. When the monasteries were disbanded in 1834, twenty monks remained, and, since Bussaco was such an isolated place, they were allowed to stay on till they died off, the last of them giving up the ghost in 1860. When the palace was built, between 1888 and the beginning of the twentieth century, a good part of the monastery was destroyed, notably the library. But the hermitages remain, as well as the cloisters of the monastery and the chapel. No sign there now certainly of monkish discipline and meditation, only of popular religion. On an altar of the virgin Mother are littered, as *ex votos* of thanks or as prayers for protection, waxen figures of breasts (the large majority), legs and ears, as well as photographs. One Dutch businessman, a computer expert, I noticed, had left his business card, so God could get in touch by e-mail.

In addition to their solitude, austerity and silence, those monks also had a feeling for nature. It's there in their love of the forest, which is expressed even in the most mystic poems of San Juan, as in the *Subida al Monte Carmel* or the *Noche Oscura*. In one of them, while talking of divine aloneness, he evokes 'the wind in the cedars'. And in the Carmel Chronicles, there's the story of a hermit-monk who went even farther, he actually made friends with a magpie, teaching it to talk man-talk. Unfortunately, this began to worry him, because he felt he was breaking his vow of silence. Which is why, in a great fit of remorse, he not only decided to break off the communication, but actually blamed the poor bird for attracting him, ordering it and its like, in the name of the Lord, to leave the woods of Bussaco for ever. I hoped his Lord told him to go to hell.

In addition to the monastery and the hermitages, the monks laid out what they called 'a sacred path', being stations on Christ's itinerary from his arrest to the resurrection. At the beginning, those stations were simply marked by a cross, the monks having all the rest in their heads. But when the monks had gone, somebody took the initiative of putting up little chapels in which the various scenes are presented in a child-ishly theatrical, hyper-realistic way. Despite this, I decided to follow the path, about three kilometres in length. It's just that, where it was advised to 'consider' such or such an event, such or such a station of the Cross, I'd tend to 'consider' some tree, a light through the branches, a rock.

At the hermitage of Mount Calvary, believe it or not, after I'd come through the little oratory, and had emerged on to the terrace, looking out from the cliff over the forest and a wide expanse of land, a magpie rose up in flight from an oak tree.

'Welcome back!' I squawked.

★

That night, at dinner, in addition to the table of the Yorkshire businessmen (three of whom were puffing at cigars to show they'd really made it), and a big table of Japanese, there was the table of the Texans. I don't know what it is exactly, but American women, when in company, seem to feel they have to howl and scream with laughter – maybe in order to demonstrate to all and sundry that they have no complexes and are totally liberated beings. As for the men, they always give the impression that they want to be heard all the way from Florida to Alaska, from Minneapolis to Moscow.

Anyway, while eating my cold carrot soup and my succulent pig (a Bussaco specialty) with an excellent bottle of Bussaco Branco, I had plenty to occupy my mind with. That was because the dining-room of the Bussaco Palace is lined with scenes illustrating *The Lusiads*.

I first read Camoens, dutifully, in Glasgow, and I read him again years later, obstinately, in Macao, and on both occasions I was epically bored. But with these paintings by Joâo Vaz, every one of them accompanied by a short quotation, this was not the case. Far from it, I was enthralled.

Here's a sultry, sun-drenched beach, with white houses and palm trees: '*Terra he de Calicut, se nâome Engano.*' Here's the scene of a total becalming: '*O vento dorme, o mare as ondas iazem.*' Here's a lone ship in a great expanse of waters: '*Grande seescondia.*' Here's an empty sea and two gulls: '*Porque a lampada?*' And here's an entering, after trials and buffetings, into the quiet Tagus: '*Teio ameno.*'

The Lusiads is supposed to be about conquistadors. That's how it's been mostly put over, and that's how it's been used by the Portuguese nation. But on more than one occasion, I see, on a re-reading of the poem, there's open criticism of conquest – as in the fourth Canto where, in front of the tower of Belem, an old man cries out against 'the folly of it, this craving for power, this thirsting after the vanity we call fame, this fraudulent pleasure known as honour that thrives on popular esteem!' And this supposedly Christian enterprise is placed, in

Camoens' poem, under the protection of Venus. There's more *eros, logos* and *cosmos* in Camoens than there is martial conquest and ideological banner-waving. When Vasco da Gama is asked by the king of Calicut why he came, Vasco replies that it was neither for fame nor for conquest nor for gain, it was the desire to know 'a strange climate'. The 'regions of Aurora' evoked have a larger horizon than that of territorial conquest:

> *O Capitâo*
> *Pera as terras da Aurora se partia*

'The Captain sailed towards the regions of Aurora'

After three days at Bussaco, I betook myself to the banks of the Tagus, at Lisbon.

★

Lisbon is a labyrinth, and traffic indications in Portugal are a mess, so to get to my hotel, the Caza Lisboa, in the Lapa district, I asked a cab to guide me. My Portuguese being what it was, I asked the cabman if he spoke English. 'Yeah', he said, chewing gum, and sounding convincing. I realized later his English stopped there, but he understood what I wanted. He also understood that he could make a good thing of it for himself. He took me for what Parisian taxi-drivers, considering it a speciality of the Chinese cabmen in the city, call 'the Shanghai Road'. Which meant we went the long way round and I had to pay my gum-chewing cabbie at least twice what the trip should normally have cost (that I learned later).

If anybody tells you contemporary Lisbon is a beautiful city, you can consider that the hidden persuaders, the tourist brochure lyricists, have been at it again. Modern Lisbon is not, absolutely not, a beautiful city. It is drab and dull. After the resounding earthquake of 1755 (as far away as Malaga was heard 'a great voice coming out of the sea'), the Marquis of Plombal certainly did a great job building it up again (the royal authorities were for packing off to Brazil), but it was a great job such as the great job done by French urbanists to Le Havre after the war of 39–45: fast and utilitarian. A lot of people in Portugal realize this, and are trying to give the town a face-lift. What that means for the moment is that to the general dull drabness are added the noise and dust of countless machines.

Thank God, may it be said in passing, for the little ladies of Lisbon who continue, in this dull context, to put a little erotic logic into the atmosphere. This year, they are showing their belly-buttons, the fashion being to wear pants, often black, that don't go too high up, and tops, blouses or pullovers, that don't come too far down. Bless em all, and may their belly-buttons continue to shed light and promises of ecstacy over the dingy, dusty thoroughfares.

★

The first quarter I made for was the Chiado, because I know that was where Fernando Pessoa, the only Portuguese poet I can put up alongside Camoens, used to hang out. Writing at his best moments an oceanic, plurivocal poetry concerned with the ultimate sense of things (*The Sea of Intranquillity, Towards the Horizon of Another Ocean*: 'signs of a clearer, more limpid way of life'), Pessoa drudged, if I remember rightly, in some import–export office nearby, and would repair frequently to the café A Brasileira ('Importers and Exporters of Brazilian coffee') for a drink, a dream, a talk with other drinkers and dreamers. I had no great trouble finding the Largo do Chiado (Chiado – a sixteenth-century poet whose statue in the middle of the square makes him look like a hilarious Voltaire), and there indeed, facing some totally uninteresting official building, with no perspective at all, was the Brasileira. Pessoa was still sitting there – in bronze, and beside him an empty chair, also in bronze, on which a Japanese (Professor of Portuguese literature at Tokyo University?) was getting himself photographed. I was about to pass on, but decided to satisfy my curiosity to the full and see it all through. Inside, the Brasileira was a long, narrow coffin-shaped place, with a red and gilt roof and some pretty awful paintings slung round the walls. It may have been an attractive *art nouveau* spot at the turn of the nineteenth century, now, packed with tourists from Frankfurt, it was noisy, smoky and devoid of any attraction whatsoever. I listened for a minute to a little Portuguese, half-sloshed, talking at the bar to an intense black-bearded, silver-eyed Spanisher with a ruck-sack, about Europe: 'Portugal is not the same as Spain or France...', then went back on to the terrace where I sat down – well away from the bronze chair – and ordered a coffee. It was then a street-artist turned up. He had a Mohawk haircut, a red and white chain hanging from his belt, ten bracelets on each arm, spider webs tattooed in blue from his ears across his cheeks, and carried a bright red guitar from which he struck fierce chords while intoning what I supposed was some kind of rock-a-billy *fado*. I was moving away, fast, when I was accosted by another guy who told he was Portuguese, but from Mozambique (what they call here a *retornado*), didn't know his father or mother, was contaminated by AIDS and had a bad arm from a machine accident. It sounded a lot at one time, but I gave him a 500 escudo piece, just in case.

★

Another area I wanted to go to was the old Arab quarter, the Alfama, away at the East End.

It was raining again as I walked from the Av. Infante d'Henrique, out by the South-east Ferry Station, past the Taverna del Rey (The King's Tavern), one of the places in Lisbon best known for *fado*, up into the Alfama. A man was roasting chestnuts over a coke-burning stove, and the smell of coke and chestnuts filled the air. A tramcar clanged its way past the Café do Eléctrico (the Tramway Café). I climbed up ruinous streets paved with little black and white cobbles, past flaking façades on one of which somebody had scrawled in great letters the word NIRVANA, past houses overlooking detritus-strewn wastelands where old women fed bands of pink-footed pigeons from their windows, till I came to the ruins of the ancient Arab fort from which the eye can take in a large vista comprising the red and yellow huddle of Lisbon and the grey-green expanse of the Tagus, as well as 'the land beyond the Tagus', the Alemtejo.

After that, I came back down to the dock area where, among other converted warehouses, the Celtic Pub stands beside the Salsa Latina Centre, the Ultramar Club, the Blues Café and the Cacalao Bar, where I drank a dark oporto wine, looking at old photos of the Newfoundland fish-trade and listening to original fo'c's'le *fado*.

★

But the quarter I frequented most was the one called Bethlehem, or, as they say in Portuguese, Belem. It's there, on the river front, even as you watch the plastic bottles, the orange peel and the old newspapers being silted up on to the esplanade, even as you see practically disintegrating under your eyes the windrose given by the Union of South Africa in 1960 to commemorate the anniversary of Henry the Navigator, even as you observe the gasometers and petroleum tanks amassed on the other side of the river beside the Lisnave shipyards, you can evoke all the Portuguese movements on *caminhos do mar*, say, Nuno Tristâo's arrival at White Cape in 1441, or the days of Francisco de Mascarenhas in India, or the rocks of Ielala, 150 kilometres up the Zaïre River, on which was written the message: 'To this place came the ships of the enlightened King John of Portugal, signed by the pilots Cam, Anes and Da Costa.' Nearby stands the Monastery of the Jerônimos, which in its meditative isolation was linked to all the islands of the world, and where the memories of Camoens and Pessoa, poets of the open world, are enshrined.

★

It was at Sintra, in the Sala das Pegas of the Palace (the roof of which is decorated with *pegas*, magpies), that Camoens read the first pages of *The Lusiads* to the boy-king Sebastian who was later to lead Portugal to total disaster in North Africa, leaving the country with a dreamy myth that he would come back one day up the Tagus and recover all the lost glory of the land.

Sintra lies on hilly country west of Lisbon.

To get to it, you can go by road along the coast, out by fortresses and lighthouses and lifesaving-stations and windmills, with the ocean getting wilder and throwing spray over rocks on to a landscape of windswept dune and bare moor. I went out on that road one day, but lingered on it so long reading *The Lusiads* on the shore, that I didn't get to Sintra at all.

Or you can go by train. On my second attempt to see Sintra, that's what I did.

Decorated with blue tiles depicting country scenes, Sintra railway station is one of the daintiest little stations I've ever had the pleasure to contemplate. As you come out of it, the first building you see is the Fu Min Chinese Restaurant, its leaf-strewn terrace graced with a dozen red metal tables advertising Coca-Cola. But this is modern, workaday Sintra, where any big house you may see is abandoned, ruined, or converted into a bank. To get to old Sintra with its hoary residences, you have to walk up the hill.

A few pages back I presented the Palace Hotel of Bussaco as a prime example of architectural fantasia. Well, in Sintra, there are dozens of places like that, crazy castles and extravagant mansions, all nestling in the thickly forested slopes. The National Palace stands out among them, mainly because of its two great fat chimneys that make you think of some kind of bizarre distillery, but it has fine rooms in it: in addition to the Magpie Hall, there are the Swan Hall, the Mermaid Hall, the Chinese Room and the Council Room. It's something like the Swan Palace of mad Ludwig in Bavaria, and the surrounding landscape is similar. In fact the landscape was so wild and attractive that the aforementioned Barefoot Carmelites of the seventeenth century thought of setting up a monastery there. They finally decided against it, considering that the silly ceremonies and futile festivities of the court and the courtiers would be a nuisance. How right they were. I prefer Bussaco to Sintra by far. But the winding streets of the old town, leafy and mossy, with fountains gurgling here and there, and the proximity of the forest, certainly contain enough elements for what the poet Garrett called an *amena estancia*. Byron lived there for a while, probably limping about in elegant boredom and thinking vaguely (this was 1809) about *Childe Harold*. I wandered around for a couple of hours, thinking of nothing, just picking up images, then took the train back to Lisbon. It was in the train I realized that the image remaining deepest in my mind was that of the ruined Moorish fortress up on the highest ridge, and the mist swirling round it.

★

I haven't said much about the Caza Lisboa. That's because, apart from the fact that it had a good view over the Alcantara docks, there wasn't much to say about it. It was just a place where I slept and sometimes ate. But on the last evening I heard an amusing little conversation there between a New York Jew, maybe Portuguese in origin, and his wife. The man was saying that when he got back to New York he was going to 'organize an enjoyable little lunch for Murphy'. 'In honour of

Murphy', said his wife, thinking to echo and enhance her husband's thought. 'No, just in his memory', said the man. 'Murphy didn't know much about honour.'

On the following morning, I left for Evora.

★

At Evora I found myself quarters at a beautiful old monastery converted into a *pousada*, that is, an inn and hostelry, and went down for lunch to tables set out in the cloisters.

In the courtyard, a bewildered garden with lemon trees full of green fruit, a rose bush with one single rosy rose, a lizard, and two tortoises. One of the tortoises, after plodding along for a foot or two, stopped in the pale but still warm Autumnal sun and *started yawning*, in antediluvian contentment. I'd seen tortoises before, in all shapes, colours and sizes, but I'd never actually seen one yawning. I was engrossed in the meditation of this scene when somebody at the next table shouted out: '*Grüss Gott, Gretchen!*' and I could hardly believe my ears. It wasn't that I was surprised to come across Germans – *Mein Gott*, no, they are all over the Iberian peninsula. It was just that the phrase was so totally and deliberately German, in fact probably Bavarian, and it was so close. Was it because of some innate gregarious tendency that the Germans had sat at the table next to me, although all the other tables were empty, or was it because the waiter, disinclined to move about much, had put them there?

The Convento dos Lóios is situated on the heights of Evora, on a terrace with a wide view over the countryside, just behind the remains, four lines of fine Corinthian pillars, of a Roman temple dedicated to Diana.

These were extreme lands for a Roman (a township nearby is called exactly that: Extremos), but Evora seems to have been a fairly important agglomeration. Pliny refers to it as *Oppidum veteris Latii* ('a town of old Latium'), and it seems to have had municipal status from the times of Augustus: there's that temple, and vestiges (I saw them later in the museum) of some substantial villas. It's enough to evoke the tramp-tramp-tramp of a Roman army to hate Roman imperialism and, if I'd lived at that time in Portugal, I'd certainly have been alongside Viriato, the man from Viseu, who rose up against it. But Roman civilization did bring some good things with it. Among the elements piled, rather pell-mell, in the Roman section of the museum, I saw two really lovely sculptures: female torsos, in the local rosy marble, the breast nipples inserted with marble of a darker shade. They are among the most beautiful anthropomorphic sculptures I have ever seen, evidence of fine living in one or the other of those rustic villas in the far-flung province of Lusitania.

Evora has always been a place of stone.

In the Iberian peninsula, Portugal has many more megalithic remains than Spain, and in Portugal the greatest concentration of those old raised stones is found around Evora.

As they moved around Europe, those megalithic wanderers seemed to keep resolutely to the rim, and if they raised up stones to mark out a territory, or to create an astronomical observatory, or to indicate a route, it was maybe also because, deeper down still, they had a sheer liking for stone and an eye for its forms. The form here, as I saw at Almendres and Portela de Mogos, tends to be rounded, which is why the name among the local peasants for one place was 'the hill of winejars'.

The monastery of the Franciscans in Evora is just about as far as you can get both from movement over land and from garden pools on the edge of which are exposed Venus torsos of rosy marble. What they have rather is a Chapel of the Bones, with walls built of skulls, hung with decomposing corpses, accompanied by sentences such as *Melior est dies mortis die nativitatis* ('the day of death is better than the day of birth') or *Nos ossos qui aqui estamos pelos vossos esperamos* ('the bones lying here are waiting for yours'). Yet even in the church of those same Franciscans, amidst a wealth of religious symbolism and overwrought decoration, I saw, set in a wall, a piece of brute marble, with an intriguing pattern, there only for itself.

Evora, nowadays, is a nice little town, all white and yellow, with its Street of the Infant Jesus, its Street of the Three Lords, its Street of the Painted Houses, and its parking problems.

As for the *pousada*, you had to choose between the guff from the kitchen or the stench of disinfectant. You also had to forget the waiter howking his throat over the table. As to my room, a little monk's cell still decorated with religious pictures of Sulpician taste, the air conditioner sounded now like a rush of traffic, now like a train entering a tunnel, now like the Lisbon earthquake.

After three days, I felt like getting back out on the road again. I made for Sagres.

★

Azure blue sky, burnt sienna fields. Scatterings of grey granite boulders. A shepherd leaning on his stick and watching over his flock. Cork oaks bared darkred high up their trunks. Storks' nests on pylons. Plantations of eucalyptus. Paleblue away there to the east, the Serra de Monchique.

This, I said to myself, was what I'd ultimately come to Portugal for.

As the word Sagres indicates, it was a *sacred* place, so spoken of in many texts, from Avienus's *Ora Maritima* ('the shores of the world') on. The Phoenicians considered it so, the Greeks considered it so, the Romans considered it so. It was the outlet of the Mediterranean, the last land (last gods of the homeland, last port of Venus) before the wind-blasted, monster-filled space of the Atlantic.

In fact there are three capes down there at Portugal's land's end. There is Cape St Vincent where, according to the legend, the body of St Vincent, a Christian martyred in Spain, was brought in a boat guided by ravens, and where ravens supposedly guard over his grave. Nowadays, it's a chapel, a lighthouse, and a huddle of pedlar booths. Then there is Cape Sagres proper, where Henry the Navigator based his school of navigation and exploration. Nowadays, it's a tourist complex, with a little monument to the Infante of the Ocean and memorial plaques from South Africa and the United States Power Squadron. The third cape is, I think, the original cape hit on by the nosey Phoenicians and which became (like others, say at Biarritz) their *atalaya*, their landmark and observation point.

It's on this cape that the Sagres *pousada* is situated.

I had a large-windowed room looking out to sea. Every day I'd walk on the headland, over the stony scrubland terrain, among tough juniper bushes, and here and there a clump of little blue flowers. Out there, I'd listen to the cries of gulls, oyster-catchers and curlews. And farther out still, in the ocean silence, since it was the time of the great migration, I'd see auks and ospreys winging their long, open way from Europe to Africa.

The Lights of the Atlas

Friday is couscous day in Oujda.

I was enjoying mine, in the Couscousserie Tlemcen, watching storks flying round the minaret of the Mosque. In these parts, anyone who has made the pilgrimage to Mecca is called *haj*. Because it migrates from one place to another (it's here from January to September), the stork is also called *haj*.

★

I'd flown in to Oujda from Casablanca.

Mohammed V airport was packed. At least the central alley was. I saw a tiny Japanese walking about under a great big floppy leather cowboy hat – the lone ranger from Yamaguchi. And heard a Frenchman talking to his wife: 'Where's the East?' She pointed vaguely NNE. 'Shit, I thought it was over there' – he pointed SSW.

At Gate 4, on the other hand, things were very quiet. There were only three of us waiting. Besides myself, an old man in a thick brown jellaba, and a businessman reading a newspaper, *L'Opinion*. At one moment, the businessman got up, went to a corner of the waiting-room, laid out the sheets of his paper, took off his shoes, did his devotions (*he* knew where the East was), then picked up the sheets again, fitted them together once more, and, going back to his briefcase, resumed his economic-political reading.

It was a warm, rosy evening.

The plane was a small throbber that flew low and slow. First over flat land, then into humpier ground and finally over mountains, those of the Rif: rugged and contorted, sometimes streaked with snow. Townships here and there – scatterings of light in the thickening blue.

★

Oujda lies in the Oriental district of Morocco, close to the border with Algeria. It was founded in the year 994 by Ziri ben Athia ben Mohammed, known as Ziri the Magrawi. Some say its name means 'place of ecstasy'.

It's a great place for smuggling. Local fortunes have been

made that way. If you see a 504 (they've got a lot of space in the boot) crashing over the fields, all dusty and fuming, from the direction of Algeria, don't be astonished. 'Don't be astonished at anything in Morocco', says a modern Moroccan proverb. During my sojourn, great business was being done in petrol. All along the roads, from the edge of town out, you would see youngsters surrounded by jerrycans and jugs, giving a thumb down signal for pouring. The locals are up to all kinds of dodges. I heard of some who would make their way into Algeria by donkey, load up the donkey with contraband, fix a walkman to its ears with a recorded '*Ra ra ra ra ra tchktchktchk*', and come home themselves by bus. But that could just be an Oujda joke.

I had been told the Oujdians were very serious people, very tradition-minded. Well, they seem to take their tradition lightly. At least the ones I knew did.

It was at the Café Averroës that I made the acquaintance of 'the ones I knew'. I was sitting in there one morning, reading a French translation of Averroës' *Decisive Treatise* (*Fasl al-magal*) I'd picked up in Casablanca, when a man came up from a neighbouring table and said: '*Vous êtes Français?*' I said yes.

We started talking about Averroës, whom Dante calls 'the great commentator' (of Aristotle), born in Cordoba, for a while doctor at Marrakech, and who died, isolated, attacked by orthodox theologians, in 1198. It turned out that Khalid, for that was his name, belonged to a group that had started up a few years before in Oujda, devoted to a re-reading of the Islamic tradition in all its aspects, and in particular to a re-evaluation of its thinkers and poets. Khalid was working on Averroës, Omar on Ibn Arabi, the '*doctor maximus*', Abdelkrim on Bedouin poetry, others on Al-Ghazzali, Al-Mutarrabi, and Ibn Battuta the traveller... The Averroës was their café, but they met regularly, once a week, in the house of this or that member of the group.

I met the whole gang on the following evening.

That took place in one of those big, bare Arab *salons*, with a cushioned sofa all round the wall. They had prepared a huge meal, telling me with smiling apology that in the tradition there would be as many cloths on the table as there were courses to be served, but that, with a little concession to utilitarian modernity, they made do with one.

At that, they described, with humour, the distance between themselves and modern Morocco.

In Casablanca and in Rabat, for 'yes', you say *nam*. In Oujda, it's *wa wa*. They tell the story of the thin-skinned visitor from the west whose face was scurvy with all the rough *wa was* that had been pronounced up close to it in the eastern region.

★

One day we left on a little trip up north, to the Mediterranean coast, Khalid, Omar, Abdelkrim (Krim) and myself.

The first halt was at Beni Drar. Meat hanging from hooks at open booths, braziers burning charcoal, their acrid fumes cellophaning the air. On the pavement, oblivious to the world, two old men on their hunkers, playing draughts with bottle tops on a battered bit of cardboard.

'Watch out here', said Krim, smiling. 'If in Morocco you come across some big quarrelsome fellow, you can say he's from Beni Drar.'

A car passed by with a white flag flying – the sign of some-one leaving on the pilgrimage to Mecca.

Then it was the Beni Snasen hills, a kind of prelude to the mountains of the Rif, blue there on the horizon.

Khalid told a story about tribal warfare, and the arrival of modernity. This tribe in its skirmishing came up against a railway. Rode around it, sniffed it. A trap? At that moment, a train came along, banging right through a herd of cattle. Astounded and aghast, the tribesmen went to see their wise old man. 'What is this thing?', they asked. The venerable sage thought, and thought, then came out with a nugget of sceptical, humorous wisdom: 'All I can say is, thank Allah that thing goes straight forward and not sideways.'

Past Ahfir and the Oued Kiss, we were at Saïda on the coast: Algeria, with a line of conical hills, just there to the east behind the barbed wire fence. Men gathering mussels from the rocks, others fishing.

We went on farther along the coast road to the west – goats up on their hind legs feeding on bushes, storks flying over the reeds, out there in the haze the Islas Chafarinar. Till we came to the mouth of the Moulouya. There we had a bite to eat, sitting on the bank among oleander bushes, beside a thick blue wooden skiff that did ferry work. While we were there, a young fellow wearing jeans and a turban got himself rowed across with two goats.

We then made for Berkane, which is the city of oranges. But it wasn't the orange season now, it was the medlar season. As the saying goes: 'When the oranges go out, the medlars come in.' As we sat in the Café Riad at Berkane, drinking exquisite coffee, my companions told me the Berkane folk were as idiotic as the Beni Drar people were aggressive: they would stop at the green light, and make a mad dash at the red.

Just another Oujda joke, of course.

In the Zegzer canyon, where we went after the halt at Berkane, I saw a tree packed, absolutely packed, with storks and white herons, and as we walked along the river, a couple of turtles with half-a-dozen young ones.

Back on the main road again in the twilight, we stopped at a wayside café for a pot of tea. It was Omar who poured it, making sure it had a good 'turban', that is, froth. In Winter, they told me, the mint doesn't taste very strong, so they put in some absinthe. '*Ça étanche la soif, ça enneige le coeur*', said Omar ('it slakes the thirst and puts cool snow on the heart').

It was Krim who told the story about the man who had been invited to a marriage, but was annoyed because he hadn't been asked to pour the tea, which is considered an honour, usually conferred on the best tea-pourers, which means those who can do it from highest up. The man, in anger, went back home, got his wife to fill the biggest teapot she possessed, asked her to lay out ten glasses on the ground, went up to the terrace of their house, thirty feet up, and poured, and poured and poured.

★

I'd be wakened with the call from the muezzin, around 5 a.m. That's the traditional rising time. As Khalid told me: '*On a honte si les oiseaux sont debout avant nous*' ('We're ashamed if the birds are up before us'). I'd go to the window, seeing little donkeys and horses straining at carts piled high with fruit and vegetables.

During the day, I just wandered about the streets, or read Ibn Khaldûn, Averroës, Ibn Battuta.

Then one day, with my three companions of the first time, I

made a little trip south, down into the land where there's nothing but esparto grass and wind: '*shih was rih*'.

We passed by the Beni Oukil hills, with Jebel Metsila high on the horizon, then Guenfouda, which means 'the wife of the hedgehog', then Jerada, which means 'the grasshopper', till we came to Aïn Beni Mathar, which means the well ('the eye') of the Beni Mathar.

It was about fifty miles south of Aïn Beni Mathar that we saw the Bedouin encampment – three harsh black-haired tents, low on the ground. We'd stopped the car to have a walk about. And we were still walking about the dry, esparto-covered ground, when an old woman, very small, about five foot high, with a brown, wizened face marked by a blue tattoo, wearing a pink gown over a spangly dress, a purple turban on her head, came hirpling over towards us:

'Are you in need of anything?'

We said thanks, no, we were just looking about.

They were sheep-herders. They'd come up in a hired truck from Tendrara because of the drought, and the truck had broken down. All the men were out with the sheep looking for water, so the old woman, out of decency and convention, couldn't ask us into the tents. But, if we liked, she could bring us tea where we were.

Again we declined. We weren't going to take what was maybe the last of their water.

'We are waiting for the blessing of Allah', she said.

We for our part said we'd continue on our journey:

'While you are on earth, see the world. Afterward, you see nothing. May Allah keep you and open the ways.'

A couple of days later, I left for Marrakech.

★

It was the black cobra that intrigued me, and the grey donkey – the one with the white flash down its brow. I wondered what went on in their heads.

The cobra usually lay coiled on a dusty carpet in the middle of the Square. But, every now and then, the snake charmer would abandon the grass-snakes he'd let onlookers touch so they could feel their rippling muscles, as well as the big fat one he'd coil round tourists' necks so they could get themselves photographed, and play a little flute tune for him alone. At this, the cobra would rise and nod his head very slowly right and left. At times too, the charmer would show his teeth, up close to the cobra's head, as though daring him to bite. At those moments, the charmer's two mates would beat frantically on their drums. The cobra never made a single biting move, knowing perfectly well that if he did, he'd get his skull bashed in. It was, the cobra no doubt thought, a dull life, but who knows he might be able to slip away some quiet night...

As to the donkey, his station was just next to the Café des Arts. That's where he waited for loads, sometimes leaning his weary head against the wall. There's an Arab proverb that says: there's only one thing more patient than a donkey, and that's a tent-peg. That donkey was Patience Personified. His big rheumy eyes had centuries of workworn patience swimming in them. Sometimes I'd see him in the street, loaded with two huge panniers slung on his flanks, or ten rope-festooned canisters of butane gas, or a dozen crates of Coca-Cola. If it wasn't him, it was one of his cousins – there are thousands of them in Marrakech. But I always recognized that one, because of his distinctive white flash. I've heard of a race of donkeys that once existed in Arabia: white donkeys, that could run faster than horses. I wondered if 'my' donkey still had some trace of them.

When I spoke of 'the Square', I meant of course *the* Square: the Djemaa El Fna, once a place of execution, for many years now a permanent circus.

The Square, for me, meant first of all the Café Argane, where I took most of my meals. But all around the Square, you'll find also the post-office, La Poste, with a bunch of men sitting hunched on its steps (waiting for a letter that will never come?), a café called La Caravane des Arts, another, the Café Toukbal, and the restaurant Le Marrakchi. Then there's the Banque Al-Maghrib, an ice-cream parlour called L'Étoile, a bazaar called Le Cadeau Berbère and an institution called Le Croissant Rouge Marocain ('The Moroccan Red Crescent').

But all that's only the outer periphery.

After it, comes an inner line consisting of carts loaded with oranges and dates – and inside that line, it's difficult to say what you *can't* see, or hear, or smell.

It's a bedlam loud with drums (*harraz, tbal, bendir, aouad, llira*) and thin, high-pitched flutes, a bedlam that reeks, fumes and sizzles, with charcoal fires roasting sheep heads that grin grotesquely through the fiery smoke. There are snake charmers galore, at least a dozen of them, with snakes from all over Morocco and beyond. At various spots, dancers clashing cymbals work themselves up into at least a semblance of ecstasy. Here and there, seated under umbrellas for both shade and secrecy, fortune-tellers read lines on the palm of the hand. Here's a water-carrier, ringing a big bell, with a string of bright copper cups slung round his neck and a hairy black water-bag with a spout under his arm. Over there is a medicine-man from down the continent, an African Black dressed in a blue gandura, very quiet, contained and dignified. And here's a dentist, with six still bloody glistening teeth, the morning's work, displayed beside a big pile of old dry yellow ones.

That's '*la Place*'.

I'd made straight for there as soon as I got into Marrakech, and had found a room in a little hotel, with a window that looked down over the Square.

When Youssef ibn Tachfin, who'd bought the land from the Masmouda tribe, founded Marrakech in 1062, it was a village on the plains, looked down upon, with a mixture of contempt and desire, by the hillmen of the Atlas. Youssef had ambitions for it, bearing as he did in his head the distant mirage of Andalusia, where the sun and the moon of science, art and culture rose and set. Youssef's tomb is still there in Marrakech, under a tree near the Koutoubiya minaret, only a few hundred yards from where I was staying.

As for Marrakech, it lived on and grew: part Arabian night's dream, part historical nightmare. Palaces were built of magnificent cedarwood, their walls elaborately decorated with stucco made of plaster, crushed marble and white of egg. In them were gathered eunuchs, courtesans and concubines, making of them hives of intrigue and debauchery, rife with poisonings, knifings, all the boredom and horror of the harem. Around them settled artisans, working in metal and leather, wool and silk, stone and bone. The village grew into a town, the town into a city – imperial, commercial, cultural. In the Spring of 1147, Abd el-Moumen with the tribes of the Atlas laid siege to it. The commander surrendered, but the attackers refused to enter the darkred walls, saying: 'The mosques of your city are not correctly in line with the *kibla*.' Maybe Marrakech had been thinking more of cultural Cordoba than of religious Mecca. The commander retorted that the error of orientation, the ecclesiastical deviation, would be corrected, and the town purified: many buildings were then demolished, and, in the process, hundreds of people massacred.

In 1337, in his own hand, El Mansour, son of Abou Saïd, wrote out a copy of the Koran, had it bound, decorated with precious stones, and offered it, as a significant symbolic gesture, to a mosque in Mecca. More palaces were architectured, more colleges for the study of the Koran (*medersas*) were built, and more shops were opened. Men of destiny, having aroused and convinced this or that turbulent tribe from the hills, came and went: one short-lived dynasty followed another. All of those leaders, some no more than vicious and ambitious bandits, would claim to trace conscientiously their genealogical line straight from the Prophet. But some were downright cynical. Asked to prove his line, one man drew his sword from its scabbard, held its blade high in the air, saying: 'That's my line – any objections?' With the men of destiny came the prophets, some half-crazy, one of them so obviously crazy and an embarrassment for all that he ended up with his hands nailed to one of the city gates. In June 1638, Mohammed ech-Cheikh wrote from Marrakech to his brother in Fez: 'Victory called you to the Maghreb. Be as wary as a crow. Never attack the Bedouin in their mountains, wait for an easier way to get at them. Do not trust the word of the Arabs: attack them with troops used to pillage and merciless massacre. Close your eyes on the city merchants and their shameful business. Never recruit courtesans or civil servants among the people of Fez, those people are as vindictive as mules. Raise the palace of your power on pillars of terror.' That was the prevailing political programme. Marrakech went from glory to ruin, and from ruin to glory. Known as 'the drum of the South', it sounded its wild weird music over all the Maghreb.

With images of old Marrakech in my head culled from Gsell, Leo the African (*Histoire ancienne de l'Afrique du Nord*) and other archival historians of the Ifrikiya such as Lévi-

Provençal, I wandered through the modern city, from the souk of the tanners to the souk of the carpet makers through the souks of the dryers, the metal workers, the leather workers, the drum-makers and the jewellers, seeing intricate, exquisite details all the time.

One artisan was Ishaq, a worker in copper and tin. I was standing in front of his little booth admiring the engraving he was doing on a copper plate when he engaged me in conversation. Where did I come from, and was I enjoying my stay in Marrakech? Oh no, he did not make that many plates or trays. A merchant had come to him once, proposing to buy his work wholesale, they would both make a big profit, but he'd said no, he preferred to sell his pieces one at a time, and to people he had *talked* with. As to his designs, he used all kinds: Arab, Jew, Turkish – 'We are all the children of Adam, and Adam is the son of the earth.' He'd worked all his life, and loved his work passionately. Sure, he was a bit weak in the eyes now, but he could still work on: he saw the plate, the tray, the space to work at, the tip of his graver. When his sight failed him, he'd stop: 'When a man has had his share, he closes his eyes and leaves the dish to others.'

In another tiny booth, I met Tahar, a leather worker who made belts, babouches and cushions, drawing in the designs on them free hand, and colouring them with the green you can get from wild mint, the blue from indigo, the red from poppy and henne, the orange from saffron. He'd just received an order for 600 poufs destined for the king's palace. You might think that, with commissions like that, he could open a bigger place, spread out, put up a sign. But no. There he was in his tiny hole of a place, working away with a certificate to say he was 'a first class craftsman' hanging on the wall above his head, and perfectly content.

Apart from these trades, Marrakech stinks. It stinks of everything under the sun. But where it stinks most is the tannery. The tannery of Marrakech is like a bomb site, the bomb craters being the vats in which the skins are tanned. These vats are filled with lime, pigeon shit, flour and tannin, in that order – it's probably the pigeon shit that reeks the most. In the dyers' souk, the results of the dying process are hung out to dry in multi-coloured, fluttering lines above the street. But the actual colours are made in dim and dingy little holes, cellars and dugouts where a man all blue with the dye will be feeding wood to a fire under a tub of boiling indigo, while in another dark hole adjacent another man will be stirring poppy juice, his arms a vivid red up to the elbow.

If Marrakech stinks, it is also a place of exquisite perfumes. In one shop I liked to frequent, spices and scents were laid out on the shelves as in a library. There was argana oil, arnica from the High Atlas, orange flower oil and that sweetsmelling product of the thyroid gland of gazelles, musk. This shop sold also all kinds of materials for occult practices: snake skins and monkeys' tails which, combined with verses from the Koran, guarantee full protection from all evil.

'How much do you offer me?' he said, 'just say any price.' I said: 'One hundred dhirams.' 'One hundred dhirams is money', he said, 'but you can't buy a camel for the price of a chicken.' That was at a carpet merchant's. He'd insisted on serving me mint tea: 'it's our Berber hospitality.' I'd said right from the start I didn't intend to buy any carpets (I made a point too of moving through the souks with my rucksack on my back, so as to be taken for a dusty pilgrim rather than a wealthy tourist, and so be less hassled), but I was interested in them. Not so much in the thick dust-gatherers, as in the thin *haubel*, the 'nomad carpets', easy to transport because they fold up into next to nothing. '*Voilà un très beau ancien qui chante tout seul.*' ('There's a lovely old carpet that sings to itself.'), said the merchant as he spread out yet another splendid piece. But it was a white raw silk one that attracted me. '*Je te fais un super bon prix. Sept cent cinquante – je baisse peut-être encore un chouia.*' ('I'll make you a super-good price. Seven hundred and fifty, and I might drop it just a bit farther.') I said I'd think it over. '*Si tu réfléchis, c'est mille. Il faut battre le fer pendant qu'il est chaud.*' ('If you stop to think, it'll be up to a thousand. You have to strike while the iron is hot.') So it's not the price of the thing, I said, it's the price of the situation? He laughed: '*Le berbère il est fauché comme les blés. On discute même pour un kilo de tomates.*' ('Berbers are as poor as mice. We can spend hours discussing a pound of tomatoes.') I said I might be back, and I did go back. For that raw silk touareg carpet.

There was a kind of antiquarian bazaar too, piled high with

all kinds of gear. I fingered for a while certain boxes with silver walls, their lids made of slivers of camel bone dipped in henne. When the merchant saw me looking at some old locks, he came up to me, saying: 'It's to open the gate to Paradise.' 'Paradise' in Arabic means of course simply 'garden', but I got the same kind of linguistic shock as I did years ago in Greece when I realized that a bus-stop is a *stasis* and that you wait there for the *metaphor*.

Before leaving the souks of Marrakech, one more stop – at a jeweller's. I'd seen a very interesting, very lovely necklet in the window: dark silver, and with turquoises so old they were no longer pale blue, but green. The first day I enquired, the merchant offered me 15 per cent off. The next day, it was 25 per cent off. The next day again, he said that, since it would soon be the Great Festival of the Sheep (he drew his finger along his throat), he'd make a supreme effort, and take off 30 per cent. I was sure he was still doing me – but I really did like the look of that necklace.

★

Morocco was indeed getting ready for the Great Sheep Festival, the *El-Kebir*. Never, not even in old Mexicali films made in Hollywood, had I seen so often that gesture of pulling a knife across a throat. They all did it: bakers, tinsmiths, shoe-makers, carpet sellers, jewellers. So that Morocco might commemorate symbolically Abraham's readiness to sacrifice his son, sheep were being sold for slaughter all over town.

The sheep market in Marrakech is up by the railway station, and trade – in sheep, camels, horses and donkeys – is usually done up there on Thursdays. But now every day was Thursday, and, since every family wanted a sheep, the trade was brisk, not only at the souk, but anywhere. To sell at the souk, you have to pay a fee of so much per head, so not all sheep-sellers go to the souk. They just stop with their khaki-coloured flock in some piece of wasteland outside the darkred city walls, and wait till they get customers. Somebody will drive up in a car and bundle a big, thickly matted sheep into the boot. I saw one youngster with a poor sheep grotesquely straddled over the handlebars of his moped. Morocco was sheep-crazy, and out for blood. The family buys a sheep, the children play with it for a while, get themselves photographed riding on its back, then they slaughter it, feed on it for a couple of days and set the salted and spiced remains away for future consumption.

'*C'est la Fête*', said a man to me in a shop.

'Not for the sheep', I said.

I was sitting one morning in the New Town, in the Grand Café de l'Atlas, which stands opposite the café called Les Négociants, watching the grass growing up through the pavement stones, when I decided that the time had come to move out.

★

After the polluted paradise of Marrakech, it was good to feel the salty windy atlanticity of Essaouira.

Situated 175 kilometres west of Marrakech, 350 kilometres south of Dar Béida, which is Casablanca, Essaouira is a sunny, white-walled, African St Malo. Its name contains the Semitic root, *sour*, meaning 'rock' (as in Syria). It's built on a rocky promontory that ends up offshore in a chaos of little islands. The biggest one, used at various periods as pirates' nest, prison, leper colony and place of quarantine, is described in an old text as lying off the coast 'the distance a big crossbow can shoot an arrow'.

Close to it stretches an expanse of sand dunes, held tight at first by junipers and argania trees but, owing to careless deforestation at the hands of charcoal burners, threatening at one time to creep up on the town and choke it – till in 1918, under the French protectorate, foresters from Gascony, who'd met the same problem on the south-west coast of France, were called in to fix them.

A trade wind from the north-north-east, known locally as *Acharaqi* ('the east wind') or *Ouled El Bilad* ('native son') blows from April to October, keeping the place fresh.

Hannon the Phoenician, out from Carthage with sixty pentecontors (50-oared boats) on a mission to set up trading posts and colonies all along the west coast of Africa, came by this way in the fifth century before the Christian era. He writes about it in his periplus: 'From Soleis we waited for half-a-day, and arrived at a lagoon situated not far from the sea, covered with tall reeds. A great number of elephants and other animals grazed there. Once past that lagoon, we sailed another day, and founded colonies we called Acra, Melitta, Arambys. Then we came to the great River Lixos. On its banks nomads come to graze their herds. Above them lies the country of the inhospitable Ethiopians, a high, mountainous land full of wild beasts. This is where the Lixos has its source.' That Lixos must have been one of those rivers like the Wadi Sus, the Wadi Massa, the Wadi Nul, the Wadi Draa, that start up in the snows of the Atlas and many of which get lost in the sands of the south.

It was maybe Hannon who gave the site its original name, Mogdul, 'beacon tower', from which Europeans were later going to make Mogador. After the Carthaginians, the local Berber tribes saw the arrival of the Romans, hunting in what they called the *Insulae Purpurariae* for that violet red dye that can be got from the shellfish *purpura haemastoma* and that they employed to stunning effect on their togas. Then came the Arab navigators, travellers and geographers: Al-Bakri, with his *Description of North Africa*, Ibn Saïd al-Magribi with his *Kitab al-Ju'grafiya* (*Book of Geography*), based on the data gathered by Ibn Fatima who explored the Atlantic coast of Africa south of White Cape, not forgetting Al-Idrisi who, in his *Description of Spain and Africa*, calls Amogdoul 'a good harbour giving shelter to boats taking on board barley and wheat'. Leo the African was down there around 1500, giving detailed descriptions of the argania tree, and commenting ecstatically on the huge schools of sardines. Thereafter, it was Henry the Navigator's Lusitanians, Portuguese *adventureiros*, followed by Hornacheros from Spain, Danes of the Afrikanske Compagnie, Englishmen of the Barbary Company... Till the Sultan Mohammed ben Abdallah, deciding to make the site the chief spot for his naval politics, founded Essaouira, ordering all foreign consuls to settle there, under his authority. He it was who gave the city a Sea-Gate, as well as two fortresses, the harbour fort and the town fort, and a city wall with four great doors: the Bab Marrakech, the Bab Doukkala, the Bab Sebaa and the Bab Al Achur. He also endowed the mosque of the town with some rare manuscripts, and invited teachers to come in.

Essaouira was to be a centre of culture.

The town grew, commerce expanded, the six-petalled Rose of Essaouira (the town emblem) flourished. Mogador was in a strategic position, half-way between the heart of Africa and greedy West-European ports like Marseilles and London. Big caravans numbering a hundred to a thousand camels would come up from Timbuktu laden with ivory, gold, ostrich feathers, and go back down with textiles, cutlery, tea and sugar. Those were the days when ships of the London, Lisboa and African line could be seen riding at anchor in the bay, when the refined ladies and gentlemen of Essaouira drank tea flavoured with ambergris, when Pepe El Cubana was the soul of social life, and when artisans like El Alj father and son started producing their exquisite marqueterie work, encrusting tables, trays and musical instruments of mahogany, ebony and lemon tree with silver and mother-of-pearl.

The Sultan favoured a strictly protectionist policy, but had to yield gradually to general pressure, and, finally, to forces from France. The War of the Rif broke out, lasting seven turbulent years. Essaouira got some refugees, and at least one political prisoner was confined there. In the meantime, the bay sanded up, and trade went more and more to Casablanca and Agadir.

*

I'd seen Essaouira first from the heights above the town, beside me a nonchalantly munching camel with a multi-coloured blanket slung over its back. It was its owner who broke the silence, saying: '*Bonjour, soyez le bienvenu au Maroc.*' I was looking over an expanse of blue and sandycoloured waters, a cluster of islands, a red wall and a huddle of buildings. Dotted here and there in the back-country, many a white *marabout*, devoted as I learned later mainly to the seven patron saints of the region, among them Sidi El Jazouli (studied at Fez, became initiated into Sufism, founding in time his own order), who had been prominent in the resistance movement, the holy *jihad*, against the Portuguese.

Down in town, I found myself a room at the villa Mogdoul, a long, narrow whitewashed room overlooking the harbour, which bore on its walls a painting (lines of Berber signs) done on darkly tanned hide, a copy of an old map, the *Tabula Aphrica* I later saw in the local museum, and a framed letter from the Consul of France at Mogador to all French ship captains, dated Mogador, 7 September 1839: 'All captains of

French ships are advised that, except in the case of extreme danger of shipwreck, it is absolutely forbidden to land on the island of Mogador, or even make an approach to it.'

I laid out my things, including my raw silk nomad-carpet, and went out for a walk.

What I came upon first of all, on a little square, was the Café de France. A depressing place: a big pool table, bare tables set around it, and men watching football on TV. At one table, two young Frenchmen, trying to look native, sporting turbans, drinking beer. I went back out into the gathering dusk, returned to the Mogdoul, dined on a *tajine* of fish, and went to bed.

★

The next morning, early, I was down at the waterfront. A big sea was pounding in against the piles of spiky, fiery rock that fringe the harbour mouth. An old man was standing at the railing, gazing out to the horizon:

'Is it always so rough?' I asked.

'At Essaouira, it is always so.'

Later on, somebody else to whom I put the question said it was like that during the windy season.

'How long does it last?'

'That depends.'

I read later in a meteorological report on the coastal weather of Morocco that, around April, a cold current comes in from the Canary Islands, creates a depression, and the wind rushes in to fill it.

I passed the massive Sea-Gate, sculpted with crescent moons and scallop shells, and entered the harbour. Two men were selling fish from baskets and boxes, rockfish and sandfish: congers, mullet, whiting, giltheads, skate. Cats were vying with gulls for pickings. Further on, a bunch of beautifully shaped and very powerful looking boats: the *Sahara*, the *Golan*, the *Miraje*, were at their moorings. I passed by a restaurant, Le Coquillage, beside it stalls announcing *kalamar, krevittes*. Then it was another restaurant, Chez Sam. There I retraced my steps and settled on the terrace of the Bab Loachom which stands in front of the gate Al Achour, so as to watch Essaouira coming to life.

After a while, I went into town.

That's when I met Abdallah and Mohammed.

I'd noted the name of the shop, La Maison du Touareg, and was passing by when a voice hailed me from the other side of the street:

'Go in and look!'

'I'm not a buyer.'

'No matter. If you buy something, good. If you do not buy anything, good. We'll always have enough sugar in our tea.'

That, as I learned later, was Abdallah talking.

I shrugged and went in.

Inside was another young man, who turned out to be Mohammed:

'Look', he said. 'For the pleasure of the eyes.'

They had cases and cases of jewellery, and a display of goodlooking knives. I fingered a beautiful southern cross (from Togo, I was told), and a knife whose scabbard was of darkred leather and cobra skin. On either side of the blade's central runnel was a wavy line:

'Dunes', said Abdallah, who had come in behind me. 'That's the signature of the man who made it. It's from the Niger country.'

'Very nice', I said. 'Old?'

'Quite old.'

I didn't know what he meant by that. Was he talking in antiquarian terms? The knife certainly didn't *look* as if it had been made in Marrakech the month before – even taking into account the 'disaster effect' some antiquity fakers are expert at. It was maybe a working knife that had come up on the caravans. I liked the look and the feel of it.

'You want it?', said Abdallah.

'I told you – I'm no buyer, and I'm no knife-man either.'

I drifted away to look cursorily at other objects, many of which were superb in design and workmanship.

'Do you know Morocco?'

'No, but I'm learning.'

'Where have been in Morocco?'

'Marrakech', I said, to make it easy.

'The real Morocco is not in Marrakech. The real Morocco is in the south.'

He, naturally, was from the south – from a village near Erfoud.

I asked what they were doing so far up north, why they had left the south.

'*On suit la bouchée de pain*', said Mohammed ('We go where the bread is.')

But they would be going back home soon – for the big Sheep Festival.

'Everybody wants to go back to the family for the Feast.'

They would take a bus, then 'desert transport'.

'This is a big time for Moroccan transport.'

I asked them if they were really interested in the Sheep Festival.

'It is to show respect to the parents.', said Abdallah.

He asked me where I wanted to go after Essaouira.

'South', I said, 'into the Atlas.'

'The Atlas!' he cried. 'The country of the Atlas! I can tell you, my friend, I am a Moroccan, I know this place. But in the Atlas, I go crazy. In the Atlas, even nowadays there are people who have never seen a car, they think that cars eat human beings. The Atlas is another world. If you come down to the south, you must come and meet my people. In our house, the *barraka* is big.'

At that moment, a friend of theirs, from another shop down the road, came in to say he'd just bought a new jellaba and a new pair of babouches and had had a haircut – for the Sheep Festival.

I bade them farewell for that day, and went back down to the harbour with the intention of eating a plate of fish at Le Coquillage or Chez Sam.

After that, I thought I'd have a look at the forts. For some reason or other, or maybe for no reason at all ('That's the way it is', Abdallah had said in the shop about this or that aspect of Moroccan life), the harbour fort was closed. But there was no problem with the town fort, the *squala* or the *kasbah*.

The guns, big bronze cannons of Spanish fabrication, some bearing personal names: Ayandante, Léal, Aguareno, Cordero, Garapata, Almanzor, and at least one bearing the motto *Vigilate Deo Confidentes* ('Watch out, with trust in God'), were still lined up at their emplacements, but those emplacements, I saw, were now used by the citizens of Essaouira as meditation places. Nearly every slot in the wall had somebody hunched up in it reading a book or looking out to sea.

Finding myself an empty slot, I took my place on the ramparts with them.

Next day was Sunday. That meant guys laying out football pitches on the sand, with little metal goals.

I was more interested in the camel, whose master was offering rides for kids on his back. Every now and then he'd give a great big yawn, as though saying: to hell with all this. The only time he showed a glimmer of interest in the proceedings was when his master shared a big round sandwich with him.

A waste of dunes, blue sea, emptiness...

'I'd like, *inch'Allah*, to make bags.'

I was back at the Maison du Touareg, and Abdallah was telling me about the plans he had to export Moroccan handicrafts. He would need a partner in some foreign country, maybe France or Germany. It might be very small to begin with, but that didn't matter, he was always ready to catch on to an opportunity:

'Little chances I never let go by, *inch'Allah*.'

He went on then to tell me he'd managed, not without difficulty, to get himself a ticket on the next morning's bus to Marrakech. He'd visit an uncle of his who lived there and then go south – for, as aforesaid, the great Sheep Festival. I said I'd be leaving the next morning too, and, if he liked, I could drop him off at Marrakech on my way down into the Atlas. He said that was great, he would give his bus ticket to somebody else.

Because of the Sheep Festival again, we got on to religion:

'I am religious, at heart', he said, 'I don't drink alcohol. I respect Ramadan. But I don't do the five prayers. I'd like to practise better, *inch'Allah*, but, I tell you, my friend, what the Muslims do most of the time is not Islam.'

★

We left Essaouira at the same time as a blue bus marked SUD.

Moving back along the road to Marrakech:

Ounara – a copse of small pines, century plants.

El Hanchane – little nags with moth-eaten, mangy pelts.

Taftachte – the ploughing of stony ground, harvesting in another field with a sickle, a dusty township, white arcades with blue-tiled columns.

Sidi Mokhtar, a series of red earth kasbahs and another dusty town of the plains.

Piles of rubble, the sun glaring.

Oued Chichaoua – a thin trickle of water.

Everywhere, flocks of sheep.

Oued N'Fis.

A fluttering flock of five white herons.

At Marrakech, on a noisy, fuming square, I dropped off Abdallah, who pointed to a plastic bag he'd left on the seat of the car.

In the plastic bag was the extraordinary knife I had admired in Essaouira.

I spent the night there in Marrakech, at my little hotel off the Square.

★

Next morning, seven kilometres out from Marrakech, I had left the road to Fez and got on to the road to Ouarzazate. I was heading straight into the Atlas: those white crests in the misty blue.

Ouarzazate, 190 km.

'Ouarzazate, it's the desert', was what the driver of a Petit Taxi in Marrakech had told me.

I had a phrase in my head, culled from my erratic Arabic readings: *El-Medjabat el-Kobr*, 'the Great Solitude', that refers to somewhere down there in the south (along the Oued Draa, I think.)

Going up into the mountains was, as always, a multi-dimensional sensation. The atmosphere of the foothills was rosy grey and misty blue, with water trickling at the side of the road, here and there the red earth walls of a kasbah or a ksar and vegetation that passed through palm, olive, cactus, cypress and pine. Now and then, I'd meet on the road a flock of small, glossy brown-black goats, or thickpelted sheep, when it wasn't one or two of those little dainty-arsed donkeys trotting, trotting, trotting. Above all, the sound of the mountain, made up of wind, rock, water and silence.

Beyond the Tichka Col, I left the main road and turned into the Telouet Pass, moving among red rock by the side of a dried-up river bed. Passing then through the village of Telouet, I came up against a formidable red earth kasbah, half-ruined, with storks flying over its walls and turrets. I learned later this had been the home and fortress of Haj-Teheim El Glaoui, a

Berber pacha who had sided with Maréchal Lyautey and with France at the time of the Protectorate, later demanding pardon at the feet of King Mohammed newly returned from exile in Madagascar, and dying shortly after of cancer in Marrakech.

It was a good place to reflect on the history of those mountains.

Not so long ago, it was a history of bloody encounters, shrieking skirmishes and colourful cavalcades, with tribes roaming around in this rude chaos engaged more or less perpetually in mutual extermination when they weren't banding together to descend, 'like a shower of wasps and grasshoppers', as a poem puts it, on the warehouses of the wealthy merchants lolling in the souks of Marrakech, and, farther, on the suave and indulgent gulfs of the Mediterranean.

Along with the turbulent tribal life went what one might call *marabout* fever or *mahdi* madness. A *mahdi*, a 'master of the hour', is a privileged being who lives hidden for years and then suddenly reveals himself. A *marabout* is something of the same, distinguished likewise by his *barraka*, the manifest sign of his holiness, but being more deeply engaged in revolt against sheriffs and in hatred, blind or informed, of Christians. I don't claim to go into all the ins and outs of the categories. What is sure is that those mountains, like the desert lower down, bred prophets the way a carcass buzzes with flies, more than one of them with an itch to unfurl a banner and become another 'Prince of the Believers'. In 936 or thereabouts, there was one Hamin, who went about declaring that five prayers were unnecessary, two were enough, that it wasn't useful to go to Mecca or wash so much, and that a Muslim could safely eat *she*-pig, the Prophet had forbidden only *male* pig meat. He was crucified and his head was sent to Córdoba. Then there was one who said the fact he had a blue tooth in the front of his mouth was a sure sign of his holiness, especially as he had a hairy black patch in the palm of one of his hands. Not all of them of course were so simplistic. I'm thinking of El-Djazouli. Raised in the mountains, he studied at a *medersa* in Fez, the Zaffarin, before leaving for Mecca, where he stayed seven years. Back in Morocco, he spent fourteen years in solitude before setting up his 'house' (*zaouia*). It was from that hermitage his Word spread to the cities of the plains.

I came back to the dusty crumbling ruins. How many languages have been lost in places such as this? How much writing effaced by the sandy wind? How is it possible to follow up all the paths of a wandering Word?

I went back into Telouet the village, sat down at a table in the café Le Grand Atlas and asked for a coffee. At the table next to me, one man was holding another man's palm, touching it here and there, writing on it.

I got on the road again, following more or less the course of the Asif Imini, passing Agouine, Amerzgane and Tiffoultoute, till I got to Ouarzazate.

A fellow I met in front of the old red kasbah told me 'Ouarzazate' meant 'no noise town', adding that this was no longer the case: Ouarzazate now was a modern town, with its share of screeching, honking traffic. I went with my new companion down into the Old Town, where about sixty families still live. Blood was streaming down the beaten earth of the alleys: the Sheep Festival had begun.

★

My room at the Hôtel Touksal had an orange carpet on the floor, and windows of many-coloured glass.

I was awakened to the roar of *quatre-quatre* getting underway.

I got on to the road that runs along the Oued Dadès. The Atlas rising up there to the north, mauve and rosy, with snow on the crests. To the south, the Jebel Sarhro, craggy red and scrubby yellow.

Idelssan.

Amerhidil.

All along the valley, earth houses, ruined – earth returning to earth.

At Skoura there was a palm-grove, redolent with mimosa, and a trade in rose water: *Eau de Rose, Rosenwasser, Aqua di Rosa.*

'*Tu veux visiter un petit chouia?*' ('Would you like to visit a bit?')

El-Kelaa M'Gouna.

Zaouit El Bir.

Souk El Khemis.

The road went on and on, a thin ribbon, rubble on either side, then houses. Miles and miles of drab agglomeration: alongside the old earth-houses, crenellated neo-Berber monstrosities.

The colours of the mountain were amazing, and changed all the time: mauve, rose, plum-blue, lavender...

A stork's nest on the top of a minaret.

There to the south a fiery quarry, a furnace of elements, a volcanic fantasia.

My next stage was Boumaine. I tried out one hotel. But it had a pool around which twelve Germans – men fat-bellied, women wearing brightly coloured kaftans – were singing songs. I had a beer at the bar and made some enquiries.

That's how I got to the Kasbah Tazazert.

★

The Kasbah Tazazert seemed to be run by a bunch of enterprising young fellows who'd set it up only a few years before. Inside the compound, they had rigged up rows of harsh black goathair tents which they presented as an introduction to the 'nomad life'. They were expecting five buses and two hundred visitors that evening. There would be a big festival.

I'd noticed in the office at the entrance they also had rooms. Any available? Yes. They had troglodytic rooms, built into the rock, looking out over the valley. I rented one of these at a corner of the rectangular compound. It was a small room, but it had the great Atlas in its window. And on one wall was a map drawn up by a Frenchman, '*Le Sahara des nomades*', showing all the caravan tracks from the Niger up, indicating tribes and languages.

Would it be possible to have something to eat?

'Sure, with the Berbers, no problem.'

I ate couscous under a black tent, then made for the canyons farther up the Dades river country.

In the evening, I sat on the roof terrace of my room, looking out over the valley. The west was fiery red, the east a cool blue silkiness. Bullfrogs were calling from the oued.

I was up at dawn. The only sound was a dog barking. Two white herons were flying over the river.

'*Vous avez été très content chez nous un peu?*' ('Were you very happy with us a little?')

'Yes, thank you.'

I got out on the road to Erfoud.

★

Timadrouine.

Tinerhir.

Aït Aissa-Oubrahim.

It's red desert country: dusty, stony, scrubby. Against the red flanks of hills, black and white flocks.

Here and there along the road, fervent religious meetings. And sheep scenes: one poor animal hung by its hindquarters to a tree, being skinned; another being disembowelled on the pavement; one being led by a woman, who holds one of its legs in her hand, the sheep hopping and hirpling along; another tied to a post, waiting.

The redness of the desert fades at one point into yellow. Later on again it's an expanse of black metallic lava-like stone. Here and there, little sand tornados: sand wisping and whorling over the landscape.

At Erfoud, I go to a gas-station in order to ask the way to Merzouga.

Hearing me say 'Merzouga' a guy comes hurrying up:

'A tour of the dunes?'

'No, just the way to Merzouga.'

He's about to tell me when somebody behind him gives him an authoritative shout:

'I'm not the guide', he says hurriedly. 'I don't know the road. He's the guide. He knows the road.'

The other fellow turns up, shoves the first man brutally aside:

'A tour of the dunes?'

'No thanks.'

I get the information as to the Merzouga road from an ordinary citizen.

You had to follow the macadam right to the end. Then you went along a track marked at 100-yard intervals by small green and white poles.

Rosy dunes on the horizon.

I was making for the Kasbah Oudika.

An adobe building. Nine rooms. Roof of cedar trunks and cane. In the hallway, a cage with three parrots.

The Kasbah Oudika was run by a Frenchman, Michel. In his family, the tradition for the men was to join the 'Saharan army' of France, in the *compagnies méharistes* (camel corps). With this in mind, Michel had gone to the prestigious French military academy at St Cyr. But he had health problems and had had to give up. Never forgetting the desert, though. After some time he had managed to open, on the verge of nothingness, this guesthouse.

I was sitting in the main room, drinking coffee after my meal when an elderly Englishman came in, a brisk seventy, loud-voiced, a guide of authority, accompanied by an American tourist, a woman of about thirty-five. They sat down at a table behind me:

'At last, water – I've been thirsty all morning.'

'But there's masses of water in the boot.'

'I didn't know.'

'You didn't say you wanted water.'

'I asked where it was.'

A silence, then, tense with a slight strain in Anglo-American diplomatic relations.

At six, I was sitting out in the patio, under a fig tree, when the wind started to rise. First a breath, then a wheeze, then a howl. Soon after, the storm broke: thunder, rain, lightning. From the gateway, I could see car lights scattered out there in the grey windy mass: now single, now in a long, straggly line.

Before dinner, conversation among French folk from Perpignan:

'It's too simple to be religious, but it's too easy to say there's nothing... I can't stand people who're too sure: there is, there isn't... I think a lot... I can't help feeling there must be "something"... I don't believe in anything I can imagine... There are those who think you live and then you die, I think the cycle is more general than that... The important thing is to ask questions.'

No, lady, the essential thing is to go beyond the questions.

Into the desert.

★

I'd phoned Abdallah, the chap I'd met in Essaouira, in the afternoon. He said he'd come and pick me up in the morning to visit the dunes of the Erg Chebbi, then we would go to see Rissani.

At five o'clock the next morning, I was standing in the courtyard of the kasbah, waiting for Abdallah to turn up, and watching the sky: it was absolutely clear, and full of stars.

When Abdallah did turn up, he was accompanied by his brother, Abdelhak. It was Abdelhak who was driving, and he was a lover of American music. So that it was with the most moronic of American rock ('We love, we loove you, we looove you') pounding on the radio that we approached – along with twenty other cars, sedans, jeeps, 4X4, 2CV – the dunes of the desert.

Saying that he had 'seen it all before', Abdallah let me go into the dunes alone, while he and Abdelhak retired to a little coffee-booth.

I started walking south. It was still before sunrise. Only the wind blowing, and the tingle of sifting sand on the skin. Here and there my foot kicked against a plastic bottle left by some slob.

Then the sun rose, throbbing, throwing out its rays, casting shadows along the pure lines, scalloping the edges, the sand still sifting and smoking along the crests.

I passed an Australian – I knew he was an Australian because of the flag his tent was flying – engaged in shitting on the flank of a dune about ten yards from his abode.

In the *Book of Marvels*, Marco Polo talks about 'the song of the dunes'. Crossing the Gobi, he says he heard 'the spirits talking', as well as 'the playing of many musical instruments, especially drums'. The Touareg speak of the same phenomenon, saying it is 'the voice of the dead'. Men of the French camel corps have also said they heard it.

I didn't hear any music. Just a burning silence.

With that, I turned back.

'*Bismi elah*', said Abdallah ('in the name of God'). 'We say that', he continued, 'to create the *barraka*, make a good atmosphere.' We were seated at breakfast in the Kasbah Oudika, a breakfast laid out French style, with bowls for coffee. Abdallah looked embarrassed, as though waiting for something. At length, '*Je suis un vrai saharawi!*', he cried ('I'm really from the Sahara backlands'), explaining that, for him, a bowl meant soup – in order to drink his coffee, he was waiting for a glass.

'*Ham de elah*' ('Thanks be to God'), said his brother as we finished.

'Now we go to eat the famous Rissani pizza!', cried Abdallah.

On the way, we met up with several people carrying sheep-skins, some of them washing the skins in the river: 'They clean them – for the mattress.' And passed by the ruins of Sigil Massa: 'It's the town that fell. It's Casablanca before. The big souk: gold, silver, slaves – everything.'

As we passed under the great gateway of Rissani, Abdallah said the people here were 'rich in their pocket, but also rich in heart'. Rissani was the last palm-grove before the desert, and it had been the end-point of the long caravan trail from the Niger. He had friends here who still continued that tradition, the only ones who did. But before going to see them, he wanted to show me the mausoleum to Moulay Ali Chérif, of the Alaoui family (the family of the prophet), in Rissani's Old Town. The mausoleum was in a bad state of repair, the guardian seated at a table in a niche, behind him two black-and-white inscribed tiles, saying: 'God is one' ('No mother, no wife, no son', said Abdallah), and 'God is with those who suffer.'

We then went to the Sahara Warehouse.

We were led upstairs by a man Abdallah greeted familiarly at the door to a big room lined with multi-coloured cushions, where tea was served us. 'Berber whisky', whispered Abdallah, serving the tea from way up high: '*Saharawi* charm'. He then left me – to buy meat for the pizza, he said.

A few minutes later, another man came in, a tall, silent, solemn fellow, dressed in a blue gandura. He seated himself a couple of yards away. He didn't look as if he'd also come in for a pizza. But who knows?

Finally he broke the silence with this:

'The Berber sits low, on the floor of the earth. The Arab sits high, on a sofa.'

Not a passing remark, the opening of a dialogue.

'Are you a Berber?'

'No Berber will ever say he is a Berber. If he is from the High Atlas, he will say he is a *chleuh*, if he is from Agadir, he is a *souss*, in the Rif, he is an *amazigh*, in Algeria, he is a *kabyl*. Me, if I ask myself the question, I am Arab and Berber – Araberber', he laughed.

'What does that word Berber mean?'

'It certainly doesn't mean "barbarian", as some would like to think. That is a Roman idea. The word in Arabic is *barabira*. That means a walker on the earth (*un marcheur sur la terre*). *Br-br*, that means "earth-earth" (*terre-terre*). The Berber is a man who uses the earth, not the sea, not the sky. He walks on the earth, he works with the earth. That doesn't mean just moving about (*c'est plus que se déplacer*). It's more than walking (*c'est plus que marcher*). It's super-walking (*c'est sur-marcher*).

'That's what we do', he went on, after a pause to let the phrase sink in. It was then I realized this man was a member of the Warehouse establishment. In fact, as it turned out, he was the head of the outfit.

'In the old days, the caravans would come up regularly from the Niger to the Tafilalet. We continue the tradition. We follow the Star of the South. That is the pure life.'

I asked him how often they went down, and how – less for the actual information than just to hear his rhetoric and his logic.

'We gather a group together. We leave in trucks. Later we take to camels. And often we have to go on foot. We barter. We offer flour, tea, clothing. In exchange, we get carpets, jewellery, knives. Money is of no use in the desert.'

By this time, Abdallah had come back, saying he hadn't been able to find the meat for the pizza.

The man in blue suggested we go and look at some carpets. 'Here we go again', I thought, with memories of Marrakech:

'This one is a carpet saying welcome – it is placed at the entrance to the tent... This is a symbol of the kasbah, the sign of meeting... This is a *han-dira*, from the tribe of the Beni Ouaraïne, it is a cloak-carpet, that can be worn, with the thick hair on the outside and the short hair inside... Red is for joy. Blue is the colour of sky and sea, it means nobility, prosperity, pride of being. Green is for Islam and for hope, the great tradition of peace – it goes back to Noah's branch of olive...'

I said they were all beautiful, but I couldn't use any more carpets.

The man in blue wasn't too pleased, and showed it. He didn't even say goodbye. Just, suddenly, he wasn't there any more.

'He asked me if you would buy', said Abdallah outside on the pavement. 'I said I didn't know, *inch'Allah*.'

'French?'

'No.'

'English?'

'No.'

'German?'

'No. Russki.'

The Russki usually stumped them and made them leave me in peace. But not this informed little blighter. Back came the retort:

'You live in a cold country. Did you bring your vodka?'

It actually was quite cold in Midelt, which lies under Mount Ayachi, at the edge of the High Atlas, about two hundred kilometres north of Erfoud.

I'd come up to Midelt, stopping here and there on the way, via Zaouia-Jedida, Aoufouss, the Source Bleue de Meski, Er Rachidia, the Ziz canyon, and the Défilé N'Zaa. It was a magnificent road. Along red cliffs under an absolute blue sky. By yellow ochre flats. By sphinx-like rocks. It was geological and mineral. Whereas in the Dadès valley I had a sense of stifling, congested agglomeration, here I had a sense of openingness. Now and then, across the red flank of the hills, there would be a great straggling flock of black goats and grey sheep, bleating and mehing. But mostly it was just the rock, stony rivers unflowing, a thin line of snow on the horizon.

I had left the Tafilalet, and was now in Kehnifara province.

Coming close to Midelt, I saw writing on a hillside. I wondered what phrases could merit such a background. Given the cultural context I was in, I thought it might be a splendid sentence from the Koran... At the Kasbah Ayachi, a hotel I came across at the entrance to Midelt, I learned it was no more than birthday greetings to the king.

I settled in at the Kasbah Ayachi. It was a palegreen room with a copper lamp in the middle of the ceiling, multi-coloured carpets on the floor, and, more important, the formidable mass of Mount Ayachi looming in the window.

I thought of lunching in one or other of the dining-rooms available in the hotel – the Blue Room, the Green Room, the Orange Room (the stains on the table cloth were less visible in the Blue than in the Green or the Orange), but decided rather to look for an eating place in town.

If I was looking for a place to eat, the *restaurateurs* of Midelt were on the lookout for me and my kind. From as much as a hundred yards away, I could see the hustlers making the sign of eating. I finally found a place called L'Espoir, where I ate a couscous, then visited the souk:

'You French?'

'Yes.'

'From Bordeaux?'

'Yes.'

'We like the good red wine.'

But it was the stone-sellers I was interested in. There are several of them in Midelt.

When Sultonius Paulinus left Volubilis (the Roman name given to the territory of the Oulili) with an expedition force, Pliny (the Elder) went with him. In a text published much later, Pliny evokes 'those solitudes covered in black dust from which emerge rocks that seem burnt by fire'.

I knew exactly what he was talking about. I'd crossed those landscapes. I'd seen those stones, felt them in my hands.

Moroccans had been trying to sell me stones ever since I crossed the Tichka Pass. In order to sell stones to tourists, they're ready to commit the most heinous of geological crimes. Not only do they rip out, bludgeon out the stones any old way, they *colour* them. They'll paint quartz crystals with poppy juice or even fluorescent paint. These obscenities they hold up high in the air at the roadside, hoping to bedazzle and beguile the traveller. It works, unfortunately, otherwise they would have given up the hideous practice long ago.

But in Midelt it was different.

First of all, in my wanderings through the town, I'd come across the Geology Centre (Direction de la géologie) of the Ministère de l'Énergie et des Mines. They had a big map of the *Schéma structurel du Maroc* on the wall: the *Domaine rifin*, the *Domaine mésétien et atlantique*, the *Domaine anti-atlasique et saharien*, with detailed information on magnetism and tectonics. I had a little talk there about the whole geology of the region.

Then there were the stone-shops themselves.

The first one I visited stood opposite the Teinturerie l'Élégance. The man let me look around, and look around again. Then, seeing I was a difficult customer, he asked me if I would like to see his *secret* collection. I said I would. He took a key and opened a glass case that stood behind the counter. We admired together the splendid pieces of red erythrine, green anglesite, blue azurite and yellow vanadinite he had gathered there. 'Nature is very strange', he commented.

Another one farther down the road also had some very beautiful stones. He let me look round his shelves while he took out his prayer mat and did his devotions (I could hear him murmuring behind me), then went to fetch a tray from his back room. He had some of the most exquisite pieces of vanadinite I've ever seen.

Excited at the new stones I had acquired, I went back to my hotel to admire them in ecstatic silence.

Next day, I left for Fez.

★

'At daybreak, as I walked on the banks of the river, the moanings of a dove, perched on a tree of the garden, made me weep tears. The hand of dawn had just effaced the ink of darkness, and dew was flowing from the smiling mouths of the flowers...'

That's one of those sickening 'city poems' (*oroud el-beled*), a hundred metaphors to the mile, that were once all the rage in Fez, this one, by Ibn Omaïr, a native of Spain, being among the favourites.

Fez, which the locals pronounce *Faz*, is three towns in one. There's the French-styled Ville Nouvelle, then there's El Jedid, which was 'the new town' a few centuries back, and then there's old Fez, El Bali.

My hotel, a converted palace, was in El Bali, but I was up that morning in the Ville Nouvelle.

There are two cafés up there. One, the Café de la Renaissance, like a big waiting-room. The other, the Café de l'Empire, like a big disaffected waiting-room.

I was sitting in the Renaissance, drinking a coffee. A thin rain was falling over the intellectual city of the Magreb.

I'd left Midelt at sunrise a couple of days before. The Jebel Ayachi was all blue and rosy – absolutely superb. Thereafter I'd crossed the Arid plateau: big darkred buttes and snowy peaks on the horizon. A few miles up from Timehdit, I'd entered a forest of cedars, grey cloud drifting over them, frost melting, dripping from the branches.

Now I was back in civilization.

I'd sat in the gardens of Boujeloud, under mutilated plane-trees, beside a pool of stagnant water, plastic bottles stuck here and there in the green scum, while students walked about with notebooks in hand, learning up a lesson. I'd wandered about in the Andalusian quarter of El Jedid. I'd stood at the Northern Tower, among the Merinid tombs, looking down at the whole spread of the city over both banks of the river. There a man had come up to me offering bags of goat skin he said he made with his wife: 'You don't have to buy, chief. I'm no nuisance. My father was a soldier in France for twenty-five years.'

I'd also gone into an antiquarian shop, specializing in hand-written Korans. A lot of them were moth-eaten, worm-eaten, with back pages and covers that had been used for commercial transactions. But one or two of them were bound in gazelle skin, with gold lettering on the front cover. I showed interest. 'Two thousand dhirams', the merchant said. I smiled. He then went on: 'Forget about the two thousand. People like you bring the *barraka*. We'll come to a good price.' I said I'd think about it.

After the Koran shop, I'd gone to the Medersa Bou Inania. Grass growing among the green tiles, cats prowling among the ruins, the slit through which bread (charity from the wealthy) was passed to poor students.

It was coming out of the Medersa that I met the man in the red jellaba. There he was, with a big hood over his face showing little more than his gleaming eyes:

'Guide?'

For once, I said: 'Yes'.

I knew that what I was after now might be difficult to find.

'I want to visit the house of Ibn Khaldûn.'

'Ah, embroidery', he said.

'No', I said. 'History, philosophy, poetry...'

He looked startled, but wasn't willing to give in. He consulted a passing friend.

It transpired that, while the lower half of a certain house was still the 'Ibn Khaldûn house', the upper floor was used by an embroidery school. The Ibn Khaldûn house was supposedly closed – because of the Sheep Festival. At this, the man in the red jellaba, who looked as if he could have guided Dante in hell better than Vergil, not to be defeated, said there were other Ibn Khaldûn things to see nearby: carpets, ceramics, jewellery. I said those things had nothing to with Ibn Khaldûn. He seemed reluctant to agree, but finally did. We parted company.

The next morning, I decided I'd have a try on my own, and went off in what I took to be the right direction. I hadn't gone very far when I heard the familiar word:

'Guide?'

'I've got my book', I said, to get rid of the fellow.

The book I had under my arm was Vol. 3 of De Slane's French translation of Ibn Khaldûn's *Prolegomena*, which isn't exactly a guide to the streets of Fez.

'But books are dead!' he cried.

'Not to live minds', I said.

A bit farther on, it was a merchant who wanted to stop me:

'I'm in a hurry.'

'People in a hurry are already dead!'

'Slow people are dead before they die!'

I didn't really believe that. I just wanted to disturb all the sententious complacency.

So I wandered around on my own – but didn't succeed in re-locating the house of Ibn Khaldûn.

That's why the next day I asked the man behind the counter at the hotel to recommend me a well-informed guide. This guide was waiting for me when I came down from my room at nine. I explained what I wanted: no shops, no carpets. Obviously not considering me an interesting client at all, he immediately passed me on to what I took to be the second string man. Once again I stated my requirements. This man also estimated I wasn't interesting, and passed me on to the lowest level possible man.

That's how I got to make the acquaintance of Saïd Al-Fazi.

I told him what I wanted, and how I'd got lost the day before: 'You can't say you know Fez until you get lost in it.'

Saïd lived alone with his mother, who made belts. He'd studied linguistics, he said, at the university, and had been a guide for thirty years, liking the job: 'To see strangers makes the mind bigger.' He knew Ibn Khaldûn, a *chouia*, a little – he'd studied parts of the *Muqaddima* at the university. Saïd chain-smoked cigarettes – an American brand. When he had nothing to say, but felt something had to be said, he would say: '*Bien-venue au Maroc*', so that I must have heard from his lips 'Welcome to Morocco' about a hundred times. But he was a likeable fellow. And he took me to the house of Ibn Khaldûn, pointing out several other locations on the way: 'A sacred Jew lived there' (pointing down a little lane), or 'that's the house where a famous player of Andalusian music lived.'

There was no museum at all, said Saïd. The house of Ibn Khaldûn was now a private residence. Maybe that was why he kept well away, on the other side of the street, while I went up to the door and knocked. It was opened by a woman about 35 years old. When I said: 'Excuse-me for disturbing you, is this the house of Ibn Khaldûn?', she called out to somebody else. We were in a small patio, and she had been doing washing. She now hid behind the hung-out washing, as though behind a veil, while I talked with her son. He simply confirmed this was indeed Ibn Khaldûn's house. I said I was surprised there was no plaque on the wall to make this known to all. He said there had been one, but it had fallen off.

It was because the whole world had somehow 'fallen off' that Ibn Khaldûn started to write. The Andalusian culture was being reduced to its last stand in Granada. Mongols and Turks were threatening in the East. Science and literature had become narrow and rundown. The sources of life and thought seemed dry.

Ibn Khaldûn enquires into the causes of this decay in the world of Islam, and into the rise and decline of civilizations in general. He's usually classified as a historian. But cultural anthropology and sociology are just as much a part of his project as pure history, and what he called his new science, *Umran*, goes in fact farther out again. It's a meditation on the very notion of world. In the *Prolegomena*, Ibn Khaldûn starts off with geography – the influence of milieu. Then he goes into a comparison between nomadism (*badiya* – bedouinity) and sedentarism (*hadara* – urbanity). Thereafter he traces the contours of politics and economics. And he ends up with a long presentation of Sufi mysticism followed by poetics.

Born in the Ifriqiya (at Tunis), Ibn Khaldûn moved for years all over the Maghreb, with incursions into Spain, then in 1372 he retired to the fortress of Ibn Salima in Algeria in order to write the *Prolegomena* (prolegomena to a 'history of the world', *Kitab al-Ibar*). After that, he took to teaching, at Cairo, later in Fez, at the Carouiyine University, arousing the enthusiasm of students, at the same time as the hostility of those in more settled positions. Teaching was a dangerous enterprise. Later on, in the sixteenth century, Ibn El-Ovancharisi was teaching at the Carouiyine one evening after sunset when a band of ruffians sent by the sheriff broke into the place, pulled him down from his chair, and murdered him on the spot.

Ibn Khaldûn lived to write his autobiography, *Tarif*, but as an isolated figure. I imagine him there in that house, getting his water from the fountain close by, having his bread baked in an oven pretty much the same as the one down the street.

Alone, totally alone – but in touch with all time and all space.

★

From the terrace of my room at the Akkam Palace I had a plunging view of the Old Town, spread out over the river basin, palegold and smoky black in the late afternoon light. Here and there, the green-tiled roofs of the mosques. On the hillside, scatterings of white cemeteries.

Below, in the garden, royal palms and fountains, cacti flowering yellow, and little squares of many coloured plants.

On the terrace, and on adjacent roofs, a flying population of sparrows, starlings, blackbirds and grey-brown kestrels.

At seven, there would be the Allah Akhbar called from all the minarets, in various voices, via megaphones. At night, it would be dogs howling through the streets. Then, in the morning it would be the call again from the muezzin.

In his section on Sufism in the *Prolegomena*, Ibn Khaldûn speaks of a move from science to presence, and of the rising, via 'tastes', 'openings', 'enlightenings' and 'ecstasies', to 'the farthest horizon'.

That's what I was thinking about, there at Fez, in Morocco, on the edge of the great desert. The farthest horizon...

The Road to Rangiroa

It all began with a vague idea: that of a kind of wide-ranging mental navigation in a great ocean of emptiness. Maybe a series of Pacific Sketches that would be a sort of postscript to history. Maybe a long horizontal rock-and-roll scroll of sea, volcano and atoll to be called something like Pacific Ocean Blues.

★

The first stage was Los Angeles, arrived at after a nine hours' flight out of Paris Charles-de-Gaulle over by Hudson's Bay, then down the States, finally via Utah.

Before you can set foot on American soil, you have to fill in a green form for the US Department of Justice. On that form, you have to say, yes or no, if you're a drug-addict, if you have a criminal record, if you've ever kidnapped children, if you have been or are at present engaged in espionage, sabotage, or terrorism.

If you say 'yes' to any of these questions, they probably shoot you on sight. If you say 'no', you will be suspected of lying and they'll keep an eye on you.

You're also informed on this form that it takes six minutes on average to fill it in. If you do it in four, they offer you a job in Silicon Valley. If it takes you eight, forget it, no future, but you can always lodge a civic complaint with Washington DC (Office of Management and Budget, Paperwork Reduction Project).

There were huge Stars and Stripes hanging from the roof of LA airport, to show whose side God was on – but don't ever dare make any cracks about it; these people are not only patriots, they're believers. While you're in the vicinity, just say cheese all the time – with a capital C.

Cheese, I said to the attendant.

Cheese, I said to the baggage control man.

Cheese, I said to the cop. In fact, to him I overdid it and said it double: he looked suspicious.

★

I'd been in an off-and-on correspondence for years with this American poet, Jasper Wilkes. Wilkes lived out at Pasadena and taught Creative Writing at Cal State. He'd been at me several times to drop in on him, which I'd never done – but this time I did, just to break the journey, and, for old time's sake, to salute California, the old Barbary Coast.

I had a bedrock feeling for that territory of California, which came largely from a reading, at about the age of fifteen, up on my own west coast, of Richard Henry Dana's *Two Years before the Mast*. Of a little place on the coast, Dana has this to say: 'It was the only port for a distance of eighty miles, and about thirty miles in the interior was a fine plane country [...], in the centre of which was the Pueblo de Los Angeles – the largest town in California – and several of the wealthiest missions, to all of which San Pedro was the seaport.'

But that was in the 1830s, and times have somewhat changed. If the bedrock of the Santa Gabriel hills is still the same (for the moment), California nowadays is a place of total vapid nonentity.

The way John Kwoh, one of Wilkes's friends, put it was this: 'We've got what the sociologists call multiculturalism – but nobody's cultured.'.

Against this background, you have all the manifestations of what the local Latinos call *la vida loca* ('the crazy life'), with gangs festering viciously in the back-alleys, and streets seething legally with trigger-jittery police.

Neither bedlam nor pandemonium, nor anything interesting like that, just a nothingness full of screaming emptiness and howling automobiles going nowhere.

As to Wilkes the poet, he was a nice enough fellow, but he was so full of his 'creativity' that every time he let loose a fart he wanted to put it on the internet.

After a week, I'd had more than enough.

Which is why I found myself so quickly back at Los Angeles International Airport, saluting the Santa Monica and the Santa Ana hills, wishing them well in that glittery vacuum, as the plane got out over the Pacific.

★

A few years ago, in 1947, Thor Heyerdahl shook the world with his Kon-Tiki expedition, which had been out to provide practical proof that a simple raft could leave the coast of South

America (Callao in Peru) and reach the far islands of Oceania (the Tuamotu Group). It was the exploit that hit the headlines. But more interesting than the exploit was the whole theory behind the expedition, a theory which Heyerdahl laid out in his massive study, *American Indians in the Pacific*:

> The question to be dealt with in the present work is that of the complex origins of the Polynesian people, the easternmost islanders of the Pacific. This question is indeed neither new nor unattempted, as it arose from the European discovery of the Pacific island world and has since provoked a continual series of theories almost as rich in variety as in number. The present work is no exception in this respect, as it presents material in support of yet another diverging answer to the same old question. It differs, however, to my knowledge, from all the rest in being the first systematic attempt to turn face to the winds and examine the bordering slopes of the New World for vestiges indicating the route of man in the open Pacific.

The evidence Heyerdahl brings forth is impressive, whether it be the comparison of petroglyphs, stone images and house-posts from the north-west coast of America (Vancouver island, the Bella Coola valley) and others from Tahiti and Hiva-oa; the relationship between the pre-Inca *tici* (light, the foundation of things, the beginning) and the *tiki* of Polynesia, particularly Mavi-tiki, who, fishing in the open ocean (with human ears as bait, according to one story), caught the Polynesian islands on his hook and brought them up from the depths; the *kawa* ceremony in Polynesia and the making of *cawau* in Chile; the tradition, strong among the Kwakiutl, of the American wanderer, the solar culture-hero, Kane, Kani, who seems close to the Maori ancestor *Tane* (Hawaiian, *Kane*); the image of bird-men in Peru and Polynesia.

Heyerdahl makes a good case. But all those concordances don't necessary mean that Polynesia was peopled from America. It could simply mean that all those signs belong to one large culture-space, whatever its origin.

Leaving Heyerdahl, I come to a sharper mind, that of Ernest Fenollosa.

In his *Epochs of Chinese and Japanese Art*, Fenollosa (father from Malaga in Spain, born in Salem, studied philosophy and art at Harvard, professor of aesthetics at Tokyo, commissioner of fine art to the Japanese government) speaks of 'the unwritten odyssey of the Pacific', 'those vast silent waters', traversed by 'the carved canoes of maritime races', going on to say that 'the bulging broken contours of East Asia could not avoid the currents of waters and of men, whose relics are strewn, like wreckage, half around the globe, from the Fuegian coast of South America to the Aleutian Archipelago and from Khamskatcha southward to Tasmania.'

There, the space is radically and also rationally opened, with a sense of complex movement, and with a desire to look into the widely dispersed 'wreckage': a scattered repertoire of signs and the patterns of an art.

For Fenollosa, the salient features of Pacific art are faces more or less human, with staring eyes, and playing about those faces, bands of design. Alongside those faces, figures of fish and bird. In all of it, a great and fine sense of spacing, harmonious spacing.

Which brings me to my own little find.

In the plane there with me, during my long flight to Tahiti, I had a little figure sculpted in dark wood that had been in my possession for years. It was in the hills of Taiwan I came across it, at a place called Wulai, in what had been the territory of the Atayal tribe. It's a figure hardly two inches tall: a man squatting on his hunkers with his hands round his knees. As to the face, large in proportion to the rest, it is typically 'Polynesian': big eyes (I interpret: to scan the horizon), big ears (to hear the sounds of the world), a big mouth (to speak the great language).

All the discussion I've just evoked was concentrated for me in that little figure.

I was turning it over in my hand as we began our descent – the atoll of Rangiroa in the Tuamotu archipelago over there to the left – down towards Faaa airport.

★

Having touched down on Tahiti, I asked a taxi-driver to take me to the nearest hotel. That's how I arrived at the Tahiti Beachcomber, room 399 (I'd asked, as usual, for a lodging on the edge).

Ia orana is the salutation, meaning 'welcome', 'how do you do' and things like that.

When the baggage-man came with my luggage, barefoot, bare to the waist, a strapping lad with a wreath of leaves round his head, there was a centipede on the floor.

He made to stamp it with his foot.

'Hey', I said, 'no.'

'Are you a Buddhist or something?', he said, laughing.

'Something', I said.

As he put down my bags, I saw he had a long blue tattoo on his back:

'I gather you're no Buddhist', I said. 'But does that tattoo on your back mean anything?'

He said they were the marks of his family, which went back a long time, the tortoise and the stingray.

'Where are you from? Tahiti?'

'Bora Bora.'

He said his great grandfather was Corsican. Another great-grandfather was Scottish. All his mothers were Polynesian.

After that little religious-ethnological episode, I was on my own again.

Being at the end of the Beachcomber building, I was close to the dark lava rock. It was raining, shower after shower, hissing and whispering. Between showers, I could hear small birds in the bushes crying: *kee-wee, kee-wee*. At times, the island of Moorea would be stark on the horizon, its jagged, scalloped heights, its peaks and fangs, blue, bluegrey, then it would disappear, then again come back.

During a longer lull, I went out for a walk, and came across a gardener.

'Is the rain going to continue?', I said, more just to get the conversation going than for the sake of meteorological information.

'Oh, yes, chief, it'll take a wind to sweep it all away.'

A bird passed, looking very much like what they call in the Indian Ocean a *mynah*.

'How do you call that bird?', I asked.

'*Manoo tai*', he said.

'Meaning?'

'White blackbird. We call them 'white', because it was the Whites that brought them in. *Tai*, white, is also a family name. It's not vulgar. It goes into the depth of things. The real depth of things. Because there's a lot of people that just imagine things.'

This was almost too much. I hadn't expected to get so fast into anything that you might call, with all kinds of hesitations and reservations, 'the depth of things'. But there it was. I didn't care to insist on it, killing it with comment. So, stashing it away like a little pearl, for future contemplation, I steered the conversation back to a more superficial level.

This gardener hadn't always been a gardener. A sailor, he'd been to all the islands: the Society Isles, the Gambier, the Australs, the Marquesas, the Solomons. He'd even been as far as Australia, New Zealand, Hawaii. In addition to Polynesian and French, he could speak English, several brands of English:

'There's real English', he said. 'Then there's Australian English and all that. And then there's beach-la-mar.'

Beach-la-mar!

It was a long time since I'd heard of beach-la-mar.

It took me back to early days on the west coast of Scotland, when I was studying, among other books on linguistics, Otto Jespersen's *Mankind, Nation and Individual from a Linguistic Point of View* and his *Language – its Nature, Development and Origin*. It's in a chapter on Pidgin English that Jespersen talks of beach-la-mar, from the Portuguese *bicho de mar*, a sea-slug (the trepang), taken over into French as *bêche de mer* ('sea-spade') and imported into English as *beach-la-mar*, the seafaring trade-jargon of the Pacific, the *lingua franca* of the fo'c's'le, culling words from languages diverse and sundry, where 'know' is *savvy*, where any small axe is a *tomahawk*, where 'small' is *likkilik* (Polynesian, *liki*), where every woman is 'a Mary', where any written document is a *nusipepa*, where all tinned food is *pisupo*, where anything made of glass is *a squareface* (from the traditional square gin-bottle) and where, the vocabulary being so limited, composite expressions are a necessity, so that to evoke a piano, you have to say 'big fellow bokus you fight him he cry', and to call attention to a bald paleface, you have to say 'you savvy that fellow white man coconut belong him no grass'.

It's a pretty primary linguistic context. But at the same time, there's a kind of universality to it, and even an absurd dadaistic, pataphysical, polyglottic poetry.

The rain falling again, harder than ever, I went back up to my room, watching the surf running in a long white broken line along the reef.

★

Loaded with some exotic cash from a bank (good-looking notes and coins in FCP – 'Francs Cours Pacifique'), I'd been wandering along the waterfront and up the back streets of Papeete, the metropolis of French Polynesia, passing by the Kon-Tiki Hôtel.

The first impression you have is that you've stumbled into a society consisting entirely of sumo wrestlers. It's only after that initial general observation has faded that you begin to have an eye for varieties of human appearance and behaviour, as well as for other items of the town.

At the corner of the Boulevard Pomaré and the Rue Jeanne d'Arc, a woman was seated in the shade of a tree suckling a child, while three of those tawny 'island dogs', laid out and panting, enjoyed the same shade. Inside the red-steepled cathedral of the Immaculate Conception, a man was sleeping on a bench, turning the joss-house (beach-la-mar for 'temple') into a doss-house. Hep guys strolled about with self-conscious abdominals and cultural identity tattoos, wearing skull-fitting spandex caps or Black Power du-rags with a flap to protect the neck and a band to be tied around the forehead. Some fine-looking girls – one with a blue tattoo in the little valley of her breasts. But beware, if you see an extraordinary female figure in Papeete, it might be no woman at all, could be a *rae rae*, a transvestite, one of the specialities of the place.

Street vans were selling hamburgers, Coca-Cola and *doughnuts à la tahitienne*. And on the quay side, a huge liner, a multi-tiered monstrosity, the *Tahitian Princess*, was massively in dock.

Above it all, the smoky green gulches, the purple ridges, the great brooding basaltic brows of the Tahiti heights.

I took a seat on the terrace of the café Le Rétro.

There have been many sacred places on Tahiti, but Papeete was never one of them. In fact it existed only as a purposeless plot of marshy ground till an evangelist by the name of Crook poked up his tent and started preaching. He called the place, predictably enough, Hope Town. The people kept calling it

Vaiete, after the name of the local river. Then finally, for some hidden reason, the word 'Papeete' emerged, meaning 'water basket', and it stuck.

The first map of Tahiti was made by a navy hydrographer off the Spanish ship *Aguilla*, in 1774: a map of the *Ysla de Amát* (after the name of the viceroy of Peru, Don Manuel de Amát) or *Otaheti*, and the first European to live in Papeete was one Maximo Rodriguez, off that same ship. Which no doubt accounts for a certain Spanish influence on the early language of the town.

When Herman Melville, who had just escaped from the hell of a whaler with its weavilled meat and wormy biscuits, was housed in Papeete, it was in the hoosegow (Spanish *juzgado*, 'tribunal') known as the *Calabooza Beretani* (Spanish *calabozo*, 'dungeon'). That was in 1842, when he'd taken part in a mutiny of sailors fed up with lousy conditions and crazy captains. The Papeete calaboose was no very tough penitentiary, things were polynesianly easygoing and Melville was probably able to continue smoking his favourite Mexican cigars, as well as thinking things over metaphysically in peace. He'd just lived through the experiences (and fantasies) that were to go into his first book, *Typee*, with its painfully amateurish but also voyeuristic sub-title, 'a Peep at Polynesian Life during a Four Months' Residence in a Valley of the Marquesas'. There in the Tahitian hoosegow he found himself in the company of a rascal familiarly called Long Ghost, a Scotsman, who had been surgeon on a British emigrant ship bound for Sydney, before deserting.

This Long Ghost, a pale, bony character about six feet tall, who was always quoting Virgil ('*continuo, ventis surgentibus, aut freta ponti incipiunt agitata tumescere...*') and who had an eldritch sense of humour that tickled Melville's mind, was the son of Allan Cunningham, a poet. Few people nowadays, in this unlettered age, may have heard of the poet Allan Cunningham, but in the early part of the nineteenth century (he died in 1842) he had some reputation, and when I was a school pupil at Largs, in Ayrshire, I still had to learn by heart as part of the curriculum one of his poems: 'A Wet Sheet and a Flowing Sea', with its evocations of 'snoring breezes', 'the world of waters' and 'white waves heaving high'.

In the company of Long Ghost, Melville was able to escape

from the calaboose in Papeete and make for the island of Moorea where they had the fun together that led to Melville's second book, *Omoo – a Narrative of Adventures in the South Seas.*

While Melville was vagabondizing from port to port, more and more evangelists, Protestants and Mormons, were pouring in from whalers out of New Bedford and Nantucket to convert the Polynesian pagans and bring in the democratico-imperialistic Pax Americana to the Pacific. Since these Yankee evangelists, along with their equivalents of the LMS (the London Missionary Society), had told the naked natives that, for the saving of their souls, they must clothe themselves, the scene at the Papeete waterfront was picturesque to grotesque, with native Polynesians garbed in the rags and odd ends of toggery discarded by sailors. Behind the burlesque carnival, there was also a more sordid scene of drunkenness, prostitution, brawling and disease. Long gone were the images of paradisal innocence broadcast by Cook and Bougainville.

Beside me, there in the café Le Rétro, was a Tahitienne in black, with long black hair, in it a red hibiscus flower, who was laughing throatily as she talked into a portable phone. To my linguistically tuned ear, Polynesian sounded phonetically like Japanese. When Titava (I learned her forename later) pronounced the place-name 'Outamarao', I couldn't help hearing the name of the floating-world painter, Utamaro.

At another table a burly Hawaiian, who seemed to be playing, with some gusto and obvious enjoyment, the rôle of Cicerone to an American professor from Ann Arbor in Michigan, was saying, in English (very twangy American English), that Papeete would soon be another Honolulu. There was no more room in the town, so they'd have to grow upwards, US-style. There in Polynesia, he said, they had 'come out of the darkness into the light'. They were out to create business. Some of the other islands might want to protect their beauty, their environment, but there on Tahiti, in Papeete, they knew more and more they were a growing country. They had no choice, they had to move ahead, forge the future. Anyway, they were already 'used to this life-style', they didn't care.

A bit farther still, a Frenchman was talking to another Frenchman. He'd come over years before as technical advisor to the CEP, the Centre d'Expérimentation du Pacifique (France's nuclear research centre at Mururoa), and had fallen in love with the country. Now he sold car accessories. He was glad the island and the town had cleaned itself up a bit, but he hoped 'progress' wouldn't go too far; there was a balance, a harmony to be respected.

★

I went back out into the streets, and pretty soon found myself at the market, between the Rue François Cardella and the Rue du 22 septembre 1914, the Rue des Halles and the Rue Colette.

Here you have what I saw described in a French text as 'a concentration of Tahitianity'. The approach is by a cluster of little bazaars and stalls: chowchow shops, tinpan shops, pants-and-skirts shops, and a bedlam of fuming, honking trucks.

As to the market itself, it gathers in produce not only from the various districts of Tahiti – Faaa, Punaauia, Paea, Papara, Mataiea, Papeari, Faaone, Hitaa, Mahaena, Tiarei, Papenoo, Mahina, Arue, Pirae – but from the other Windward isles of Moorea, Maiaa, Tetiaroa, and from the Leeward islands of Maupiti, Tahaa, Huahine, not forgetting produce from still farther-flung places: the Tuamotu, the Gambier, the Australs. The fishing boats have been out all night, and they've brought in pelagic fish such as tuna (*aahi*), bonito (*auhopu*), shark (*mao*), mahimahi, as well as lagoon, coral or reef fish, such as carangas, catfish, parrotfish (*aati*), moonfish, napoleons and flying fish (*marara*). The vegetables of the traditional Tahitian diet – taro, breadfruit (*uru*), sweet potato, plantain (*fei*) and other bananas – are all there, along with mangos, pineapples, papaya, kava, coconuts, yams – and pork, and chicken. But there are also Chinese ready-made dishes (*maa tinito*), such as *ham soy*.

The place is crowded, and there is a great variety of people. But what is surprising, for anyone who knows the markets of, say, the French West Indies, is the *silence*. Here, there is no hustling, no shouting, no joking, no altercation. Over it all, one hears only an ambiance song, provided by loudspeakers, and every time I was in that market, that day and the days to come, the song was that well-worn Italo-American chestnut: *Che sera sera*.

After roaming again about the harbour for a while, noting

the names of other cruise-ships in dock: *Wind Star, Legend of the Seas, Crystal Symphony*, alongside some inter-island cargo-boats (the *Mareva Nui*, the *Maris Stella*, the *Rairoa Nui*, the *Aranui*) and a slim, sleek ship discreet in military grey, I went back to the Rétro, just in time to take refuge from another long shower of rain.

Ordering a rum, I let myself drift into another freewheeling Melvillean meditation.

After *Typee* and *Omoo*, Melville was surfing on a great tide of success, but he was getting billed more and more as an exotic travel-writer, as an adventurer among cannibals, and such a categorization did not please him, because it did not correspond at all to what he felt lay dormant in the farther reaches of his mind.

'Damn the bitch-goddess', he thought, 'I have to follow the path, the multiple, meandering paths of my wayward genius.'

That's when he started working on *Mardi* (as in Mardi Gras).

The scene was still Polynesia, but the atmosphere was no longer ethno-lyrical, it was cosmo-philosophical.

In order to limber up intellectually, in order to develop his cervical muscles, Melville started off by plunging into the metaphysical archives of the world, reading Plato, Seneca, Thomas Browne, Coleridge, Carlyle.

This time, it's not with a romantic Toby Green that he deserts, as in *Typee*, or with an erratic Long Ghost, as in *Omoo*, but with one Jarl, supposedly a Hebridean post-Viking sailor from the Isle of Skye, who has, significant detail, lost all sense of a mother tongue, be it English or Scottish, but talks a wild cosmopolitan lingo, a kind of super beach-la-mar.

Another significant detail. In the two earlier books, Melville-author deserted to an island: Nuka Hiva in the Marquesas, Tahiti in the Society Archipelago. Here, he deserts in the open sea, on the open ocean. We're no longer concerned with adventures among strange lands and savage tribes, but with lonely speculation about man-in-society, man-in-the-universe.

The Mardi archipelago consists of fifteen islands: Valapee, Juam, Okonoo, Mondolfo, Maramma, Padulla, Diranda, Dominoza, Vivenza, Hooloomooloo, Serenia, Flozella-a-Nina... Every one of them presents an aspect of civilization, the whole constituting an account of human progress. Some present certain States (Britain, America), others represent types of humanity (dreamers, criminals), others again states of being (pensiveness, platitude), the conclusion being that it's all madness (*hooloomooloo*), and the only 'solution' a kind of sad tranquillity (*serenia*). At one point in the book, Babbalanja, another of the author-traveller's companions, says that he is looking for the essence of things, the precious pearl in the rough, rude shell. But he does not find it, and despite the recommendation of a stoical 'sad tranquillity', the search continues, in an open ocean, in an endless vagabondage...

The rain was still falling over the waterfront at Papeete, and I was well into my third rum. Finishing it, I made to leave, not forgetting to leave a little extra with the price of my drinks, according to the big notice in the café Rétro: *Tips are not tabu* (this for the benefit of readers of old guide-books in which it is stated that to offer money for service is an offence to the Tahitian sense of hospitality – the times, my friend, have changed).

I took a truck back to the Beachcomber. A 'truck' here is a lorry converted into a bus, with two benches on each side and another bench running down the middle. *Prix fixe:* 130 FCP. Night rate: 200.

★

It had been a beautiful morning: pearl-coloured, paleblue, palerose. I'd been up even before the birds, the white blackbirds with their screeching, the ground doves with their throaty *coora-coora-loo*. I'd gone for breakfast early too, to the hotel restaurant, hoping the mush-music might not yet be started up. But there it was, awful stuff, omnipresent, never-ending, the same slush, whether in English, French or Polynesian.

There were a lot of Japanese in the restaurant. California used to be la-la-land for the Japanese till crime started to escalate. Now they're saying 'sayonara Los Angeles' and going to Polynesia.

It was while drinking my second espresso, watching the cheeky, yellow-beaked mynahs pirating among the tables, that I decided to spend the day moving round the island.

My first stop was at the house of the man who wrote *Mutiny on the Bounty*, the book that gave birth to something like a quintuplet of films. They all feel they have to do it. Clark Gable did it, Marlon Brando did it. If Errol fuckin' Flynn didn't do it, he must have nearly done it. And so on. I liked it when I was ten. I've become a bit harder to please since, but I don't mind a backward-looking little pilgrimage now and then.

When I arrived in the garden after coming up the path, it was to find about twenty people sitting or hanging around, talking French and looking abysmally bored.

I went on in.

It was a fine house, spacious and graceful, and the library wasn't bad at all (it had a copy of *Purchas, his Pilgrims*, at least). As to the productions of Mr Lane, they were destined for Hollywood. His son, just as present in the house, became a cameraman there, which is genealogical logic. When I saw the photograph of a cameraman looking very pleased with himself sitting on the back of a turtle, I left.

The party of twenty French folk were still hanging about. It turned out they were participants in a symposium at the University of French Polynesia on 'Exoticism in Art and Literature'. One man, sitting under a tree, a philosopher as became immediately apparent, was talking, and continued talking for ten minutes non-stop, about the phenomenology of the coconut. OK, why not? It's at least as interesting as *Mutiny on the Bounty*. It's just that the object he was phenomenologizing about wasn't a coconut at all, it was a breadfruit.

★

'Is that for decoration or for meaning?', I said.

'Meaning', he said.

I was referring to the circular tattoo on the guy's left leg.

'So what does it mean?'

'It's not finished yet.'

'And when it's finished?'

'Serenity, love of country – things like that.'

I asked him when it would be finished.

'It takes a long time', he said. 'Unless you're very brave.'

This was at Venus Point, on Tahiti's north shore, a spit of land at the top of Matavai Bay. We were sitting on a rock beside a little beached outrigger, a *vaa*.

Venus Point is so-called not for libidinous reasons but for astronomical ones. On 26 August 1768, the good ship *The Endeavour*, with one James Cook, later Captain, in command, left the English port of Plymouth. Cook's mission was to find an appropriate spot in the Pacific island group to observe the passage of the planet Venus across the sun. On 26 January 1769, he rounded Cape Horn. On 10 April he anchored in Matavai Bay. It was at the point thereafter called Venus, on 3 June, that he was able to observe the celestial phenomenon that was the main purpose of his journey.

The first thing you see when arriving on the promontory is a sturdy white lighthouse tower, one of the many constructed round the world by the Northern Lighthouse Company of Scotland. When he stood there in 1888 during his Pacific cruise on the *Casco*, Robert Louis Stevenson remembered his early days in Edinburgh: 'Great were the feelings of emotion as I stood with mother by my side and we looked up on the edifice designed by my father when I was sixteen.'

Beyond the lighthouse, there's a monument to celebrate the arrival of the Evangel on the islands (Matavai Bay, 5 March 1797), with this declaration, in French: 'The people of Tahiti accepted the Evangel and carried it to the furthest archipelagoes of the Pacific Ocean, following the royal road of the setting sun.'

In his *Polynesian Researches*, William Ellis, of the London Missionary Society, then based on Huahine, talks of the new laws brought into the islands around 1820: thou shalt not steal pigs, thou shalt not have two women, and so on. One of them was against tattooing. According to the new legislation, to mark your body wasn't in itself a sin against God, it was just that it brought the whole pagan field and all its bad habits back in with it. So, if you got yourself tattooed, the punishment would be roadwork: twenty yards for the first tattoo, forty for the second, and so on.

Further on along the promontory, I met up with another young fellow also sporting a blue tattoo, this time on his right arm:

'What's that?' I said.

He hesitated for a moment, then answered:

'A head-crusher.'

'That means you're a tough guy and the other fellows better watch out, eh?'

'Yeah', he said, laughing.

He'd had it done when he was fifteen. It was, he said, a tradition in his family. Some people get it done at twelve. And some parents will have their infant tattooed right after birth – a little thing on the leg or the back, for luck.

★

Just after the village of Papeari stands a little museum devoted to Paul Gauguin.

It traces the life of Paul Gauguin, from Paris to Brittany, from Brittany to Paris, Panama, Martinique, Tahiti and the Marquesas.

There at Papeari, Gauguin studied what he could find about Polynesian culture, notably in the pages of Moerenhout's *Voyages aux Îles du Grand Océan*. While trying to get on with his painting (that intellectual and sensual 'synthesis' he was after), he soon found himself totally at odds with the local colonial administration as well as with the religious authorities. He had come to Tahiti looking for cheapness, peace and ecstasy. What he found himself in was a nest of degenerate, perverted hornets. That's why he left for the Marquesas. But he found them across his path there too.

I'd thought of going up to the Marquesas. I'd learned that one of the inter-island cargo-boats I'd seen in Papeete, the *Aranui*, took on passengers. Then in Le Rétro one morning, I heard a commercial traveller telling about the trip he was going to make, on the *Aranui*, to the Marquesas – to replenish the local stocks of chewing-gum and Coca-Cola. That kind of put me off. Especially as there was also something else. About a century after Gauguin, a Belgian popular singer decided to spend his last years on the same island where Gauguin worked, and he's a blot on the landscape. You can no longer see a reference to the Marquesas without some mention of 'the two artists'. But the 'two artists' just don't belong to the same category. This kind of confusionism makes the context a lot less attractive.

I decided to give the Marquesas the go-by. Gauguin would

have finally left them anyway – for Spain, or maybe, once more, Brittany.

★

Emerging from the little Gauguin museum, I made for the Museum of Tahiti and the Islands.

This has none of the cogency, the coherence and the kind of cultural perspective that Gauguin was out for, and that he would have liked to see in a Museum of Oceanic Art. It is nothing like the museum that Victor Segalen, who was moving about these islands before leaving for China, would have liked to found in Pekin. But it's interesting enough, with a mix of geology, archeology, ethnology and sociology.

And it was there I saw the more or less exact replica of the little 'Pacific' figure I'd picked up on Taiwan. Made, not of wood, like mine, but of human bone, this figure was catalogued as an *iui po'o*, a 'tube ornament', an *ornement tubulaire*, its site 'the Marquesas', its date 'nineteenth c. or earlier'.

★

Having gone round Tahiti, the next thing to do was to go into it.

That night, in room 399 of the Beachcomber, I took out my detailed map of the island and had a good look. Even nowadays, there's only one road, or maybe rather a track, that goes right across the island. It's the Papenoo Trail, from Papenoo in the north to Otiaroa in the south, following, to begin with, the valley of the Papenoo River.

After consulting the map, I had a look at bits of information I'd picked up in Papeete, and phoned up a man who ran a landrover service.

That's how on the following morning at nine o'clock I was all set to cross Tahiti.

The Papenoo (*pape*, same as in Papeete, 'water') Road is a rough mountain track being cleared, solidified and widened by the French army. At the rate they're going, it'll take them about half-a-century to make it to the other side. Which is OK by me.

All around, scatterings of black lava boulders.

To the left, the rushing green waters of the Papenoo, fed into farther up by the Maaituhine, the Mareiati, the Vaituoru

212

and several others. To the right, the Plateau of Atohei and Mount Taatehau.

Nowadays, 80 per cent of the population of Tahiti lives in a little arc around Papeete, and valleys like the Papenoo have practically been abandoned. But you can see remnants of cultivation if not habitat here and there: patches of yam, banana, sweet potato, kava, plantain, taro.

It was a pretty rough ride, but beautiful.

Big cliffs on the right, with cascading waterfalls.

Away up in the high valley, only cloud whispering over the flanged edges of the caldera...

I stayed a couple of days up there, at a mountain resort called the Relais Maroto, reading Moerenhout's *Voyages*, walking along the River Maroto. On the second morning, I found an orchid on the river bank, on the branch of a tree, with green translucid flowers such as I'd never seen before anywhere. I spent a long time with it, fascinated.

'The more a traveller extends the circle of his knowledge', says Moerenhout, 'the more isolated he becomes, alone with the universe.'

★

The murena eased its way, very slowly, very precautiously, out of its hole in the coral. There was a coral head just below the deck of my bungalow, frequented also by a school of flickering blue fishlets.

It was daybreak on the island of Huahine, with a frenzied screeching of birds in the palm-grove.

I'd been up before dawn, listening to the roar of the surf on the reef. When the light came, it was a rosy flush, with Raiatea palegreen on the horizon. The rain clouds of the night were drifting west. Fish were leaping in the lagoon's still waters, and terns were fishing. Then smoke began rising from the little row of houses farther along the shore. A man paddled out to an outboard-motor boat, and started bailing. Little outrigger piraguas appeared here and there. The workaday world really began when a lad started spurting along the sands on a mo-bike.

I came back to the blunt-nosed, dusky brown murena, gently swaying in the water, letting a little blue fish swim in and out of his mouth.

A quick shower fell from one of the retreating clouds, giving rise to a glistening rainbow.

It was three days since I'd left Tahiti.

I saw myself again sitting in the domestic flights section of Tahiti Faaa airport, under a huge colourful mural of a fish-hunt with spears: frantic movement, excitement, the mad gaping mouths of the fish. Eight in the morning. The boarding time for the flight to Huahine was 8:30.

At Huahine airport, a taxi was waiting to take guests to the Transfert Base (written so: a mix of French and English) for the boat-trip to the hotel. There were a couple of Americans with me in the taxi: the guy burly, grizzle-haired, in shorts and stockings, the woman frizzle-haired, peak-nosed. From San Francisco. The driver said he was going to put on the clim 'to give a breeze'. 'It's snow I want', said the American.

At the hotel, after filling in forms to the accompaniment of a cocktail in the lounge, we were led to our bungalow, the American couple to one in the garden, myself to one of those on piles over the water. The advantage of these bungalows on piles, apart from the width of their view, is that they're free from mosquitoes and those *nono* that can really make life uncomfortable.

Huahine (151° longitude west, 16°30 latitude south) consists of two islands sharing the same lagoon, a second volcano having come to life in the caldera of the old one. The two islands are separated by Maroe Bay. It's maybe because of this bay that the island is called Huahine, which could mean 'vagina'.

So you have two volcanic piles, rising on the little island to mounts Pohue Rahi and Mou'a Toru, and on the larger island to mounts Turi, Mato Ere Ere ('the black cliff'), Tapu (taboo), Pa'eo and Vahi, and a reef with five passes: Avamoa, Tiare, Farerea, Araara, Avapeitu.

The main village is Fare, which means simply 'house'. On the notice board of the townhall (*Fare Oire*), I saw that according to the census of 1996, the population was 5,417, and that in 2002 it was 5,757.

The very afternoon of my arrival I went to look for a grave.

This was the grave of the American naturalist Andrew Garrett, who lived on Huahine in the 1880s, after years in the islands collecting specimens of shells, fish and birds, and drawing them.

The owner of a shipping company in Germany, Johann Caesar Godeffroy, whose boats plied between Hamburg and ports on the west coast of South America (Conception, Valparaiso), and who had started up a museum in Hamburg, got wind of Garrett, offering to buy a vast quantity of his drawings and paintings for five hundred Chilean pesos along with free lifetime travel on his boats. Godeffroy later published a large selection of Garrett's work in three volumes, *Fische der Südsee*. How I got hold of one of these volumes in a second-hand Antiquariat shop in Stuttgart is a long story that doesn't belong here. Suffice it to say that I've spent hours, in my Breton library, looking at Garrett's paintings of surgeonfish (*acanthurus dussumieri*), longfins (*caranx ciliaris*), porcupinefish (*diodon bleekeri*), scorpion fish (*scorpaena paripinnis*), and firefish (*pterois radiata*).

But to get back to Garrett. He died here, on Huahine, of face-cancer, in 1887, and was buried in or near Fare. That much I knew. The rest I hoped to find out.

Passing by a big church in the village, *Te Ekalesia a Iesu Mesia i te Feia Mo'a i te Mau Mahana Hopei Nei* ('The Church of Jesus-Christ and the Latter Day Saints'), I thought I'd make enquiries there. They'd never heard of Garrett, but they said, probably just to get rid of me, there was a 'family grave' just down the road. I wasn't sure exactly what a 'family grave' meant. What I did know was that, if he had mistresses in a good few islands, who did shell-collecting for him when he wasn't there, Garrett had never burdened himself with a family. So I was a bit sceptical. But trekked on nonetheless in the heat. About a mile farther on, I came to this derelict patch of ground at the roadside and went in through the long grass. There were graves there, sure enough, in a dilapidated state, overgrown with creeping plants, but still legible:

IN MEMORY OF
FAATENE WEET
DIED
SEPT. 22 1888

JOHN FLEMING
DIED
JANUARY 3 1886

The dates were about right, but still no Garrett.

I came back out on to the road.

On the way into the village, I passed by a shack sporting the definition Tabac-Café and calling itself Chez Gégé.

I decided to pursue my investigations there.

Gégé, for it was the man himself I had before me, was a little bloke with a bulging belly, a blue tattoo on his arm and a Marseillais accent you could cut with a hatchet. He was living the great life, there, Gégé: no taxes, no rules and regulations, nothing. In addition to his café-shack, he had a Polynesian wife, a garden and a television. What more could a man want? Sure, he'd been an avid and faithful supporter of the OM, the Olympique de Marseille football team. But you can't have everything, can you? As to graveyards, there were no graveyards on the islands, people buried their dead in the garden. I said I'd just seen a graveyard. 'They must have been foreigners', said Gégé.

I kept looking.

And finally, a couple of hours later, found what I was looking for, in an old Protestant Cemetery close by the shore, a stone bearing these words:

IN MEMORIAM
ANDREW GARRETT
(CONCHOLOGIST)
BORN AT ALBANY, NEW YORK STATE
9TH APRIL 1823
DIED ON THIS ISLAND 1ST NOVEMBER 1887

I saluted the man, as I'd wished, and went to have a closer look at Fare.

★

The supermarket, the *Fare Nui* ('the Big House') was rocking and rolling, telling all and sundry to BUY COCA-COLA. Just along from it, there was a conglomeration of trucks selling burgers, pizzas, all kinds of ready-made grub, with braziers sending acrid columns of blue smoke into the air. A poor dog, so mangied it showed pink, loped and limped around, hoping for some goodies, at least a sign of affection, and not often getting it. Farther on, there was a handicrafts centre, with stalls and booths selling shell jewellery, hats and baskets, coconut oil. Four fellows, fat, with flowery head wreaths, standing behind a table laden with food, were doddling and bobbing their bodies to music played with great enthusiasm by a Tahitian band. The tune I heard was vaguely familiar, but I couldn't place it. Then suddenly I realized it was a Polynesian version of 'The Yellow Rose of Texas'.

I went into Gynette's.

There, from radio or cassette, a voice, female, was wailing: 'Take me to your heaven, take me to your heaven.'

At one table, a little lady with a packet of Marlboro and a portable phone looked as if she'd given up that idea a long time ago.

At another, there was talk of some French film that had been shot on an island near by. All the material, jeeps and so on, had been brought over by cargo. '*Ça a coûté des milliards*' ('it cost billions').

Farther on was the table with the American: the American with the blotched face, the sagging crop, the pigtail, and the tattoo on the right leg; the American wearing a baseball cap, a loose T-shirt, and flowery shorts. I learned later that this character was known locally as Ru Au ('the Old Man'). Apparently he had something to do with the hotel I was staying at. Whether he was one of the owners or had acted as an intermediary during its construction (interrupted for lack of funds, but then re-started with money from the French government) was never clear to me.

Anyway, I had other things on my mind than local business.

★

The days started early, and the evenings lasted long. In fact, sometimes I'd lie out on the deck of the bungalow all night, watching the multitude of stars, listening to dogs barking in the dark.

Red sundowns over Raiatea.

Mornings – the glistening silk, the shimmering satin, the nacreous green of the lagoon water, dragonflies skimming over it, shoals of *nate* fish swimming with heads in the air.

And always the quiet, duskybrown murena.

Now and then, a black or white tipped shark.

I was reading a lot: books I'd picked up in Papeete. In addition to Eliot's *Researches*, the memories, for example, of Arii Taimai as recounted by the American writer Henry Adams (author of a nine-volume history of the US that had left him numb as a mummy), after talks with her on Tahiti in 1891 to 1892, and published by him in 1901. At first, Adams had undertaken these talks simply out of boredom, but he'd got more and more interested.

Here's Arii Taimai talking about her ancestors. Her family, she said, the Teva family, were descended from Shark. First of all there was a chief, Temanu, who married a chiefess, Hototu. While Temanu was away on a long voyage to the Tuamotu, a strange man turned up out of the blue at their place, and, according to the laws of hospitality, Hototu had to welcome him. This character was half-man, half-shark. After they'd been intimate some time, the shark-man saw Hototu fondling her dog. That got on his nerves. 'You betrayed your husband for me', he said. 'Who says you couldn't cheat on me now for your dog?' And he made back for the sea in a huff.

But as a parting word he said that if she had a child by him, which was very probable, she was to call him Teva. The birth of the child would be accompanied by wind and rain, and wherever he went, wind and rain would announce his coming. 'Even to this day', said Arii Taimai to Adams, 'the Teva never travel without the wind and the rain. That's why they're called the wind-and-rain people.'

Writing this book, Adams said he realized just how much he loathed American civilization. 'Tahiti is totally poetic', he said. 'America has no poetic conception at all.'

★

Some archeologists will tell you, a certain Japanese professor, for example, that the island of Huahine has some of the oldest sacred sites, *marae*, in the Society Islands. Maybe true, maybe not. Anyway, where sacrality's concerned, what's a few centuries this side or that?

The sacred sites of Huahine lie mainly along the shores of

Lake Fauna Nui: great blocks of coral, white-grey-black, with coral chunks and other stones interspersed.

Others were raised on the heights above, so I started to climb up Matairea Hill.

Ground strewn with coconuts and mangos, the smell of rotting mangos in the air.

A greenblue lizard on a boulder.

Tree trunks entwined by wild vanilla.

The yellow flowers of *miro*, which is rosewood (*thespesia populnea*).

Ironwood, which is *casuarina equisetifolia*.

Pandanus tectorius, which is Polynesian *fara*.

The orange flowers of the *tou*, which is *cordia subcordata*.

Ora, in Polynesian, which is the banyan.

The first place at which I stopped on the heights, Marae Tefano, had a huge, aged banyan at one corner of its precinct.

I kept climbing up, through sun and shadow.

At the top, I arrived at a site of lava stones overlooking the lake and lay out on it for a while, like a lizard myself, taking in the view...

Back at the bottom of the path, I came across a party of workmen, employed by the municipality of Fare to clear and clean the area.

One I saw had a tattoo on his back: an outrigger and a *marae*.

Seeing my interest: 'We were travellers', he said.

Another had travelled a bit. He'd worked on the docks at Concarneau in Brittany. But he'd found the pace of work demented.

'Wait till the Japs and the Yanks come in', I said, 'and France will seem like paradise.'

He looked startled.

I felt a bit sorry for having made this little prophecy, but in history, if there's anybody who's always right, it's Cassandra.

I continued on my way.

A strand with bits of broken coral, coconuts and plastic refuse.

Blue-eyed eels in a still pool.

A place, at the southern tip of the island, around Bay Mahuti, where the tarmac becomes a crab-walk, thunder rolling, and a woman up to the waist in water, fishing.

Rain gouging ravines in red earth.

A couple of days later, I left my floating hotel for an Air Tahiti flight to Tahaa, via Bora Bora and Raiatea.

★

I got tattooed on Tahaa – on the left breast and the left thigh, in red.

Here's how it happened.

It had been a beautiful, mid-day flight from Huahine to Uturoa airport on Raiatea, via the peaks and pinnacles, the darkblue emeraldgreen waters of Bora Bora. From the airport, a boat takes you across the Te Area Rahi passage to Tahaa, which shares the same reef with Raiatea but is a totally separate island.

Where I was making for was a very little palm-packed *motu* ('islet') on the Tahaa reef.

While waiting for another couple of passengers arriving from another flight, I talked with the boatman. He was saying that, with the opening of the new hotel, people who had gone to look for work elsewhere, to Bora Bora or Tahiti, were coming back home, back to the *fenua*. On Tahaa, only about 10 per cent of the people had jobs with salaries, but they got by. A lot of folk cultivated vanilla. Tahaa was 'the vanilla island' – the conditions there were special. Of course there was vanilla on other islands too, but it was not like the vanilla of Tahaa. Tahaa was a lovely island. Naturally, there were changes, like everywhere else. In the old days, the people used to grow flowers all along the roads. Now the roads have been macadamized, they don't do it any more.

The boat yamaha'd its way over the Te Area Rahi, past Pointe Toamaru, Pointe Apoo Pahi, Pointe Tiamahana, Pointe Tepari, up towards Tapuamu Bay, from where it crossed to the little *motu* of Tautau.

I had one of those overwater bungalows again, out on the edge.

To the left, the south-east, lay Raiatea. To the right, the south-west, rose the darkblue mass of Bora Bora. From the south, out of the bluegreen empty space with the broken white line, a gentle breeze was blowing. A couple of frigates hovered over the lagoon, a black tern flew over the roof.

I spent the afternoon lost in that absolute stillness, then, towards evening, decided to go out to the reef and swim down the pass I'd heard about on arriving.

Pretty soon I'd left the bounds of the hotel behind me – a notice made it clear that from now on you were on your own.

It was a jagged coral-strewn shore but, surmising it might be so, I was wearing sandals, so that was no problem. A black heron rose up into startled flight and flapped away over the waters. At the pass, I put on flippers and goggles and got into the water. It was shallow and there was coral everywhere, but I thought I could make it. That's where I was wrong. Within a couple of minutes, I had coral gashes on breast and thigh. Deciding that this was going to be no pleasure (maybe if you were a Moray eel you could make it down that pass unscathed, otherwise no), and that it would be as well anyway to see to the gashes right away (if you don't do something about it, the polyps can eat their way down to the bone), I made my way back to the hotel, got some lemons (Marquesan lemons, extra strong, I was told) and rubbed the juice into my skin that had, yes, by now, something like a tattoo, meaning roughly this: Swam-down-the-pass-at-a-bad-time-and-got-badly-scraped-serves-me-right.

Sunset was palerose and greeny yellow, with an almost full moon. I ordered a room-service dinner, and had another look at my map.

The Raiatea–Tahaa reef is the shape of a keyhole, with Raiatea in the bottom part. Raiatea used to be the religious centre of the Society Islands, with the biggest *marae*, Taputapuatea, in all French Polynesia. Nowadays it has the biggest port-town after Papeete: Uturoa, with a very strong Chinese business community. As to Tahaa, it's quieter. No big town at all, only little villages: Tapuamu, Patio, Hipu, Faaha, Haamene, Vaitoare, Poutoru, Tiva.

On the following morning, I took the boat to the 'mainland', intending to move round Tahaa.

★

Port of Tapuamu, early in the morning. Smells of gasoil, rotting mango and baking bread. A little shack back of the harbour selling lollipops, Coca-Cola and hiring out a couple of cars.

'Popaa, can I borrow the Vespa?', calls a dusky young damsel to the French owner. 'For how long?' 'Just a minute.' '*D'accord.*'

Tapuamu is a church (*Makedonia – Fare Pureraa no Tapuamu*), a Chinese we've-got-it-all shop, Chong Out (this was where the baking bread smell came from), a string of houses, and a community that has its problems. In big letters on a billboard, I read this:

MELISSA

VOLEUSE DE MEC

SALOPE-PÉTASSE-PROSTITUEUSE

SIGNÉ: SPU

– indicating that SPU did not like Melissa at all, accusing her of being a man-stealer, a bitch, a slut and a whore, in that order.

Round Tapuamu Bay, it's swampy ground, littered with coconuts, lumps of dead coral and lava rock. In those marshy wastelands, marked at times with a notice: '*TABU – propriété privée*', there will be a nondescript modern house, but now and then an old cabin, with walls of wood or woven matting, and roof of thatched pandanus leaves or corrugated iron. On the shore side, it's houses on stilts, with outriggers on stilts beside them.

Along the way to Patio, roadwork was going on, watery areas being filled in with coral soup and macadamized areas being re-tarred.

At Haamene, at mid-day, two island dogs lay panting in the shade of a mango tree beside the red corrugated-iron roof of the church while Tahitian music was wafted from an establishment called Shack Mac China.

After Haamene, I followed the north shore of Hurepiti Bay to Tiva. It was just beyond Tiva I came to a restaurant Chez Loulou.

★

The approach was down a concrete path to the main body of the restaurant, which opened out on to a terrace over the lagoon, with Bora Bora, a solid blue, on the horizon.

Not a soul in sight.

Thinking I'd made enough noise for someone to turn up, I let my eye rove round the room again: flowery plastic cloths, red and yellow, on the tables; a black amplifier, Ha-Shun, Super Speaker System, in one corner...

'*Il y a quelqu'un?*' ('Anybody home?')

It was then Loulou appeared from behind a curtain, a fat old warty harridan, rubbing her eyes and yawning.

'Is it possible to eat?' I asked.

She said, *bien sûr*, it was just that it was the low season, and at mid-day there had been no customers at all, so she'd decided just to go for a sleep. Sleep's as good an occupation as any other, she went on. Besides, she had low blood-pressure and had to take things easy. In fact, she said, she was a mess. Total hormonal dysfunctioning. 'None of my clocks keep time.' She'd given up smoking, but she had haemorrhages.

Before she went into more clinical details, I asked if I could see the menu.

'It's all chalked up there on the board.'

I had a look at the board.

'These are my specialties', said Loulou. 'Hellish stuff, all of it.'

What I'm translating here as 'hellish stuff' was Loulou's French '*des plats salement dégueulasses*'. This is very popular French, in fact almost a caricature of popular French, and you don't often hear that kind of French in Polynesian mouths.

I remarked on that.

Yes, she said, she knew her French was special too, hot stuff. That was because she'd lived for seventeen years in New Caledonia. That was a faster life. When she came back from among the *Caledoches* to Papeete, she found the Tahitians too relaxed, too cool.

'Swordfish and rice will do me fine', I said.

While we'd been talking, a buxom girl of about twenty had come out from behind the same curtain as Loulou, rubbing her eyes and yawning.

She started laying the table, in slow motion.

Then a fellow about the same age as the girl appeared, and shambled his way to the kitchen behind the bar.

'Swordfish', said Loulou.

It was at that moment the music started up.

'We put on the music to convince ourselves the world exists', said Loulou.

While I was eating, she told me more about her haemorrhages. I tried to steer the conversation around to other themes.

Oh, yes, there were a lot of foreigners came through Tahaa now. She got a lot of back-packers recently, from Czechoslovakia. And then there were the Japanese. They always gave big tips.

'I thought it was an insult to Polynesian hospitality to give tips', I said, just to tease her out.

'That's what we used to think', said Loulou. 'But now we know it's not an insult, it's to express thanks.'

'Don't you believe it', I said. 'The guy who does it just wants you to think he's a big man.'

'Yeah? I never thought of that', said Loulou.

'What are you going to do now?', I said, finishing my meal.

'Back to sleep, what else?'

★

Followed a series of long days and great space.

Pacific meditations, based on next to nothing:

The blue-rosy heights of Bora Bora.

The roaring of the reef and the silence of the lagoon.

The reef's broken white line.

Now and then I'd go for a walk around the *motu*, following the path I'd taken on my first evening, amidst the clink of dead coral, alongside coconuts with new sprouts bursting out of them and taking root. However quiet and unobtrusive I tried to be, I always disturbed the black heron. He'd fly out over the sea and then come back to hunch on his perch as soon as I'd moved on.

Sometimes I'd swim up the pass, which is to say against the current, among the coral heads. There were different kinds of fish, but the main occupants of the territory were black urchins, whole colonies of them, with long black spikes (*echinotrix diadema*; in Polynesian, *vana*).

Then one morning I realized I had neighbours. What I saw first was the bottle of Pepsi and the packet of cigarettes on the railing of their deck. Then I saw and heard them. A young English couple. They spent their time smoking, drinking Pepsi, feeding breadcrumbs to the fish, and shouting at each other.

I was about to look for a change of bungalow, away on the other side of the island, when I heard in the restaurant that a hundred Japanese tourists were about to arrive, all in one group.

Time to move on.

★

It was a late morning in early April in the little port of Vaitape, administrative centre of the island of Bora Bora.

Vaitape is a huddle of buildings that includes an evangelical temple (*Église Évangélique de Polynésie Française – Ebene Ezera de Vaitape*), a Catholic church (*Église Saint-Pierre-Célestin*), a Chinese-owned general store, Magasin Chin Lee, and a post of the Black Pearl Trading Company.

In the shade of two pandanus trees, bunches of bonitos were strung out for sale, and a fellow in long shorts with a blue tattoo running down his left arm was flitching at them with a leafy twig to keep off the flies. Farther along the street, two sturdy women stood silent behind a stall piled high with chiquita bananas, alongside it great knobbly stalks of taro tied in bundles.

In another patch of shade, two dogs, one tawny, one white, lay gasping.

It was already hot, sweltering hot.

I found myself a café, ordered a bottle of Hinano, the local beer, and did a little recapitulation.

When the boat from Motu Mute airport and harbour on Bora Bora had deposited me on the Motu Tevairoa, where my hotel was situated, I was shown to my bungalow, this time (I'd thought I'd change) not an overwater bungalow, but a garden bungalow, which turned out to be in a wooded area, inside a palisade of bamboo, a spacious room looking out on to a garden and to a little hut-like structure that looked like the nearest you could get to a Japanese tea-hut outside Kyoto. There was an inhabitant in the room before me. I could hear him, a lizard, going *chuck-chuck, chuck-chuck-chuck*. I said *chuck-chuck* back, but I obviously didn't have the right accent, because he clammed up on me.

At six, I wandered over to the bar.

It was Happy Hour.

There was a big notice to this effect, saying the second drink was half-price, announcing also a Polynesian dance demonstration.

The place was dead empty.

That's why I was overwhelmingly welcomed, not only by the waitress, but by the barman himself.

The barman had to be seen to be believed. He was the kind of homosexual you expect to find only in vaudeville. A fat guy, he minced, cavorted and giggled about. Add to all that physiology the sartorial fact that, round his forehead, he had a thick leaf wreath, slightly tilted, making him look like a punch-drunk Bacchus.

While he supplied me with the cocktail list, the waitress tried to get me interested in the dance demonstration. We'd all dance together on the floor with her, and then the best man and the best woman would be chosen. 'Great', I said, and made for the far corner of the bar, facing the shore.

I was consulting the cocktail list when an American dandled in with his wife.

'Happy Hour', he read aloud, adding, as the waitress came up to him: 'Not very happy.'

She assured him it would all happen later on.

I was still engrossed in the cocktail card.

There was what they called a Taurearea, made of white rum, Get 27, coconut cream, pineapple juice and green lemon. Uh-huh. Then there was the Te Moana: white rum, blue curaçao, coconut cream and pineapple juice. Hmmm. After that, I studied and weighed up the composition of the Bora Bora Sunset, before fixing on the Maitai: white and dark rum, triple sec, cocoa liqueur, orange, pineapple and lime juice.

I made a sign to the barman.

Up he rolled, positively quaking with delight.

'*Un Maitai. Oui, monsieur. C'est très bien, monsieur. C'est un très bon choix, monsieur.*'

I sipped my multi-layered Maitai, looking out over the rosy twilight waters of the lagoon.

There was something interesting going on down there on the sands. A black heron was stalking up and down, elegant and graceful, lord of the beach, cousin to the night...

It was then the Musical Trio turned up, with a Tahitian ukulele, a Hawaiian *kamaka*, and a blue guitar from Los Angeles.

'Come back to Tahiti', they sang: *A hoi mai i Tahiti*. Then they did a song about Bora Bora: *Te mihi nei au ia oe*. To be followed by one about the Tuamotu archipelago: *Fakateretere*.

The thing about Polynesian, especially Tahitian, is the vowels. There are so many of them you're absolutely desperate for a consonant. If you want consonants, you have to go to the Marquesas. But I wasn't going away over to the Marquesas just for a consonant.

Giving a little salute to the musicians, with whom I'd talked a bit, I wandered behind the bar into what was called the Library. It wasn't a library, as I'm sure you've guessed, it was a collection of unmentionable crap. But I did come across a copy of Melville's *Pierre* – in Japanese. That put the Japanese tourists up a peg or two in my estimation. I mean, *Pierre* is pretty heavy reading even in English, in Japanese it must be total purgatory. I could imagine Mr Ishimura with a half-bottle of champagne at his elbow wondering at the tenth page if he hadn't picked the wrong book. What's sure is he didn't take it back with him to Nagasaki.

And so, back to my bungalow.

The lizard was back at his *chuck-chuck, chuck-chuck-chuck.* Mr Gecko, or Monsieur Margouillat, at home. Greygold, with little black spots. I'd seen his country cousin that afternoon as I wandered about the wood of coconut palm, filao and pandanus, a fast little bluetailed fellow, with three gold stripes on his head: *lygosoma cyanurum.*

Chuck-chuck-chuck. Goodnight.

★

It was in the café at Vaitape that I met Serge Le Gall, from Bordeaux, but whose ancestors, as his name indicated, were Breton, from around Paimpol. Serge had been kicking about the islands for years. He'd been a cook on Tahiti, a diving instructor on Moorea, he'd worked on a pearl fishery on the Tuamotu, now he ran a catamaran on Bora Bora.

We made a date to go round the island on his boat.

He picked me up at nine, and we cruised slowly, quietly, up north along the island, past Pointe Tereia and the heights of Apooyara, densely darkblue against the azure of the sky, up to Pointe Taihi, seeing frigates wheeling high and, lower down, blue-beaked gannets.

Beyond Pointe Taihi, we started swimming along the coral ridge.

Among the fish encountered were two very slim and elegant remoras, flat-headed, lower lip protuberant, grey, sometimes mauve-grey and paleblue at the tip of their fins, who accompanied us for a long and silent time.

The heights of Bora Bora had been absolutely blue when we went out in the morning. When we returned in the afternoon, they were shrouded in misty cloud.

★

Rangiroa, one of the largest atolls in the world, its name meaning 'the big sky', lies 350 kilometres north-east of Tahiti. It was to it I made my way from Bora Bora.

When I'd settled into my bungalow, named Mahinui, which is the stingray, I stood at the rail of the deck looking over the lagoon. Just below the stairs of the deck, a shoal of *nate* were passing, bobbing up their heads and diving down again with a *plop* and a *splash*. A little farther off, a black-tipped shark glided ghostily by. When I went into the water myself half-an-hour later, I met up with a band of blue chromies, a big-bellied parrotfish, paleblue, rosy under the neck, a trumpetfish and a slinky, dusky murena.

The Tuamotu are a strange, outlying zone.

In Polynesia, among the island groups of the Pacific in general, the habit is to distinguish between 'high islands' and 'low islands'. Both have their origin in lava welling up from the submarine mountain chain of the Pacific Ridge. The 'high islands' are younger, having known as yet little erosion and subsidence. The 'low islands' know it all, they've been around for a longer time. All they've got in the end is an atoll: a ring of coral (with earth) usually interrupted by passes, but not always.

All this makes for disconcerting territory. The regular trade winds go crazy there, and the currents are an inextricable maze.

Such are the Tuamotu.

★

When the Scotsman Robert Louis Stevenson and the Frenchman Victor Segalen were around these parts in the late nineteenth and early twentieth century, the Tuamotu weren't called the Tuamotu at all, they were called the Pomotu. With the very limited Polynesian at my disposal, I take the syllable

228

po to mean something like dark, nocturnal, dangerous.

If the Pomotu were considered dangerous, it was because of geographical and meteorological conditions, but also because of their inhabitants, reputed to be barbarous and rank with superstition.

Stevenson revelled in this. When he was on Fakarava, another atoll in the Tuamotu archipelago, just down from Rangiroa, in 1888–1889, he immersed himself in the local ghost stories. The actual physical reality of the islands inspired in him a kind of horror. The first sight of multi-coloured fish seen from the deck of the *Casco* had delighted him, but when he came to know about ciguatera poisoning (he doesn't use the word but describes the phenomenon), he lost his enthusiasm. Even the coral bothered him: it wasn't 'honest rock', but an organic mass, half-alive, half-putrescent. It looks as if he turned to the human psychology and sociology, ghost stories included, as a kind of relief, so as not to go off the edge.

Take the story about the night of wind and storm around the house of a certain M. Donat with a sick child in it. Suddenly a bird, a cock, is blown by the wind against the wall. The father puts it back into the yard. A quarter of an hour later, the same thing happens, but this time the cock sings. The father puts it back in the pen. After that, there's a sound, a noise, a strange noise, something between a wail and a whistle, that strikes terror into everybody. Then out of the dark comes a chief, a bold man to be out so late at night, but he must have had a lantern (no Pomotuan will be out in the dark, says Stevenson, between sundown and 4 a.m., the time when the spirits are abroad). 'Your child', says the chief, 'is surely going to die. The evil spirit of the island is getting ready to eat the souls of the new dead.' And he goes on to describe the habits of this spirit. Usually it didn't operate in such an obvious and noisy way, like some Tahitian or Marquesan spirits. It just perched in silence on the roof of the house and waited, in the shape of a bird. The people inside taking care of the dying person or keening over the dead body would never suspect anything. But in the morning, there would be *drops of blood on the wall...*

Stevenson says he loved that idea of the blood on the wall. It was the kind of touch he liked himself. Well, I leave him to it.

I like Stevenson well, but I'm more interested in Segalen's attempts to get out of human narrative entirely and really walk the edge. When Segalen was up here in what he called the Archipel des Paumotou, a place outside history, in January 1903, as a navy doctor aboard the *Durance*, it was to bring help to people whose homes had been devastated by a cyclone. But even in the midst of all these human events, he has an eye to the islands themselves, their topography, their topology (outlines of form, deep lines of growth). If an island, he says, can be defined as land surrounded by water, an atoll, paradoxically, is water surrounded by land. And he describes the 'yellow line of coral' becoming incandescent when the sun is high. That's another line entirely.

Rambling literary reflections in the house of the Stingray around midnight...

★

Next morning, going for breakfast, early, I met Fisher – Fisher Fallstrom, from Tahaa, whose father was from the Cook Islands, and whose grandfather had been a Swede. He had a labyrinthine spread of blue tattoo on his body and I asked him about it. He said it was all about his personal life, about what he had done and where he had been, he himself. He wanted to get away from the weight of the ancestors. 'There are people on these islands who want to bring back the dead.' Especially there on the Tuamotu, the folk were very superstitious, they believed in evil spirits; every time something strange happened, they thought it was the spirits. Oh, they were superstitious all right, the Tuamotu people. And *fainéants* too, lazy. They'd work for three days, then down tools and spend all their wages on drink in a few hours.

Fisher was the 'activities man' at the hotel, and he dutifully rattled off a list of them. Seeing I wasn't at all interested, he made an addition to it: 'You could shoot the pass', he said. What did that mean? The pass was one of the three passes on the Rangiroa Atoll, the Tiputa. When the time was right, the ocean waters that had piled up outside came rushing in through the coral gate and you could swim with the flow. How many people will be there? I asked. Depends, he said – six or eight. I said I'd like to do it on my own. No chance with the hotel, he said, but he had a friend who had a boat, he might be able to arrange it. He'd just ask me to sign a note taking all responsibility off his shoulders in case something happened – it wouldn't, but you never know.

Later that morning, he told me it would be possible at 3 o'clock, 15:00, the following day.

The next day at 14:50, I was at the embarcadero. There was a boat, which I presumed to be *the* boat, but no one in sight. Then after a while Fisher appeared coming down the planks in the company of his friend, Raumati, the boat-owner.

'What do you think of the boat?', said Fisher.

'Great', I said.

'He made it himself', said Fisher. I tried not to look alarmed. We moved out.

I had my fins and goggles. Now Raumati told me that the hotel boat also provided diving-suits, because of the jellyfish. What kind of jellyfish? I said. He didn't know the French or English word, but from the description he gave they sounded ominously like Portuguese men-of-war. I must admit I felt like turning back. Portuguese men-of-war can make a hell of a mess of you. 'There probably won't be any', said Raumati, no doubt seeing my dismay, 'it's not the season.' I just hoped he was right.

Once we were out at the pass, I dropped off the boat.

This was nothing like the little pass at Tahaa. No risk of scraping yourself on coral. The depth must have well been over a hundred feet. A big barracuda passed me by on the left, long-snouted, gleaming, giving me the look-over. Then a band of white-tipped sharks came in sight. Normally, nothing at all to worry about, and everything to admire. But with that damned shark-feeding they practise all over Polynesia to treat the tourists, you never know. Apart from the fact that it disturbs the fishes' habits, rhythms and system, it makes them associate the presence of human beings with food, and if you haven't got any grub with you to satisfy their expectations, they can justifiably feel a little riled... That band wasn't riled, they probably knew they could get a better meal later on. The flow was strong, no need to do any flipping, except maybe to change direction a bit now and then. Among fluttering clouds of smaller fish, six more barracudas to starboard. The depth was diminishing all the time, maybe only something like twenty feet now. No jellyfish in sight, thank the Lord. Green turtle (*cleconia Mydas*) to larboard. A black-tipped shark. Another couple of barracudas. And then, in quiet waters, the biggest Moray eel I've ever seen, swimming in great brown coils.

Raumati had been following me at a distance with the boat, and I clambered up on board again.

'OK?'

'OK.'

As I'd swum up to the boat, I'd noticed the name, and asked Raumati what it meant in Polynesian: '*La fleur de couronne de la femme*', he said ('the crown flower of woman'). I wasn't sure if that meant clitoris, mound of Venus, or head-dress, but didn't pursue the matter. 'If you don't have a boat here, you can't live', went on Raumati. A lot of people had a little motu somewhere round the atoll, and to get there, you have to have a boat. He himself had a motu, a family motu, it went way back. He still had the house there. He dried copra, would hire people to split the nuts, but sometimes went over there himself: 'Over there, there's a big silence.' Some film director from Los Angeles had come to Rangiroa wanting to buy a motu to build a hotel. He offered millions, but nobody would sell. He himself would never sell his motu. He had his copra, then he had another little spot with lemon trees, he got by. He'd thought once of getting into the black pearl trade, but he wasn't sure. He knew of some up there on the Tuamotu who'd got rich quick that way, but they also went rotten quick; black pearls can drive you mad.

I wasn't ever likely to get mad about pearls, but I'd gradually got interested in them. Enough to know that black pearls aren't black – they're grey-blue, silvery, greenish, aubergine. It's the oyster shell that's black, *pinctura margaritifera*. There were plenty of these shells in the Tuamotu – the locals in the old days would eat the flesh and spit out the pearls the way you might spit out the pippins of an orange. It was the Japanese who came in to develop the business, and although the Polynesians had finally caught on, the specialists were still mainly Asiatic. It was a delicate operation to place the nucleus (compacted calcite or whatever), along with a bit of the black *manteau*, into the gonad, the 'pearl pocket', and let that foreign body irritate the flesh into developing a nacreous growth. I'd looked very closely at a lot of pearls, from Tahiti out.

But it was another idea that was growing now in my head. I'd gathered from Raumati's talk that his house on the motu was empty most of the time. Could he maybe rent it to me for two or three days? I fancied being out there entirely on my own with the big sky and the open sea for a while. He said he'd think about it.

Meanwhile, he was going to beach the boat for the night.

'You don't anchor it?'

'No. I pull it up on the beach, so it will sleep well. You never know here. The weather changes fast.'

★

On the following day, I got a phone call from him. He was willing to rent me the house on the motu for two nights. He'd take me out, and pick me up on the third day. He'd also see to provisions. We agreed on a price.

As we headed out towards the motu a couple of days later, there was a bank of grey-white cumulus in the big sky, and rain was falling here and there in fringed curtains along the horizon. At one point in the crossing, we saw a large band of noddies collected over the sea: 'Must be a lot of good fish there', said Raumati. Like everybody else on the atoll, he did a lot of fishing. At the right time (that depended on the wind and on the sky), he'd be out on the reef, with a lamp, for lobsters: 'You see their eyes', he said.

When we got to the motu, Raumati anchored the boat and we started over land, sometimes wading in channels up to the waist, crossing beaches where there would only be a little *mikimiki* bush or two, till we came to the coconut grove and then, at the far side, on the shore, the house.

Raumati opened the basket of provisions he'd brought and we had a meal. While we were eating, he made a rough sketch of the island for me, telling me it was highly unlikely I would meet anyone, I would be all on my own. At that, he pointed over the water in the direction of another motu. There used to be a whole village there, he said, but now it was abandoned. It lived on copra, but the schooners picking up the copra often foundered on the coral heads, so they'd finally stopped coming. The people had gone away to look for jobs elsewhere.

With these few words, Raumati left me to my own devices.

'OK, *maururu, nana*', I said ('thanks, I'll be seeing you').

I spent the rest of the afternoon just wandering about the house and the coconut grove, reserving a reconnaissance of the whole island for the day following. During the night, there was torrential rain, with heavy thunder and vigorous lightning, and me thinking to myself that, if ever there was a cyclone in these parts, I'd had it, quite definitely had it.

Well, there are worse ways of putting a final stop.

I awoke to a great welter of wings, to the screaming of terns and the *craik-craik-craik* of noddies, while a white heron (*tara*) stalked along the sand. The sea was calm again, the wild weather had gone. But the sky was still a bit overcast. A faint orange sunrise was creeping up over the horizon.

There isn't much to see on an atoll. Some would say there's nothing to see at all. Walking across the island, I had the impression of going from one vacancy to another, from one silence to another, but always full of life.

It had started with the birds. Then, when I came out of the house, it was the crabs. Thousands of them. Hermit crabs. Red. Going places, in all directions.

But what impressed me most was the outer reef. It was a fantastic coral-landscape there, the shapes ferociously baroque, brown or white at base, then grey-black.

Empty sea, dark jagged coral, bird cries.

Behind the outer ridge, there were small pools of water, warm, fed into by the ocean in irregular rills; I lay in them, letting the ocean come in over me.

In the passes, I swam. I wasn't alone. A band of seven small black-tipped sharks swam with me. And clam shells, with great purple, blue or green gubs, great gaping saw-toothed mouths, opened and shut when I passed: the big ones dangerous-looking, the small ones seeming to be giving me a wink.

When I raised my head I'd see frigates (*otaha*) high in the sky.

I mentioned back there my lack of interest in ghost stories. They're only a diminished and contorted human expression of the real *panic* thing, that sense of total being, both plenitudinous and empty, that can seize hold of you in these parts.

It was that *panic* sensation, along with a mass of lines and colours, that was my last gift from Polynesia.

Maururu.